The Art of Illuminating As Practised in Europe From the Earliest Tymes

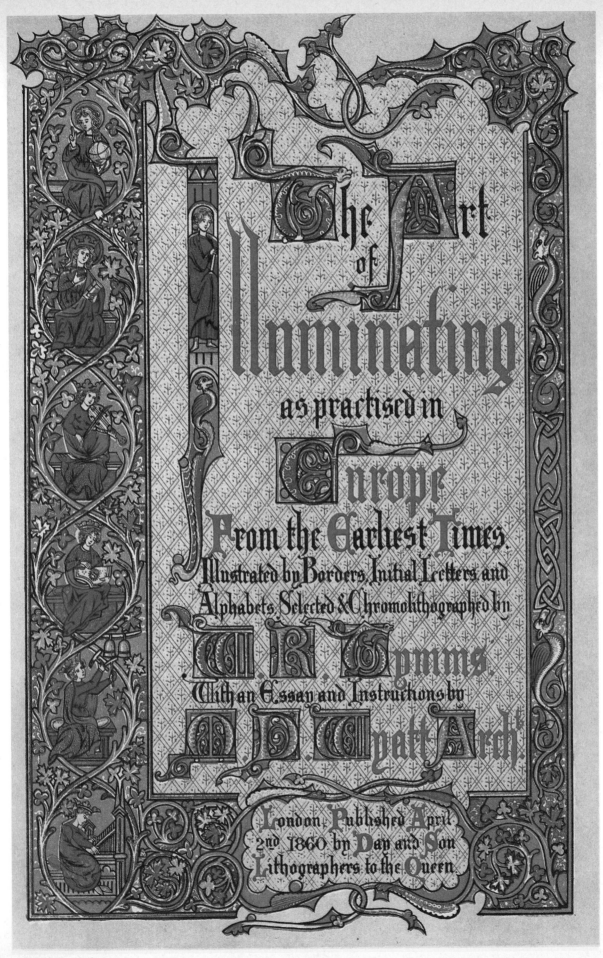

The Art of Illuminating as practised in Europe From the Earliest Times. Illustrated by Borders, Initial Letters and Alphabets, Selected & Chromolithographed by W R Tymms With an Essay and Instructions by M D Wyatt Arch.

London, Published April 2nd 1860 by Day and Son Lithographers to the Queen.

Studio Editions
London

This edition published 1987 by Studio Editions
a division of Bestseller Publications Limited,
Princess House, 50 Eastcastle Street,
London W1N 7AP, England

Copyright © Studio Editions, 1987

ISBN 1 85170 045 5

Printed and bound in Yugoslavia

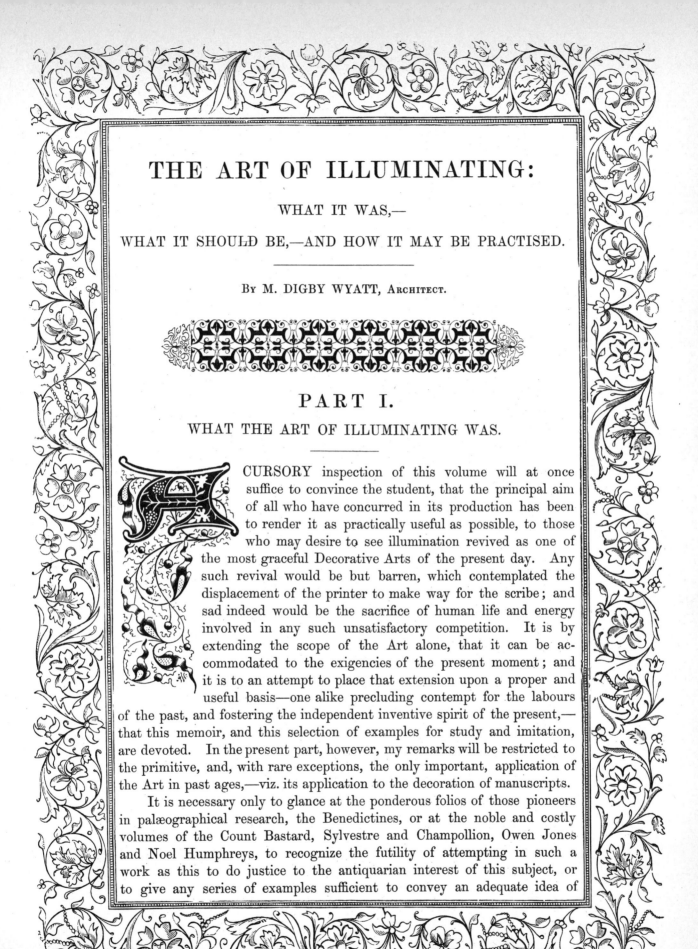

THE ART OF ILLUMINATING:

WHAT IT WAS,—

WHAT IT SHOULD BE,—AND HOW IT MAY BE PRACTISED.

By M. DIGBY WYATT, Architect.

PART I.

WHAT THE ART OF ILLUMINATING WAS.

CURSORY inspection of this volume will at once suffice to convince the student, that the principal aim of all who have concurred in its production has been to render it as practically useful as possible, to those who may desire to see illumination revived as one of the most graceful Decorative Arts of the present day. Any such revival would be but barren, which contemplated the displacement of the printer to make way for the scribe; and sad indeed would be the sacrifice of human life and energy involved in any such unsatisfactory competition. It is by extending the scope of the Art alone, that it can be accommodated to the exigencies of the present moment; and it is to an attempt to place that extension upon a proper and useful basis—one alike precluding contempt for the labours of the past, and fostering the independent inventive spirit of the present,—that this memoir, and this selection of examples for study and imitation, are devoted. In the present part, however, my remarks will be restricted to the primitive, and, with rare exceptions, the only important, application of the Art in past ages,—viz. its application to the decoration of manuscripts.

It is necessary only to glance at the ponderous folios of those pioneers in palæographical research, the Benedictines, or at the noble and costly volumes of the Count Bastard, Sylvestre and Champollion, Owen Jones and Noel Humphreys, to recognize the futility of attempting in such a work as this to do justice to the antiquarian interest of this subject, or to give any series of examples sufficient to convey an adequate idea of the magnificence and peculiarities of the rich store of monuments of art, treasured in the great public and private libraries of Europe. Men of the profoundest learning have devoted, some whole lives, and many of them long years, to the study of those precious pages, on the decoration of which the highest efforts of the illuminists of old were lavished; and have yet, one and all, confessed the partial and incomplete mastery of the subject which they, with all their labour, have been enabled to acquire, or in elaborate disquisitions to record for the benefit of posterity.

With works produced with such preparations, such energy, such devotion, it would be presumptuous to suppose that this little essay could for one moment compete; it can but aim at the humble merit of endeavouring, firstly, to draw the attention of the unlearned to the interest and practical value of the Art it illustrates; and, secondly, to direct the student to those sources of information from a careful study of which alone any proper knowledge of the archæology of the subject can be acquired.

The reader being thus forewarned of the elementary nature of the information he is likely to derive from a perusal of the following notes, I at once proceed to take up the first section of my theme.

The books of the ancients were scarcely books in the modern acceptation of the term. From Egypt, where a rude form of illumination had been practised from the most remote period, they obtained leaves of the papyrus, converted into a kind of paper by gluing them together in two thicknesses,—generally with the muddy water of the Nile,—the fibres in the upper leaf being placed so as to cross those of the lower at right angles. Pliny[1] describes the manufacture, and how the sheets, limited in size by the dimensions of the papyrus-leaf, were cemented end to end, until nearly twenty having been so connected, they were fit to form the scapus, or roll, which constituted the usual Grecian and Roman books. Eumenes, king of Pergamus, being unable to procure the Egyptian papyrus, through the jealousy of one of the Ptolemys, who occupied himself in forming a rival library to the one which subsequently became so celebrated at Pergamus, introduced the use of parchment properly "dressed" for taking ink and pigments; and hence the derivation of the word "pergamena" as applied to parchment or vellum; the former substance being the prepared skin of sheep, and the latter of calves.[2]

The sheets of parchment were joined end to end, as the sheets of papyrus had been, and when written upon, on one side only, and in narrow transverse columns across the breadth of the scroll, were rolled up round

[1] Lib. xiii. cap. 11.

[2] M. Gabriel Peignot, in his "Essai sur l'Histoire du Parchemin et du Vélin," Paris, 1812, and in his paper on the same subject in "Le Moyen Age et la Renaissance," vol. ii. Paris, 1849, produces evidence of the use of parchment for writing upon anterior to the age of Eumenes; and consequently limits his interpretation of Pliny's words, "Varro membranas Pergami tradidit repertas," to an assertion of the discovery of improved processes by which parchment was rendered more available for writing upon than it had been previous to the accession of Eumenes.

staves and bound with strings known as "umbilici," to which bosses of metal, or "bullæ," were attached.[1]

The custom of dividing books into pages is said by Suetonius to have been introduced by Julius Cæsar, whose letters to the Senate were so made up, and after whose time the practice became usual for all documents either addressed to, or issuing from, that body, or the emperors. As that form subsequently crept into general use, the books were known as "codices;" and hence the ordinary term as applied to manuscript volumes. All classes of books, the reeds for writing in them, the inkstands, and the "capsæ" or "scrinia," the boxes in which the "scapi" or rolls were kept, are minutely portrayed in ancient wall paintings and ivory diptychs. The inkstands are generally shown as double, no doubt for containing both black and red ink, with the latter of which certain portions of the text were written.[2]

Nearly two thousand actual rolls were discovered at Herculaneum, of course in a highly-carbonized condition, and of them some hundreds have been unrolled. None of them appear to have been embellished with illumination,[3] so that for proof of the practice of the art in classical times, we are thrown back upon the classical authors themselves. The allusions in their writings to the employment of red and black ink are frequent. Martial, in his first epistle, points out the bookseller's shop opposite the Julian Forum, in which his works may be obtained "smoothed with pumice-stone and decorated with purple." Seneca mentions books ornamented "cum imaginibus." Varro is related by Pliny to have illustrated his works by likenesses of more than seven hundred illustrious persons. Pliny, again, informs us that writers on medicine gave representations in their treatises of the plants which they described. Martial dwells on the editions of Virgil, with his portrait as a frontispiece. The earliest recorded instance of the richer adornments of golden lettering on purple or rose-stained vellum, is given by Julius Capitolinus in his life of the Emperor Maximinus the younger. He therein mentions that the mother of the emperor presented to him, on his return to his tutor (early in the 3rd century), a copy of the works of Homer, written in gold upon purple vellum. Whether derived from Egypt or the East, this luxurious mode of embellishment appears to have been popular among the later Greeks, a class of whose scribes were denominated "writers in gold." From Greece it was, no doubt, transplanted to Rome, where, from about the 2nd century, it, at first slowly, and ultimately rapidly, acquired popularity. St. Jerome, indeed, writing in the 4th century, in a well-known passage in his preface to the Book of Job, exclaims:

[1] The appearance of these rolls when closed, and the manner of holding them to read from, are very clearly shown in a painting in the "house of the surgeon" at Pompeii, where a man is represented evidently engaged in deep study.

[2] A good representation of a scrinium and scapi, from a painting in the "Casa Falkener," described in the "Museum of Classical Antiquities," vol. ii. p. 54, is given in one of the cubicula of the Pompeian Court at Sydenham.

[3] See Gell's "Pompeiana" Appendix; and the "Memoir of the Canonico Iorio."

"Habeant qui volunt veteres libros vel in membranis purpureis auro argentoque descriptos vel uncialibus, ut vulgo aiunt, literis, onera magis exarata quam codices ; dummodo mihi meisque permittant pauperes habere scedulas, et non tam pulchros codices quam emendatos."

This almost pathetic appeal of the great commentator was scarcely necessary to assure us that such sumptuous volumes were executed for the rich alone, since the value of the gold and vellum, irrespective of the 'labour employed, must necessarily have taken them, as he indicates, altogether out of the reach of the poor. Evidence indeed is not wanting, that many of the Fathers of the Church laboured with their own hands to supply themselves with writings, which no golden letters or purpled vellums could make more valuable to them or their primitive followers : thus, Pamphilus, the martyr, who suffered in the year 309, possessed, in his own handwriting, twenty-five stitched books, containing the works of Origen. St. Ambrose, St. Fulgentius, and others, themselves transcribed many volumes, precious to themselves and most edifying to the faithful. Whatever ornaments or pictures these volumes contained, no doubt reproduced the style of art fostered, if not engendered, in the Catacombs.

Roman illuminated manuscripts would appear, therefore, to have been mainly divisible into two classes ; firstly, those in which the text, simply but elegantly written in perfectly-formed, or rustic, (that is, inclined) capitals, mainly in black and sparingly in red ink, was illustrated by pictures, usually square, inserted in simple frames, generally of a red border only ; and secondly, the richer kind, in which at first gold letters, on white and stained vellum grounds, and subsequently black and coloured letters and ornaments on gold grounds, were introduced. The first of these appears to have been the most ancient style, and to have long remained popular in the Western Empire, while the second, which, as Sir Frederick Madden has observed, no doubt came originally to the Romans from the Greeks, acquired its greatest perfection under the early emperors of the East.

Of both styles there are still extant some invaluable specimens, which, although not of the finest periods of art, may still be regarded as typical of masterpieces which may have existed, and which fire or flood, Goth or Vandal, may have destroyed. Before proceeding, however, to an enumeration of any of these, it may be well to define certain terms which must be employed to designate the peculiarities of character in which the different texts were written, some slight knowledge of which is of great assistance in arriving at an approximate knowledge of the dates at which they may have been executed. Such a definition cannot be more succinctly given than in the following passage, extracted from Mr. Noel Humphrey's interesting work "On the Origin and Progress of the Art of Writing :"—[1]

"Nearly all the principal methods of ancient writing may be divided into square capitals, rounded capitals, and cursive letters ; the square

[1] P. 113. Ingram, Cooke, & Co., London, 1853.

capitals being termed simply *capitals*, the rounded capitals *uncials*, and the small letters, or such as had changed their form during the creation of a running hand, *minuscule*. Capitals are, strictly speaking, such letters as retain the earliest settled form of an alphabet; being generally of such angular shapes as could conveniently be carved on wood or stone, or engraved in metal, to be stamped on coins. The earliest Latin MSS. known are written entirely in capitals, like inscriptions in metal or marble.

"The uncial letters, as they are termed, appear to have arisen as writing on papyrus or vellum became common, when many of the straight lines of the capitals, in that kind of writing, gradually acquired a *curved* form, to facilitate their more rapid execution. However this may be, from the 6th to the 8th, or even 10th century, these uncials or partly-rounded capitals prevail.

"The modern minuscule, differing from the ancient cursive character, appears to have arisen in the following manner. During the 6th and 7th centuries, a kind of transition style prevailed in Italy and some other parts of Europe, the letters composing which have been termed *semi-uncials*, which, in a further transition, became more like those of the old Roman cursive. This manner, when definitively formed, became what is now termed the minuscule manner; it began to prevail over uncials in a certain class of MSS. about the 8th century, and towards the 10th its general use was, with few exceptions, established. It is said to have been occasionally used as early as the 5th century; but I am unable to cite an authentic existing monument. The Psalter of Alfred the Great, written in the 9th century, is in a small Roman cursive hand, which has induced Casley to consider it the work of some Italian ecclesiastic."

To return from this digression on the character of ancient handwriting, to the examples still extant of the two great sections into which the manuscripts of classical ages may be divided, I would observe, that, first in importance and interest of the first class may certainly be reckoned the Vatican square Virgil with miniatures, which has been referred by many of the best palæographers to the 3rd century. It is written throughout in majuscule Roman capitals, which, although MM. Champollion and Sylvestre[1] describe them as of an "elegant but careless form," appeared to me, when I examined the volume minutely in 1846,[2] to exhibit great care and regularity. The miniatures, many engravings from drawings traced from which are given in D'Agincourt's "Histoire de l'Art par les Monuments,"[3] are altogether classical, both in design and in the technical handling of the colours, which are applied with a free brush, and apparently in the true antique manner, *i.e.* with scarcely any previous or finishing outline.

[1] "Universal Palæography," London, Bohn.
[2] Through the kindness of the late Mr. Dennistoun, of Dennistoun, and Cardinal Acton, who obtained the requisite facilities for me.
[3] Tome v. pl. lxv. ; tome iii. p. 29.

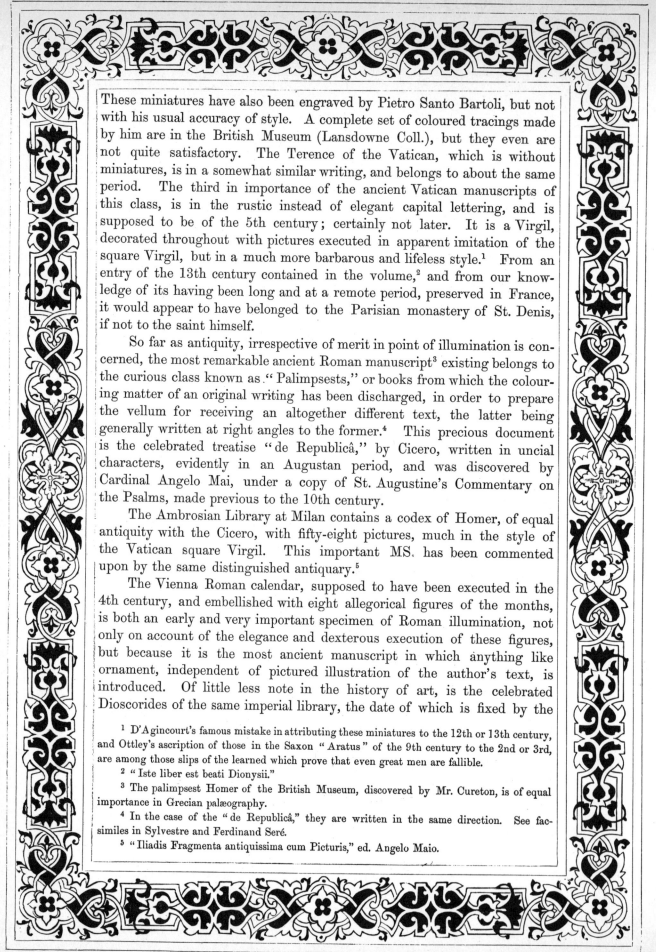

These miniatures have also been engraved by Pietro Santo Bartoli, but not with his usual accuracy of style. A complete set of coloured tracings made by him are in the British Museum (Lansdowne Coll.), but they even are not quite satisfactory. The Terence of the Vatican, which is without miniatures, is in a somewhat similar writing, and belongs to about the same period. The third in importance of the ancient Vatican manuscripts of this class, is in the rustic instead of elegant capital lettering, and is supposed to be of the 5th century; certainly not later. It is a Virgil, decorated throughout with pictures executed in apparent imitation of the square Virgil, but in a much more barbarous and lifeless style.[1] From an entry of the 13th century contained in the volume,[2] and from our knowledge of its having been long and at a remote period, preserved in France, it would appear to have belonged to the Parisian monastery of St. Denis, if not to the saint himself.

So far as antiquity, irrespective of merit in point of illumination is concerned, the most remarkable ancient Roman manuscript[3] existing belongs to the curious class known as "Palimpsests," or books from which the colouring matter of an original writing has been discharged, in order to prepare the vellum for receiving an altogether different text, the latter being generally written at right angles to the former.[4] This precious document is the celebrated treatise "de Republicâ," by Cicero, written in uncial characters, evidently in an Augustan period, and was discovered by Cardinal Angelo Mai, under a copy of St. Augustine's Commentary on the Psalms, made previous to the 10th century.

The Ambrosian Library at Milan contains a codex of Homer, of equal antiquity with the Cicero, with fifty-eight pictures, much in the style of the Vatican square Virgil. This important MS. has been commented upon by the same distinguished antiquary.[5]

The Vienna Roman calendar, supposed to have been executed in the 4th century, and embellished with eight allegorical figures of the months, is both an early and very important specimen of Roman illumination, not only on account of the elegance and dexterous execution of these figures, but because it is the most ancient manuscript in which anything like ornament, independent of pictured illustration of the author's text, is introduced. Of little less note in the history of art, is the celebrated Dioscorides of the same imperial library, the date of which is fixed by the

---

[1] D'Agincourt's famous mistake in attributing these miniatures to the 12th or 13th century, and Ottley's ascription of those in the Saxon "Aratus" of the 9th century to the 2nd or 3rd, are among those slips of the learned which prove that even great men are fallible.

[2] "Iste liber est beati Dionysii."

[3] The palimpsest Homer of the British Museum, discovered by Mr. Cureton, is of equal importance in Grecian palæography.

[4] In the case of the "de Republicâ," they are written in the same direction. See facsimiles in Sylvestre and Ferdinand Seré.

[5] "Iliadis Fragmenta antiquissima cum Picturis," ed. Angelo Maio.

fact of its being enriched with a very graceful portrait of the Empress Juliana Anicia, for whom it is known to have been written at the commencement of the 6th century. Both Lambecius[1] and D'Agincourt give various facsimiles (omitting colour) of the fine illustrations which decorate this remarkable volume.

Another 5th century Virgil of remarkable purity in the text, although without miniatures, is the well-known "Medicean" of the Laurentian Library at Florence. The Paris Prudentius, in elegant rustic capitals of the 6th century, is another fine codex of the same type. There are, in addition to those already cited, various other early texts of the classics contained in the different public libraries of Europe; and it is singular to remark, that (so far as I have been able to ascertain) none of them are embellished with those richer decorations, which appear to have been reserved after the end of the 5th century, for the great text-books of the Christian, and more particularly of the Eastern Church. Of these sacred volumes, that which is generally supposed to be the oldest complete version of the Bible in Greek,[2] is the Codex Alexandrinus of the British Museum, attributed, by consent of all the best Palæographers, to the commencement of the 5th century. It is without gold altogether, and has no other illumination than the occasional contrast of red and black inks, and a line slightly flourished, at the close of each book.[3] The next fragment of the Scriptures, in point of probable date, is the once celebrated Cottonian Genesis, or at least its ghost, for unfortunately a few charred and shrunken fragments are all that have been saved from the disastrous fire which destroyed so many of Sir Robert Cotton's precious volumes in 1731. In its original state, as we know from several collations made previous to the fire, it contained, on 165 pages, no less than 250 miniatures, each about four inches square. Astle[4] has given a facsimile of a page which, on comparison with the existing shrivelled fragments, proves that in their present state they are just about one half their original size. The paintings are in all respects antique, and correspond in general character with cotemporary secular miniatures. Dr. Waagen[5] remarks that "only the hatched gold upon the borders, the glories, and the lights on the crimson mantle indicate the commencement of Byzantine art." The great rival to the "Codex Cottonianus Geneseos" is the "Codex Vindobonensis Geneseos," which consists of twenty-six leaves with eighty-eight miniatures. It forms one of the four great lions of the Vienna Imperial Library. These two remarkable versions of Genesis are supposed to be of nearly equal date, and

---

[1] Petri Lambecii "Commentaria de Bibliotheca Vindobonensi," vol. ii.

[2] The Bible formerly belonging to Theodore Beza, now at Cambridge, and one in the Vatican, are rival claimants to this honour.

[3] It was given to Charles I. of England, by Cyrillus Lucaris, Patriarch of Constantinople.

[4] In his "Origin and Progress of Writing."

[5] "Treasures of Art in Great Britain," vol. i. p. 97.

correspond as to the character of the truly antique miniatures very fairly; the fact, however, of the text of the English version being in black ink with very regularly-formed letters, while that of the Vienna one is, for the most part, written in gold and silver, and in less evenly-distributed characters, induces a fair presumption in favour of the greater antiquity of the Cottonian fragments. In the more gorgeous details of the Vienna Genesis, coupled with its square and unadorned classic pictures, we may thus clearly recognize the transition from our first or Latin class of ancient illumination, to our second or purely Byzantine style. We especially designate this class as "Byzantine," because as art in illumination, as in all other branches, declined in the seven-hilled city, it rose in the seat of empire founded in the East by the first great Christian emperor. It is true that ideal art degenerated almost contemporaneously in the capitals of both empires; but in decorative art, at least, there can be no question but that Byzantium gained, as Rome lost, ground. The former no doubt drew fresh inspiration from her close intercourse with the Persian and other nations of the East, while the latter was content to produce little, and that little in slavish reminiscence of the past. Italy no doubt fed the earliest monastic libraries of Western Europe with the quantities of texts of ancient authors we know them to have contained; but we may fairly assume those texts to have been but rarely illustrated, since the original styles of illumination produced in those countries to which the classic volumes travelled, would unquestionably have betrayed an antique influence more strongly than they did, had the means of deriving that influence been brought copiously within their reach.

I proceed now to a slight notice of the second class of ancient codices, that on which the ultimate splendour of the Byzantine school was founded. Fortunately, time has spared to our days several brilliant specimens of the richest of these quasi-classic manuscripts. Of such, the principal are, as Sir Frederick Madden observes,[1] "the celebrated Codex Argenteus of Ulphilas, written in silver and gold letters on a purple ground, about A.D. 360, which is, perhaps, the most ancient existing specimen of this magnificent mode of caligraphy; after it, may be instanced the copy of Genesis at Vienna," already mentioned, "the Psalter of St. Germain des Prés, and the fragment of the New Testament in the Cottonian Library, Titus C. xv., all executed in the 5th and 6th centuries."

The first-named of these contains, on about 160 leaves, a considerable portion of the four gospels, and is now preserved in the Royal Library of Upsal, in Sweden. It is the earliest version of any part of the sacred writings in the Mœsogothic or ancient Wallachian dialect.[2] The second of Sir Frederick Madden's notabilities has been alluded to as of transition

[1] Text to "Shaw's Illuminated Ornaments," page 4.
[2] For a full description, with references to numerous commentators, see Westwood's "Palæographia Sacra Pictoria," cap. 49.

character. The third, the Psalter of St. Germain des Prés, is ascribed by M. Champollion Figeac, who has given a portion of it in coloured facsimile in the "Moyen Age et la Renaissance"[1] to the 6th century. It is unquestionably a beautiful specimen of gold writing on purple, but neither in the size of the letters nor in the ample spacing of the lines, will it bear comparison with the, no doubt, earlier example, the Cottonian, Titus C. xv. Our greatest authority upon all matters connected with early illuminated versions of the Holy Scriptures, Mr. Westwood, remarks, in speaking of this last-named manuscript, that "Codices purpureo-argentei are much rarer than those in golden writing, the latter material being used not only on purple, but also on white vellum; whereas the silver letters would not easily be legible except on a dark ground. The writing is in very large and massive Greek uncials; the words denoting God, Father, Jesus, Lord, Son, and Saviour, being, for dignity's sake, written in golden letters. The colour of the stain has faded into a dingy reddish purple, and the silver is greatly tarnished and turned black. This fragment is stated by Horne to be one of the oldest (if not the most ancient) manuscripts of any part of the New Testament that is extant, and is generally acknowledged to have been executed at the end of the 4th, or, at the latest, at the beginning of the 5th century; although Dr. Scholz refers it to the 7th or 8th. Casley, however, whose knowledge of the age of manuscripts has never been surpassed, considered that it is as old, or older than the Codex Cottonianus Geneseos; and Mr. Baber is inclined to give it chronological precedency to any previously-named MSS. Dr. Dibdin[2] states, that the writing is executed in the largest Greek capitals which he had ever seen; the Bodleian Library, however, possesses a noble manuscript, written in still larger but narrower characters. The Vatican codices 351 and 1522, of which specimens are given by Blanchini, are also written in larger letters; but these are much more recent than the Cottonian MS."

The Vienna gold, silver, and purple Gospels, the lettering of which corresponds closely with that last described, may be regarded as certainly next in importance, and are of about equal antiquity. In none of these relics of magnificence are we enabled to trace the Eastern or Persian influence, which unquestionably imported a previously unknown originality and character into the art of Byzantium during the reign of Justinian the Great, A.D. 527 to 565. It is, no doubt, true, as Dr. Waagen remarks,[3] that "the style of painting up to his time, both in conception, form, and colour, was much the same as that which has been preserved to us in the paintings at Pompeii; while the spirit of Christianity, operating upon the artistic Greek nature, stimulated it anew to beautiful and original inventions. In a few single instances this style of Art was maintained until the 10th century; but, generally speaking,

[1] Tome ii. article "Manuscrits," fig. 15.　　[2] "Bib. Decam." i. p. 68.
[3] "Treasures of Art in Great Britain," vol. i. p. 96.

a gradual degeneracy ensued, which may be dated from Justinian's period. The proportions of the figures gradually became exaggerated, elongated, the forms contracted with excessive meagreness, the motives of the drapery grew paltry, appearing either in narrow parallel folds stiffly drawn together, or so overladen with barbaric pearls and jewels as to exclude all indication of form. The flesh assumed a dark tone, the other colours became heavy, gaudy, and hard, while in glories, hatchings, and grounds, gold was called into requisition. In these qualities, united to a gloomy and ascetic character of heads, consist the elements of the Byzantine school." But, on the other hand, it is ever to be remembered that the mortification of the old flesh was but a symptom of the more active life beneath it, sloughing off the Pagan tradition, and gradually replacing it by that new and healthy Christian vigour which, for many centuries, nourished and aided the northern and western nations of Europe in their efforts to organize those national styles of Christian Art which are commonly designated as Gothic.[1]

To return to Justinian, and his direct influence on the change of style which took place during his reign, it may be noted as a curious fact, that the year in which the great Church of Sta. Sophia was commenced was the very year in which he concluded an eternal peace with Chosroes Nushirvan, king of Persia. In one or two reigns antecedent to his, Greek artists had been employed in Persia, and there had been a friendly communication between the two countries. It may be therefore assumed, that when Justinian proposed to build this structure in so short a time, he not only enlisted the ability of those about him, but that he recalled those straying Greeks who had gone to seek their fortunes in other countries. He most likely, indeed, employed not only his own subjects, but foreigners; and in that way probably a considerable portion of what no one can fail to recognize as Oriental Art, was mixed with that known as Byzantine. Certain it is that in many of the mosaic ornaments of Sta. Sophia a very marked Oriental character is still to be traced.

On a close comparison of these mosaics[2] with the unique Eusebian Canons on an entirely gold ground, two leaves of which, painted on both sides, are preserved in the British Museum (Addit. No. 5111), and from which the ornaments engraved in our second plate[3] have been copied, the student will certainly, I think, be induced rather to agree with Sir Frederick Madden, in ascribing them to the 6th century, than with Dr. Waagen, who considers that they " can scarcely be older than the 9th century." To the

[1] Dr. Kugler ("Handbuch der Kunstgeschichte," p. 401), in speaking of Anglo-Saxon illuminated manuscripts, observes, "dass wir diese Arbeiten als ein der ersten Zeugnisse des germanischen Kunstgeistes in seiner Selbständigkeit, und zugleich als das Vorspiel oder als den ersten Beginn des romanischen Kunststyles, zu betrachten haben."

[2] As represented in the plates to Salzenberg's fine work, " Alt-Christliche Baudenkmale von Constantinopel, vom V. bis XII. Jahrhundert." Folio, Berlin, 1854.

[3] The whole are given in Shaw's " Illuminated Ornaments," plates 1, 2, 3, and 4.

practical illuminator, these fragments are of far higher importance than all the others to which we have as yet alluded, since, while of equal archæological interest, they constitute the earliest specimens from which really decorative illumination can be studied.[1]

Another illustration of the Eastern influence brought to bear upon Christian manuscripts of the age of Justinian, is furnished by the celebrated Syriac Gospels of the 6th century, written in the year 586 (one-and-twenty years after the emperor's death) by Rabula, a scribe in the monastery of St. John, in Zagba, a city of Mesopotamia, and now preserved in the Laurentian Library at Florence. Mr. Westwood regards this as "so important a manuscript in respect to the history of the arts of illumination and design in the East," and by reflection in the West, that he is induced[2] to give an elaborate description of its embellishments, from which the following is a short extract:—

"The first illumination represents Christ and the twelve apostles seated in a circle, with three lamps burning beneath a wide arch supported by two plain columns, with foliated capitals, and with two birds at the top. The second illumination represents the Virgin and Child standing within a double arch, the columns supporting which are tessellated, and the upper arch with several rows of zigzags, and peacocks standing at the top. The third represents Eusebius and Ammonius standing beneath a kind of tent-like canopy, supported by three columns, with undulated ornament, two peacocks with expanded tails standing at the top. The nineteen following plates are occupied by the tables of the Eusebian Canons, arranged in columns, between pillars supporting rounded arches, generally enclosed between larger and more ornamented columns supporting a large rounded arch, on the outsides of which are represented various groups of figures illustrating scriptural texts, plants, and birds. In some of these, however, the smaller arches are of the horseshoe character. The capitals are, for the most part, foliated; but in one or two they are composed of human faces, and a few of birds' heads. The arches, as well as the columns by which they are supported, are ornamented with chevrons, lozenges, nebules, quatrefoils, zigzags, flowers, fruit, birds, &c.; many of which singularly resemble those found in early Anglo-Saxon manuscripts, especially in the columns supporting the Eusebian Canons in the purple Latin Gospels of the British Museum (MS. Reg. I.E. 6). There is, however, none of the singular interlacing of the patterns so characteristic of the Anglo-Saxon and Irish manuscripts."

I have dwelt thus in detail upon these Greek pictorial and decorative features, because there can be no doubt that the exportation of books so adorned, by the early missionaries, who carried Christianity and a degree

[1] It is on this account that we have refrained from giving any specimens of manuscripts anterior to the 6th century.

[2] "Palæographia Sacra Pictoria," cap. Syriac MSS.

of civilization to the Northern and Western countries, supplied the original types from which, however barbaric the imitations, the first attempts were made to rival, in the extreme West, the arts and spiritual graces of the East. On this plea, I hope I may be pardoned for dwelling yet further upon some of the leading distinctions between the Byzantine and Latin (that is, between the Eastern and Western) modes of working out religious conceptions, which were, that in the Western or Latin mode symbolism was universal ; the art of the Catacombs was followed distinctly, though frequently remotely, developing itself in mythical and ·sentimental forms, and systems of parallelism between type and prototype. In the Greek Church, the exposition of faith, through art, took a more tangible form. Symbolism was avoided on all possible occasions, and the direct representation of sacred themes led to a partial transfer to the representation of the adoration due to the thing represented. Iconoclasm was the reaction to this abuse. In the advanced periods of Greek art, this realistic tendency led to a painful view of the nature of religion, more particularly in connection with the martyrdom of saints, and the physical sufferings of our Saviour and his followers, which are frequently represented in the most positive and often repellent forms.[1]

Long, however, before Byzantine Art had time to deviate much from its ancient traditions, and even while it maintained an easy supremacy over the Western empire, the Lombard kingdom, and all the Visi- and Mœso-Gothic and Frankish races, a formidable competitor for the leadership in the Art of Illumination, had sprung up in the extreme West, in the island homes of the Celtic races.

[1] The artistic peculiarities which specially characterize the march of Greek intellect in the caligraphic direction, have been admirably indicated by Dr. Kugler, in his " Handbook of Painting." " Many of the representations of Byzantine art," he observes, " may be traced back even to classical antiquity (particularly the representations of allegorical figures), and not unfrequently contain very significant and clever motives. But the particular knowledge of nature, that is of the human form, is entirely wanting : this is apparent in the drawing of the naked, and in the folds of drapery, which follow no law of form, but succeed each other in stiff lines, sharp and parallel. The heads do not want character, but the expression is not merely defective, —they have in common something of a spectral rigidity, indicating, in its type-like sameness, a dull servile constraint. The figures are long and meagre in their proportions, and so lifeless in their movements, that they set at defiance even the common law of gravity, and appear to totter on level ground.

" In the Byzantine manuscript miniatures, the execution is generally distinguished by extreme finish, though not by particular harmony of colour. A prevailing greenish-yellow dull tone is peculiar to them : this has been attributed to a more tenacious vehicle,[1] which has also produced a streakiness in the application of the pigment : another peculiarity is the frequent use of gold, particularly in the grounds, which are entirely gilt. This was not the case with the early Italians, who also made use of a lighter and more fluid vehicle."

[1] " Bindemittel.—The technical term for the more or less fluid medium, of whatever kind, with which the colours are mixed, or which serves to dilute them. The two *vehicles* described by an early Florentine painter, Ceunini (· Trattato della Pittura,' p. 70), and which are known to have been very anciently used, would quite account for the difference above alluded to. The Greek paintings on panel were partly done with wax, if an analysis recorded by Morrona ('Pisa Illustrata') was accurate. See Rumorh, ' Ital. Forsch.' i. 312."—Note by the editor, Sir C. L. Eastlake, P.R.A.

It is not necessary now to prove, what historians have freely admitted, that Ireland was certainly christianized for a long time previous to the date of the mission of Augustine to England. The disputes which arose between the followers of that saint and the Irish priests, so soon as they clearly apprehended the nature of the supremacy claimed by the Church of Rome, assure us of their early isolation in the Christian world. Even in their at first entire, and ultimately partial, rejection of the Vulgate text of the Gospels, and their retention of the older versions, from which no doubt their formulas of faith were derived, they steadily maintained their Ecclesiastical freedom from the dogmatism of Rome. As their creed was independent, so was their Art original; nothing resembling it can be traced previous to it. "Thus," as Mr. Westwood declares, "at a period when the fine arts may be said to have been almost extinct in Italy and other parts of the Continent, namely, from the fifth to the end of the eighth century, a style of Art had been established and cultivated in Ireland, absolutely distinct from that of all other parts of the civilized world. There is abundant evidence to prove that in the sixth and seventh centuries the art of ornamenting manuscripts of the Sacred Scriptures, and especially of the Gospels, had attained a perfection in Ireland almost marvellous."

Before proceeding to examine the precise form assumed by this "marvellous perfection," it may be well to remind the student that, with the exception of a few manuscripts decorated in the style of the Laurentian Syriac Gospels and the British Museum golden fragments, the general character of the decoration of all writings, previous to the origination of the Celtic style in Ireland, had been limited to the use of different-coloured, golden, and silver inks, on stained purple and white vellum grounds, to the occasional enlargement of, and slight flourishing about, initial letters; to the introduction of pictures, generally square, or oblong, enclosed in plain, or slightly bordered, frames; and, occasionally, to the scattering about, throughout the volumes, of a few lines and scrolls. Let us now see — in the words of Mr. Westwood, who has done more than any previous writer had done to vindicate the honour of the Irish school of caligraphy[1] — what features of novelty it was mainly reserved for that school to originate. "Its peculiarities,"[2] he states, "consist in the illumination of the first page of each of the Sacred Books,—the letters of the first few words, and more especially the initial, being represented of a very large size, and highly ornamented in patterns of the most intricate design, with marginal rows of red dots; the classical Acanthus being never represented. The principles of these most elaborate ornaments are, however, but few in number, and may be reduced to the four following :—1st. One or more narrow ribbons, diagonally but symmetrically

[1] O'Conor and others were of course earlier in the field.
[2] "Palæographia Sacra Pictoria," Book of Kells, page 1.

interlaced, forming an endless variety of patterns. 2nd. One, two, or three slender spiral lines, coiling one within another till they meet in the centre of the circle, their opposite ends going off to other circles. 3rd. A vast variety of lacertine animals and birds, hideously attenuated, and coiled one within another, with their tails, tongues, and top-knots forming long narrow ribbons irregularly interlaced. 4th. A series of diagonal lines, forming various kinds of Chinese-like patterns. These ornaments are generally introduced into small compartments, a number of which are arranged so as to form the large initial letters and borders, or tessellated pages, with which the finest manuscripts are decorated. The Irish missionaries brought their national style of art with them from Iona to Lindisfarne in the seventh century, as well as their fine, large, very characteristic style of writing; and as these were adopted by their Anglo-Saxon converts, and as most of the manuscripts which have been hitherto described are of Anglo-Saxon origin, it has been the practice to give the name of Anglo-Saxon to this style of art. Thus several of the finest facsimiles given by Astle as Anglo-Saxon, are from Irish manuscripts; and thus Sylvestre, who has copied them (without acknow-ledgment), has fallen into the same error; whilst Wanley, Casley, and others, appear never to have had a suspicion of the existence of an ancient school of art in Ireland."

The monks of Iona, under the great Irish saint and scribe Columba, or Columbkill, and their Anglo-Saxon disciples at Lindisfarne, under his friend St. Aidan, together with the Irish monks at Glastonbury, spread Celtic ornament in England, from whence it had, to a great extent, retired with the expulsion of the ancient British. St. Boniface, the principal awakener of Germany to Christianity, carried with him his singularly-ornamented book of Gospels, which is still preserved as a relic at Fulda. Similar evidence of the transmission of the Art prevalent during the early centuries of the Church in Ireland, to other lands, by means of the missionaries who left her shores, is to be found in the books of St. Kilian, the apostle of Franconia, still preserved at Wurtzburg; in those of St. Gall, now in the public library of St. Gall, in the canton of Switzerland which still bears his name; and in the very important series, of which Muratori has given an interesting catalogue, connected with the monastic institution founded by St. Columbanus, at Bobbio, in Italy, and now principally in the Ambrosian Library at Milan. Many of these pious men were themselves scribes, and their autograph copies of the Holy Gospels are still in existence, with the name of the writers, in some cases, identifying the volumes, and absolutely fixing their date. Thus we have the Gospels of St. Columba, the Leabhar Dhimma, or Gospels of St. Dhimma MacNathi, and the MacRegol Gospels in the Bodleian Library. All of these are anterior to the 9th century, and are distinguished by an elaborate style of ornament unlike any other European type. The extent of influence exercised by these eminent men and the "Episcopi Vagantes," or missionaries, is strongly insisted upon by M. Libri, unquestionably one of the most eminent and correctly-informed bibliographers of the present day. Speaking of the latitudinarianism of some among these Christian men, he observes, "No doubt certain pious but narrow minds hoped to open the door to ecclesiastical literature only; but the exclusion sometimes pronounced against the classics was never general amongst writers who, even in their rudeness, always showed themselves imitators of antiquity. Thus we find that the celebrated manuscript of Livy, in the Imperial Library at Vienna, belonged to Sutbert, an Irish monk, one of those wandering bishops who, towards the close of the seventh century, had gone to preach Christianity, and, as it would seem also, to teach Roman history in Belgium. One cannot help remarking, that the most celebrated of these pious missionaries, St. Columbanus, laid the foundations at Luxeuil in France, at St. Gall in Switzerland, and at Bobbio in Italy, of three monasteries which afterwards became famous for their admirable manuscripts, in many of which the influence of the Irish and Anglo-Saxon schools can be recognized at a glance. The library of St. Gall is too celebrated to require mention. The Bobbio manuscripts are known everywhere by the discoveries which have been made in the *palimpsests* which once belonged to that collection. As for the manuscripts of Luxeuil, they have been dispersed; but the specimens of them which are to be found in the Libri collection, joined to what has been published on the subject by Mabillon, O'Conor, and others, prove unanswerably that in this abbey, as well as in that of Stavelot in Belgium, and other ancient monasteries on the Continent, a school of writing and *miniature* had sprung up as remarkable for the beauty of its caligraphy, as for the care applied to reproduce the forms of the Anglo-Irish schools."[1]

In delicacy of handling, and minute but faultless execution, the whole range of palæography offers nothing comparable to these early Irish manuscripts, and those produced in the same style in England. When in Dublin, some years ago, I had the opportunity of studying very carefully the most marvellous of all—"The Book of Kells;" some of the ornaments of which I attempted to copy, but broke down in despair. Of this very book, Mr. Westwood examined the pages, as I did, for hours together, without ever detecting a false line, or an irregular interlacement. In one space of about a quarter of an inch superficial, he counted, with a magnifying-glass, no less than one hundred and fifty-eight interlacements, of a slender ribbon pattern, formed of white lines, edged by black ones, upon a black ground. No wonder that tradition should allege that these unerring lines should have been traced by angels.[2] However "angelic"

[1] Catalogue of the Libri collection of MSS., Introduction by M. Libri, pages xiv. and xxvi. London, 1859.

[2] Giraldus Cambrensis, speaking probably of this very book, says, "Sin autem ad perspicacius

the ornaments may be, but little can be said in favour of the figure subjects occasionally introduced. In some manuscripts, such as the Book of Kells, in pose and motive it is generally obvious that some ancient model has been held in view; but nothing can be more barbaric than the imitation; while in the other specimens, such as the so-called autograph Gospels of St. Columba, or Columbkill, who died A.D. 594, two years before the advent of St. Augustine—the Book of St. Chads, or the Gospels of MacRegol, — no·such evidence of imitation is to be met with, and the figures are altogether abortive.

I was enabled some years ago, by the kindness of the Rev. J. H. Todd, the learned librarian of Trinity College, Dublin, to compare the so-called autograph Gospels of St. Columba, with the Book of Kells, which is traditionally supposed to have belonged to that saint, and remained strongly impressed with the superior antiquity of the former to the latter. The one may have been his property, and the other illuminated in his honour after his death, as was the case with the Gospels of St. Cuthbert. In none of them, at any period, were shadows represented otherwise than by apparent inlayings under the eyes and beside the nose; and yet, at the same time, the ornaments were most intricate, and often very beautiful, both in form and colour. The purple stain is frequently introduced, and is of excellent quality; but gold appears, so far as I have been able to observe, only in the Durham Book, and in that even most sparingly.[1] From that precious volume several of the subjects on our plate 7th Century, No. 3, and all upon 7th Century, No. 4, have been taken. It is the most celebrated production of the Anglo-Hibernian monastery of Lindisfarne, founded by St. Aidan and the Irish monks of Iona, or Icolumkille, in the year 634.

St. Cuthbert, who was made bishop of Lindisfarne in 685, was renowned as well for his piety as for his learning; he died in 698, and, as a monument to his memory, his successor, Bishop Eadfrith, caused to be written this noble volume, generally called the Durham Book, and known also as St. Cuthbert's Gospels, now in the British Museum. This manuscript, surpassed in grandeur only by the Book of Kells, in the same style, was greatly enriched by Æthelwald, bishop of Lindisfarne, who succeeded Eadfrith in 721, and caused St. Cuthbert's book to be richly illuminated by the hermit Bilfrith, who prefixed an elaborate painting of an Evangelist to each of the four Gospels, and also illuminated the capital letters at the commencement of each book. The bishop caused the whole to be encased in a splendid binding of gold, set with precious stones; and

intuentum oculorum aciem invitaveris, et longe penitus ad artis arcana transpenetraveris, tam delicatas et subtiles, tam actas et arctas, tam nodosas et vinculatim colligatas, tamque recentibus adhuc coloribus illustratas, notare poteris intricaturas, ut vere hæc omnia angelica potius quam humana diligentia jam asseveraveris esse composita."

[1] It is more abundantly used in Vesp. A 1, which, as we shall have occasion to notice hereafter, is in a very mixed style.

in 950, a priest named Aldred rendered the book still more valuable by interlining it with a Saxon version of the original manuscript, which is the Latin text of St. Jerome.

Want of space alone prevents our following Simeon of Durham in his touching narrative of the circumstances which attended the translation of this volume, together with the body of the much-loved saint, to Durham Cathedral, in which both were long and profoundly venerated. The peculiar importance of this volume in the history of Illumination, consists in its clearly establishing, by its coincidence with earlier examples, the class of caligraphy practised by that primitive Church[1] and people, to whom Gregory the Great despatched St. Augustine, at the end of the 6th century. With the mission, which reached its destination, and effected the conversion of Ethelbert and of many of his subjects, in the year 597, Gregory forwarded certain sacred volumes, of which the following were long preserved with the greatest veneration :—A Bible in two volumes; two Psalters; two books of the Gospels; a book of Martyrology; apocryphal Lives of the Apostles, and expositions of certain Epistles and Gospels.

The first — the Bible—which was beautifully written on purple and rose-coloured leaves, with rubricated capitals, was certainly in existence in the reign of James I. Mr. Westwood ("Palæographia Sacra," 1843-45) looks upon the magnificent purple Latin Gospels of the British Museum (Royal Library, 1 E 6) as "no other than the remains of the Gregorian Bible." In this, with the utmost respect for his opinion, I cannot concur, since the fragment exhibits far too many genuine Saxon features to have been possibly executed in the Eastern or Western empires, previous to the date of the mission of St. Augustine. That it may have been produced in this country, in imitation of the more classical original, by the immediate followers of the saint, is, I consider, very highly probable; and from the tenour of Mr. Westwood's recent writing, in the "Archæological Journal," 1859, it may be inferred that his opinion may have been modified since the issue of his profoundly valuable work — the "Palæographia Sacra Pictoria."

The second—the two Psalters—have disappeared. Several learned men have indeed looked upon the British Museum Cottonian MSS. Vesp. A 1, from which our plates 7th Century, Nos. 1 and 2, have been taken, as one of these celebrated books, but, as I venture to think, erroneously; for it is difficult to believe that ornaments, so entirely of the Anglo-Irish school of Lindisfarne, as those we have engraved, could have been executed at Rome during either the 6th or even

[1] Bede expressly says, that at Augustine's synod, held at the commencement of the 7th century, the bishops and learned men attending it, "after a long disputation, refused to comply with the entreaties, exhortations, or rebukes of the saint and his companions, but preferred their own traditions before all the churches in the world, which in Christ agree among themselves."

the 7th century. Nothing is more probable than that, out of the forty persons who are believed to have constituted Augustine's mission, several should have been skilled, as most ecclesiastics then were, in writing and in the embellishment of books; and in any school, established by St. Augustine for the multiplication of those precious volumes, without which ministrations and teachings in consonance with Roman dogmas could not be carried on in the new churches and monastic institutions founded among the converts, it is most likely that the native scribes, on their conversion, should be employed to write and decorate the holy texts, with every ornament excepting those of a pictorial nature. In the execution of these, they could scarcely prove themselves as skilful as the followers of St. Augustine would, from their retention of some classical traditions, be likely to be. Thus, and thus only, as I believe, can we account for the singular combination of semi-antique with Saxon writing, and of Latin body-colour pictures, executed almost entirely with the brush, and regularly shadowed (such as David with his Attendants, in the Vespasian A 1 Psalter), with ornaments of an absolutely different character, such as the arch and pilaster, engraved on our plate 7th Century, No. 2, Fig. 9, which form the framework for the picture of King David. Another argument, which weighs greatly in my mind against the probability of such a Psalter as Vespasian A 1 being a prototype, is the fact, that the Utrecht and Harleian Psalters, to both of which I shall have occasion again to allude, in their pictorial illustrations, present us with evident copies, in outline, of some classic coloured original; just, in fact, of such a manuscript of the Psalms as the celebrated Vatican Roll[1] is of the book of Joshua. What more likely than that one of the venerated Psalters brought from Rome should have been such a manuscript, and should have been the very one copied in the case of the Utrecht Psalter, in the "rustic capitals" of the original, and in the later Harleian replica in the current Saxon uncial?

As respects the third class of Augustinian books—the Gospels—the case is far different; for the accredited and traditional originals are, in every respect, such as would be likely to have been produced at Rome or at Constantinople, but most probably the former, during the pontificate of Gregory the Great. Fragments of the most important of these Gospels are preserved in the library of Corpus Christi College, Cambridge. They are written in black ink generally, with occasional lines in red, in the ancient manner. Two pages only of illuminations are left, though it is evident that the volume once contained a large and complete series. The most important of these represents St. Luke, clad in tunic and toga, seated under just such a triumphal arch as is frequently to be met with in the Roman Mosaics of the 5th and 6th centuries.[2] The second illuminated

---

[1] D'Agincourt, "Painting," plates xxviii. xxix. xxx.
[2] This precious volume and its illustrations were first figured and described by Mr. Westwood.

page comprises a series of small square pictures, framed round with the simple red line of the oldest Latin manuscripts.

The other Augustinian fragmentary Gospel is to be found among the Hatton manuscripts in the Bodleian Library, Oxford: it is without any other illumination than the contrast of red and black ink, and a few ornaments about some of the initial letters. The evidence, upon which it may be assumed that these volumes were either brought to this country by St. Augustine, or formed some of the "codices multos,"[1] sent by Gregory the Great to the mission on its establishment, rests not only upon the antiquity and purely Latin character of the fragments, but on the fact that both Gospels contain entries in Saxon of upwards of one thousand years old, connecting them with the library of the Abbey of St. Augustine at Canterbury; and, furthermore, they correspond with the description given by a monk of that monastery, who, writing in the reign of Henry V., dwells upon the "primitie librorum totius Ecclesie Anglicane" preserved in that library, as the very Gospels in the version of St. Jerome, brought to England by St. Augustine himself.

The Martyrology, the apocryphal Lives of the Apostles, and the Expositions which completed the series, cannot be now identified.

To rapidly multiply copies of these text-books of the Church of Rome, was, no doubt, one of the first and most important duties of the monks of Canterbury; and from the traces we may detect in various manuscripts of the Anglo-Saxon mode of writing and ornamenting writing, combined with paintings such as the Anglo-Saxons were incompetent to execute for some time after the close of the 6th century, we may safely infer that the monks both worked themselves and largely employed the native scribes. Thus, as Mr. Westwood observes in a recent article in the "Archæological Journal," "We have sufficient evidence that, soon after the settlement of the followers of St. Augustine, there must have been established a *scriptorium*, where some of the most beautiful manuscripts were written in the purest uncial or rustic capitals, but decorated with initials in the Anglo-Saxon or Irish style. Of such MSS. we can now record—

"1. The purple Gospels at Stockholm, written in very large uncials, but with illuminated title-pages, with pure Anglo-Saxon ornaments, and grand figures of the Evangelists in a mixed classical and Anglo-Saxon style.

"2. The Utrecht Gospels.

"3. The Gospels in the Cathedral Library, Durham; Astle's " Origin and Progress of Writing," pl. 14, fig. B, p. 83.

"4. The Utrecht Psalter.

"5. The so-called Psalter of St. Augustine, MSS. Cotton., Vespasian, A 1; Astle, pl. 9, fig. 2.

[1] "Life of Gregory the Great," by Johannes Diaconus, lib. ii. cap. 37.

"6. The Bodleian MS. of the Rule of St. Benedict, Lord Hatton's MSS., No. 93; Astle, pl. 9, fig. 1, p. 82.[1]

"Were it not for the initials, and other illuminations in the genuine Anglo-Saxon style, not one of these MSS. would be supposed to be executed in England. They are, nevertheless, among the finest specimens of early caligraphic art in existence."

One of the most important of this interesting class of manuscripts is, unquestionably, that of the Psalms, now preserved in the public library at Utrecht. It was formerly in the possession of Sir Robert Cotton, and should be now with the rest of his library in the British Museum. The volume contains, besides the Psalms, the "Pusillus eram," the Credo, and the Canticles, with a few leaves from the Gospel of St. Matthew. It is written upon vellum, and each psalm has a pen-and-ink illustration, in the same style as those in the Harleian Psalter, No. 603, which was written in the 10th century; and similar also to those in the Cambridge Psalter of the 12th century. The writing in the Utrecht Psalter is executed in Roman rustic capitals; it is arranged in three columns in each page; and the elegance with which the letters are formed, would place the manuscripts amongst those of the 6th or 7th century: but the illustrations before mentioned, with the large uncial B, heightened with gold, in the Saxon interlaced style, which commences the first psalm, would give it a later date, certainly not earlier than the 7th or 8th century; and the pen-and-ink drawings were probably executed a century later.

Mr. Westwood, to whose highly interesting "Archæological Notes of a Tour in Denmark, Prussia, and Holland," published in the "Archæological Journal," I am indebted for the above information, tells us that the date of the few pages of the Gospel, mentioned as being bound up in this volume, is as uncertain as that of the Psalter; the text being written in a style which would place it amongst the works of the 6th or 7th century, whilst the word "Liber," with which it commences, is written in large square Roman capitals, in gold, with the remains of ornament similar to that in the Psalter of St. Augustine. Mr. Westwood says, that the title-page and inscriptions are "written in eight lines, in uncials even larger than those of the Psalter of St. Germain des Près, but enclosed within an ornamental circle, with an interlaced pattern, in the interstices of which is inscribed, ✠ ΑΓΙΑ ΜΑΡΙΑ ΒΟΗΘΗΡΟ ΤΩ ΓΡΑΨΑΝΤΙ."

That which gives, however, its greatest value to the Utrecht Psalter, is the remarkable freedom and cleverness of the pen-and-ink drawings with which it is embellished. In them may be recognized, I believe, the earliest trace of those peculiar fluttered draperies, elongated proportions, and flourished touches, which became almost a distinct style in later Anglo-Saxon illumination. So different is it, both from the Anglo-Hibernian

[1] I trust that ere long Mr. Westwood will add to this list the supposed fragment of the "Biblia Gregoriana," alluded to at page 17 of this essay.

work, prevalent in England up to the advent of St. Augustine, and from the contemporary imitation of the antique, practised by Byzantine, Latin, Lombard, or Frankish illuminators, that the conclusion seems, as it were, forced upon us, that it can have been originated in no other way than by setting the already most skilful penman, but altogether ignorant artist, to reproduce, as he best could, the freely-painted miniatures of the books, sacred and profane, imported, as we know, in abundance, from Rome, during the 7th and 8th centuries.

To so great an extent do antique types and features prevail in the earlier specimens of this class of Anglo-Saxon volumes, that, until comparatively recently, the catalogue of the Utrecht Library has designated the illustrations of the Psalter now under notice, as evidently productions of the reign of Valentinian;[1] while the outline subjects, in a similar style, and of considerably later date, which are introduced in the British Museum "Aratus," were attributed, by even Mr. Ottley's critical judgment, to a somewhat similar period.

The Harleian Psalter (No. 603), to which allusion has been already made, page 18, although written in later characters, is decorated with many pictures, all but identical with those in the Utrecht manuscript, thereby demonstrating, with comparative certainty, that both were taken from some popular prototype, possibly one of the Augustinian Psalters already alluded to.[2]

The Bodleian Cædmon's, or pseudo-Cædmon's, "Metrical Paraphrase of the Book of Genesis," written and illustrated in outline,[3] during the 10th or 11th century, and the Ælfric's Heptateuch of the British Museum, "Cottonian, Claudius B iv.," of a somewhat later date, afford excellent illustrations of the enduring popularity of this peculiar mode of outline drawing. The striking difference may, however, be noted between these later and the earlier specimens in the same style, that whereas the types of the latter are, with scarcely any exception, antique, those of the former are comparatively original, and exhibit that strong inclination to

[1] The words are, "quæ omnia illustrantur Romano habitu, figuris, et antiquitate. Imperatoris Valentiniani tempora videntur attingere." This mistake of the old librarian has been corrected with much care and learning by the Baron van Tiellandt.—See his "Naspeuringen nopens zekeren Codex Psalmorum in de Utrechtsche Boekerij berustende, door W. H. J. Baron van Westreeinen van Tiellandt."

[2] The MS. department of the British Museum possesses some tracings from the Utrecht Psalter, and on confronting them with the Harleian 603, it requires a sharp eye to detect the slight differences existing between several of the illustrations to each of the volumes. In the Harleian volume, all the subjects have not been filled in; some are left out altogether, spaces being reserved for them in the text, and others are faintly traced with a leaden or silver point, preparatory to inking in : very few artists of the present day could block in the general forms in so peculiar a style with greater freedom or more complete conveyance of expression, by similarly slight indications.

[3] The whole of the illuminations are given in the twenty-fourth volume of the "Archæologia." The manuscript stands in the Bodleian Catalogue, "Junius, No. II."

caricature, which has always formed one of the leading features of English illumination.

While, in this class of Anglo-Saxon manuscripts, the influence of Latin art may be traced on the original Hiberno-British school of scribes, a corresponding change was effected, through the introduction into this country of specimens of the more brilliant examples of Byzantine execution or derivation. Thus, as Sir Frederick Madden observes,[1] "The taste for gold and purple manuscripts seems only to have reached England at the close of the 7th century, when Wilfrid, archbishop of York, enriched his church with a copy of the Gospels thus adorned; and it is described by his biographer, Eddius (who lived at that period or shortly after), as 'inauditum ante seculis nostris quoddam miraculum,'—almost a miracle, and before that time unheard of in this part of the world. But in the 8th and 9th centuries the art of staining the vellum appears to have declined, and the colour is no longer the same bright and beautiful purple, violet, or rose-colour of the preceding centuries. It is rare, also, to meet with a volume stained throughout; the artist contenting himself with colouring a certain portion, such as the title, preface, or canon of the mass. Manuscripts written in letters of gold, on white vellum, are chiefly confined to the 8th, 9th, and 10th centuries. Of these, the Bible and Hours of Charles the Bald, preserved in the Royal Library at Paris, and the Gospels of the Harleian collection, No. 2788, are probably the finest examples extant. In England, the art of writing in gold seems to have been but imperfectly understood in early times, and the instances of it very uncommon. Indeed, the only remarkable one that occurs of it is the Charter of King Edgar to the new minster at Winchester, in the year 966. This volume is written throughout in gold."

Although but few books were thus gorgeously written, many were sumptuously decorated; and, indeed, there exist no more brilliant volumes than some of those produced by Anglo-Saxon scribes. Of these many exist; but if two or three only are noticed, it will be quite sufficient to establish the leading characteristics of the school, which appears to have been organized under St. Ethelwold, bishop of Winchester, at New Minster, or Hyde Abbey, near Winchester, during the 10th century. The names of several leading masters of that great nursery of illumination have been handed down to us. Thus Ethric and Wulfric—monks—are recorded as having been "painters;" but Godwin is spoken of as the greatest of all. Fortunately, a magnificent specimen of his art is preserved in the celebrated benedictional of St. Ethelwold, in the library of the Duke of Devonshire, and engraved *in extenso*, with great care, in the twenty-fourth volume of the "Archæologia."[2] This is one of the most sumptuous

[1] Introduction to Shaw's "Illuminated Ornaments," pages 4 and 5.

[2] The following inscription, written in letters of gold on the reverse of the fourth leaf and the bottom of the recto of the fifth, identifies both the artist and the patron under whose

manuscripts which has been executed in any age by any scribe, and differs widely from the Anglo-Saxon MSS. previously described. The text is generally enclosed within a rich framework, formed by wide and solid bars of gold, about and over which twine and break elegantly-shaded masses of conventional foliation. In the initial letters, and occasionally in the ornament, the peculiarly Saxon interlacing and knotwork is retained; but, in most of the embellishments, a reaction can be traced from the Carlovingian manuscripts themselves, originally acted upon, as will be hereafter seen, by the Saxon school of caligraphy.[1] The figure subjects in this volume are cramped in style and action, exhibit but little classical influence, and possess, as a leading merit, only a singularly sustained brilliancy of tint and even execution throughout.

Next to this great masterpiece, and from the same fountain-head, come the following, several of which are exceedingly beautiful: — The two Rouen Gospels; the Gospels of King Canute, in the British Museum, Reg. D 9, (plate 10th Century, No. 4); the Cottonian Psalter, Tib. C vi.; the Hyde Abbey Book, lately in the Stowe Library; and the Gospels of Trinity College, Cambridge. The ornaments in all these volumes are painted in thick body-colours, and with a vehicle so viscid in texture, that Dr. Dibdin[2] infers from its character, as evidenced in the Benedictional, "the possibility or even probability of oil being mixed up in the colours of the more ancient illuminations." In this opinion I do not concur, as I believe the peculiar body and gloss of the pigment to be produced by the use of white of egg.

I have dwelt in some detail upon Saxon illumination, for two reasons: firstly, because it is a theme on which some national self-gratulation may be justifiably entertained;[3] and, secondly, because it is one on which,

auspices the volume was executed, between the years 970 and 984, the term of Ethelwold's occupation of the see of Winchester :—

"Presentem Biblum jussit perscribere Presul
Wintoniæ Dñs quē fecerat esse Patronum
Magnus *Æthelwoldus*   *   *   *
*   *   *   *   *   *   *

Atque Patri magno jussit qui scribere librum hunc
Omnes cernentes biblum hunc semper rogitent hoc
Post meta carnis valeam celis in herere
Obnixe hoc rogitat Scriptor supplex *Godemann*."

[1] If the celebrated coronation book of the Anglo-Saxon kings (see plate 9th Century, No. 1), should turn out to have been written and illuminated in this country, it would afford a striking illustration of this reaction. The general opinion, however, appears to be, among the learned, that it may have been given to Athelstan by Otho of Germany, who married his sister, and by Matilda, Otho's mother. The arguments in favour of, and against, the Anglo-Saxon origin of the volume would be too long to discuss in this place. The writing is mainly Carlovingian.

[2] "Bib. Dec." vol. i. p. cxxii.

[3] It is to be regretted that the propriety of those just and learned remarks of Muratori, in which he exhibited himself as one of the earliest foreign scholars inclined to do justice to the

although much has been written, comparatively little light has as yet been thrown. Before leaving it, however, some general observations should be made upon the classes of books most in demand, and the means by which they were multiplied in this country; and, indeed, with slight local differences, on the great continent of Europe as well, — Byzantium, Ravenna, Rome, Monte Cassino, Subiaco, Paris, Tours, Limoges, Arles, Soissons, Blois, Aix-la-Chapelle, Cologne, Hildesheim, Worms, Treves, Glastonbury, Canterbury, Winchester, York, Durham, Lindisfarne, Wearmouth, Jarrow, Croyland, and Peterborough, being the great centres of production.

From the earliest period religious zeal was much shown in its offerings to the Church, by laymen, more or less pious, — the least pious being, in fact, sometimes the most liberal donors, — and very large sums were expended in illuminating and ornamenting manuscripts for that purpose. Many of these books were remarkable for the extreme beauty of the paintings and ornamental letters enriched with gold and silver, which decorate them, as well as for the execution of the writing, the most precious bindings frequently adding greatly to their cost. Gospels, books of anthems, and Missals, were most frequently chosen for such gifts; but they were not confined to sacred subjects, including occasionally the best writings of Greece and Rome, which were eagerly sought after as models of eloquence, and, still more, as often being supposed to contain prophecies of the coming of Christ, and proofs of the truths of his doctrines.

The piety of individuals often led them to expend large sums in the preparation of their offerings to the Church; the finest and best parchment which could be procured, being used for manuscripts. When black ink was used in liturgical writings, the title-page and heads of the chapters were written in *red ink;* whence comes the term Rubric. Green, blue, and yellow inks were used, sometimes for words, but chiefly for ornamental capital letters; the writers and miniature-painters exercising their own taste and judgment in the decoration, and heightening its effect with gold and the most expensive colours, such as azure and the purest cinnabar.

The greater part of these works were intrusted to monks and their clerks, who were exhorted, by the rules of their order, to learn writing, and to persevere in the work of copying manuscripts, as being one most acceptable to God; those who could not write being recommended to learn to bind books. Alcuin entreats all to employ themselves in copying books, saying, " It is a most meritorious work, more useful to the health than

ancient Irish and British schools,—" Neque enim silenda laus Britanniæ, Scotiæ, et Hiberniæ, quæ studio liberalium artium eo tempore antecellebant reliquis occidentalibus regnis; et cura præsertim monachorum, qui literarum gloriam, alibi aut languentem aut depressam, in iis regionibus impigrè suscitarent atque tuebantur " (Murat. " Antiq. Ital." diss. 43),—should have been impugned by the Rev. Mr. Berington in his " Literary History of the Middle Ages," pages 180, 181.

working in the fields, which profits only a man's body, whilst the labour of a copyist profits his soul."[1]

Home production could, however, by no means suffice to multiply books, and especially religious books, with sufficient rapidity to satisfy the eager demand for them. Long journeys appear to have been taken to foreign countries, by learned ecclesiastics, for scarcely any other purpose than the collection of manuscripts; while quantities were imported into England from abroad. Thus Bede tells us, that Wilfrid, bishop of Wearmouth and Jarrow, and Acca, Wilfrid's successor, collected many books abroad for their libraries, at the end of the 7th century. Thus Theodore of Tarsus brought back an extensive library of Grecian and Roman authors, on his return to Canterbury, in 668, from a mission to Rome; and thus, as we are told by Mr. Maitland,[2] when "Aldhelm, who became Bishop of Schireburn in the year 705, went to Canterbury, to be consecrated by his old friend and companion Berthwold (pariter literis studuerant, pariterque viam religionis triverant), the archbishop kept him there many days, taking counsel with him about the affairs of his diocese. Hearing of the arrival of the ships at Dovor during this time, he went there to inspect their unloading, and to see if they had brought anything in his way (si quid forte commodum ecclesiastico usui attulissent nautæ qui e Gallico sinu in Angliam provecti librorum copiam apportassent). Among many other books, he saw one containing the whole of the Old and New Testaments, which he at length bought: and William of Malmesbury, who wrote his life in the 12th century, tells us it was still preserved at that place."

How deeply must all lovers of illumination regret the infinite destruction of books that has prevailed in all ages! Of all this "librorum copiam," how few survive. Even in the days of Alfred the Great, the Danes had destroyed the majority of them; for, as that great royal Bibliomaniac exclaims, in his preface to the "Pastoral of Gregory,"—"I saw, before all were spoiled and burnt, how the churches throughout Britain were filled with treasures and books."

I now leave our own country for a while, and return to the general continent of Europe; having, I trust, satisfactorily established

[1] These pious monks, until probably some time after the Norman conquest, generally worked together in an apartment capable of containing many persons, and in which many persons did, in fact, work together at the transcription of books. The first of these points is implied in a curious document, which is one of the very few extant specimens of French Visi-Gothic MS. in uncial characters, of the 8th century. It is a short but beautiful form of consecration or benediction, barbarously entitled "Orationem in Scripturio," and is to the following effect: "Vouchsafe, O Lord, to bless this Scriptorium of thy servants, and all that dwell therein; that whatsoever sacred writing shall be here read or written by them, they may receive with understanding, and bring the same to good effect, through our Lord," &c.—See Merryweather's "Bibliomania in the Middle Ages."

[2] "Dark Ages," second edition, p. 193.

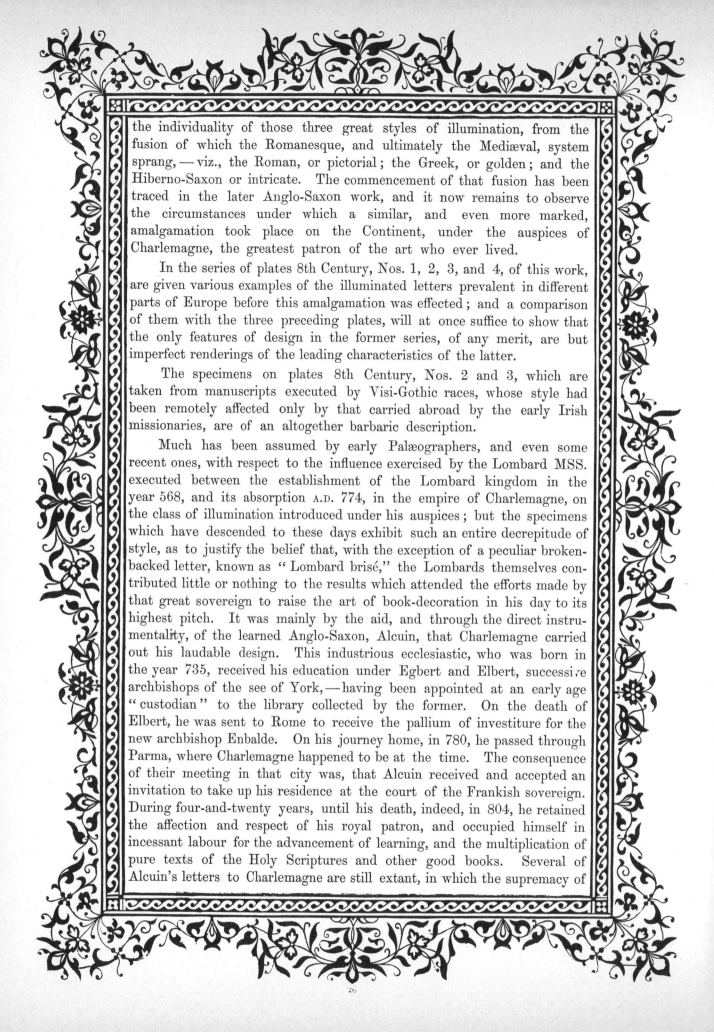

the individuality of those three great styles of illumination, from the fusion of which the Romanesque, and ultimately the Mediæval, system sprang, — viz., the Roman, or pictorial; the Greek, or golden; and the Hiberno-Saxon or intricate. The commencement of that fusion has been traced in the later Anglo-Saxon work, and it now remains to observe the circumstances under which a similar, and even more marked, amalgamation took place on the Continent, under the auspices of Charlemagne, the greatest patron of the art who ever lived.

In the series of plates 8th Century, Nos. 1, 2, 3, and 4, of this work, are given various examples of the illuminated letters prevalent in different parts of Europe before this amalgamation was effected; and a comparison of them with the three preceding plates, will at once suffice to show that the only features of design in the former series, of any merit, are but imperfect renderings of the leading characteristics of the latter.

The specimens on plates 8th Century, Nos. 2 and 3, which are taken from manuscripts executed by Visi-Gothic races, whose style had been remotely affected only by that carried abroad by the early Irish missionaries, are of an altogether barbaric description.

Much has been assumed by early Palæographers, and even some recent ones, with respect to the influence exercised by the Lombard MSS. executed between the establishment of the Lombard kingdom in the year 568, and its absorption A.D. 774, in the empire of Charlemagne, on the class of illumination introduced under his auspices; but the specimens which have descended to these days exhibit such an entire decrepitude of style, as to justify the belief that, with the exception of a peculiar broken-backed letter, known as "Lombard brisé," the Lombards themselves contributed little or nothing to the results which attended the efforts made by that great sovereign to raise the art of book-decoration in his day to its highest pitch. It was mainly by the aid, and through the direct instrumentality, of the learned Anglo-Saxon, Alcuin, that Charlemagne carried out his laudable design. This industrious ecclesiastic, who was born in the year 735, received his education under Egbert and Elbert, successive archbishops of the see of York, — having been appointed at an early age "custodian" to the library collected by the former. On the death of Elbert, he was sent to Rome to receive the pallium of investiture for the new archbishop Enbalde. On his journey home, in 780, he passed through Parma, where Charlemagne happened to be at the time. The consequence of their meeting in that city was, that Alcuin received and accepted an invitation to take up his residence at the court of the Frankish sovereign. During four-and-twenty years, until his death, indeed, in 804, he retained the affection and respect of his royal patron, and occupied himself in incessant labour for the advancement of learning, and the multiplication of pure texts of the Holy Scriptures and other good books. Several of Alcuin's letters to Charlemagne are still extant, in which the supremacy of the English schools and libraries is distinctly recognized, as well as the direct influence exercised by them on Frankish literature, and, as in those days literature and illumination were inseparable, on illumination also. Thus, in one place he begs his master to give him "those exquisite books of erudition which I had in my own country by the good and devout industry of my master Egbert, the archbishop." Again, referring to the same "treasures of wisdom," he proposes, — "If it shall please your wisdom, I will send some of our boys, who may copy from thence whatever is necessary, and carry back into France the flowers of Britain; that the garden may not be shut up in York, but the fruits of it may be placed in the paradise of Tours."

One of the evidences of the eagerness with which this task of multiplying the sources of learning was carried on, is to be found in the attempts made to abridge and expedite labour. Thus, as M. Chassant[1] observes in his useful little manual of abbreviations[2] used during the Middle Ages, the texts of all documents of importance were comparatively free from contractions from the period when Justinian the Great banished them, by an imperial edict, from all legal instruments, until the accession of Charlemagne, "during whose reign, either to save time or vellum, the scribes revived the ancient Roman practice of using initials, and frequently arbitrary signs, to represent whole words of frequent recurrence."

It is, however, in the quality, rather than the quantity, of Carlovingian MSS. that the reader is most likely to be interested; and I therefore hasten to note two or three of the most imposing specimens. The earliest of the grand class is believed to be the Evangelistiarium, long preserved in the Abbey of St. Servin, at Toulouse, and ultimately presented to Napoleon I., on the baptism of the King of Rome, in the name of the city. From contemporary entries, it appears to have been completed, after eight years' labour, in the year 781, by the scribe Godescalc. Of whatever nation "Godescalc" may have been, the volume[3] exhibits far too many composite features to justify the belief that any one individual, or even many individuals of one nation, could have executed the whole. The paintings are probably by an Italian hand, being executed freely with the brush, in opaque colours, in the antique manner. Many of the golden borders are quite Greek in style, while the initial letters, and others of the borders, are thoroughly Hiberno-Saxon. A nearly similar dissection would apply to most of the manuscripts executed for Charlemagne's descendants, to the third generation. The volume contains 127 leaves, every leaf, not entirely filled with illumination, being stained purple, with a white margin, and covered with a text, written in golden initials, in two columns,

[1] Librarian of the town of Evreux. [2] Cornemillot, Evreux, 1846.

[3] Du Sommerard, in "Les Arts du Moyen Age," has given copies of all the illuminations, and Mr. Westwood a page of specimens.

separated by very graceful and delicately-executed borders. Our plates 8th century, Nos. 5 and 6, give a good idea of the nature of the ornament usually employed in similar MSS. to fill up such borders and initial letters.

From Charlemagne's "Scriptorium," which was no doubt the head-quarters of the best artists of all nations in his time, proceeded many other volumes of scarcely less interest and magnificence. Among these, the most noteworthy are, the Gospels of St. Medard de Soissons,[1] so called because believed to have been presented by Charlemagne to that Abbey;[2] the Vienna Psalter, written for Pope Hadrian; the Gospels preserved in the library of the arsenal at Paris, and formerly belonging to the Abbaye of St. Martin des Champs;[3] the Gospels found upon the knees of the Emperor on opening his tomb at Aix-la-Chapelle; the Harleian MS. No. 3788, known as the "Codex Aureus;[4] and last, not least, the Bible, known as that of San Calisto, preserved in the Benedictine monastery of that saint at Rome, and formerly in the monastery of San Paolo fuori le Mura. The frontispiece to this volume, which is no less than one foot four inches high, by one foot one inch wide, represents a sitting emperor holding a globe, on which are inscribed various letters, arranged in the peculiar form adopted by Charlemagne in his signs manual.

The learned have disputed hotly whether this portrait is intended for that of Charlemagne, or of Charles the Bald, his grandson. Whether this manuscript, which, in all respects, except beauty in the figure-subjects, I look upon as the finest I have ever seen, was executed in the days of the former or latter monarch, is of no very great moment, as its leading features would harmonize very well with accredited reliques of either. It still contains no less than 339 pages, and is one blaze of illumination from the first page to the last.[5] The large initial letters are quite Saxon in form; the borders, of which there are endless and beautiful varieties, are more strictly classic in character than is usual in Caroline manuscripts; and the pictures are in an indeterminate style, between Greek, Latin, and that original Frankish, which subsequently absorbed in Western Europe all previous tradition, and grew into the peculiar type of French 12th century work—the progenitor of the pure Gothic of the 13th.

Ample materials happily exist for tracing the gradual development of this Frankish element; at first through the works of the immediate

[1] Count Bastard gives no less than six grand facsimiles from this volume, which is one of the greatest lions of the Bibliothèque Impériale at Paris.

[2] One of the most curious illuminations in the book, the celebrated "fontaine mystique" of the church, is altogether antique in style and execution.

[3] The colouring in this MS. is very elegant, being mainly restricted to gold, purple, white, and a little very brilliant vermilion ;—the forms are principally Saxon.

[4] Described at length by Dr. Waagen, "Treasures of Art in Great Britain," pages 104—106.

[5] Many illustrations, but unfortunately without colour, are given by D'Agincourt, "Pittura," plates 40 to 45 inclusive.

descendants of Charlemagne, and subsequently through various liturgical works, collected from suppressed abbeys, and preserved for the most part in the Imperial library at Paris. Of these, some of the most important are, the Bible of Louis le Debonnaire, executed in the eighth year of his reign;[1] the Gospels of the same monarch;[2] and the Sacramentaire de Metz,[3]—all produced for sons of Charlemagne. The first-named is of the barbaric style, on which Alcuin and others improved; the second contains some very curious symbolic initial letters; and the third, a good deal of originality, both in ornaments and figures.

The principal volumes still preserved, once belonging to the grandsons of Charlemagne, appear less original in several respects, than do those executed for his sons. Thus, in the case of Louis le Debonnaire's eldest son Lothaire, whose Gospels,[4] written and decorated at the Abbey of St. Martin, at Tours, exhibit a mixed Latin and Saxon style, with but little specifically Frankish work,—and thus also in the person of Lothaire's youngest brother, Charles the Bald, whose two celebrated Bibles, the one known as the Bible of St. Denis, and the other as that presented to the monarch by Count Vivien, abbot of the same monastery at which the Gospels of Lothaire were executed,—illustrate a similar composite, but scarcely original, style. The former manuscript is illuminated with intertwined lacertine monsters, knotwork, single (but not the three-whorl) spirals, and rows of red dots following many of the leading outlines, all of which may be regarded as distinctive features of the Hiberno-Saxon school; while the latter, with several of the above peculiarities freely introduced, combines an unmistakable classicality, shown in the various figure-subjects, and especially in the arcading which encloses the Eusebian Canons at the commencement of the volume.[5]

We can feel but little surprise at the production of such works at the Abbey of St. Martin, at Tours, for it was within the walls of that "Paradise," as Alcuin calls it, that the Saxon sage gave all the latter years of his life to the recension of the Holy Scriptures,[6] and to the organization of a "scriptorium" worthy of his affectionate patron.

[1] See plates 9th Century, No. 2, figs. 1, 2, 3, 4, 5, 6.
[2] See plates 9th Century, No. 3.
[3] See plates 9th Century, No. 4, figs. 1, 2, 3, 5.
[4] See plates 9th Century, No. 3; and 9th Century, No. 5, fig. 7.
[5] The specimens engraved on plate 10th Century, No. 1, from the fragments of a Bible illuminated for Charles the Bald, and preserved in the British Museum (Harl. 7551), are completely Saxon in general form and style.
[6] The folio Vulgate (B. M. Addl. MSS. No. 10546) purchased by the British Museum authorities from M. Speyer Passavant, of Basle, in 1836, for £750, was considered by its late possessor to have been the original transcript "diligently emended" by Alcuin himself, for presentation to Charlemagne on his coronation as Emperor of Rome, in the year 800. It is a very fine and interesting volume, but has been referred by more recent authorities to the reign of Charles the Bald. Mr. Westwood, however, considers that "it appears to have better claims than any of the several Caroline Bibles now in existence, to be considered as the volume so

The impulse given to the Art of Illumination in that celebrated establishment was speedily communicated to rival scriptoria in other localities; thus from the abbeys of St. Martial, at Limoges, from Metz, Mans, St. Majour in Provence, Rheims, St. Germain and St. Denis at Paris, issued, from the age of Charlemagne to the 13th century, an almost uninterrupted series of highly-illuminated volumes, many of which still remain to attest the vigorous efforts by which the foreign elements were gradually thrown aside in France, to make way for that expressive and original outline style [1] which achieved its greatest power in the early part of the 13th century. The throes and struggles by which this was achieved, are singularly well shown by a page engraved in Count Bastard's splendid work from the "Apocalypse of St. Sever," written during the first half of the 11th century. The page presents a curious emblematical frontispiece, the general form of which is perfectly Oriental; the border ornaments are founded on Cufic inscriptions; the animals which decorate the Arabian framework are classical; and the interlacing fretwork of several portions of the design is purely Saxon.

Many Byzantine features were brought into French illumination through the schools at St. Martial's and the other abbeys of Limoges, but it was at Paris itself that the greatest changes and improvements were effected; thus, at St. Germain and St. Denis were produced, during the first half and middle of the 11th century, two volumes, still existing in the Imperial Library of France, which distinctly show the germination of "Gothic." The St. Germain "Mysteries of the Life of Christ" is illustrated by many original and very spirited outline compositions, some of which are slightly coloured; while the "Missal of St. Denis," of a few years later, displays that peculiar grace and *naïveté* in the action and expression of the figures, together with that soft elegance in foliated ornament, which for several centuries remained a dominant excellence in the best French illuminations.

As classical tradition and Hiberno-Saxon intricacies died out in France to make way for the true Mediæval styles, so did they, although somewhat more slowly, in England, Germany, Spain, and the Netherlands. In Italy, a degeneracy occurred, from which the revival at length, under Cimabue and Giotto, was as rapid and brilliant as the previous collapse appears to have been fatal. [2]

presented." Its chief rival is the great Bible of the Fathers of Sta. Maria, in Vallicella, at Rome. Sir Frederick Madden has entered into a minute analysis of the claims of the Speyer Passavant volume, in a series of most learned articles in the "Gentleman's Magazine" for 1836. See also Westwood's "Palæographia Sacra," and the pamphlet, by its late possessor, J. H. de Speyer Passavant, "Description de la Bible écrite par Alchuine, &c." Par. 1829, pp. 112.

[1] It is singular, considering how generally Hiberno-Saxon ornament was adopted by continental illuminators, that the peculiar Saxon *fluttering* outline never obtained a footing.

[2] The learned and most eloquent author of the "Poésie Chrétienne," M. Rio (from whom it was my privilege, while yet a youthful student, to receive many a valuable lesson), in noting this

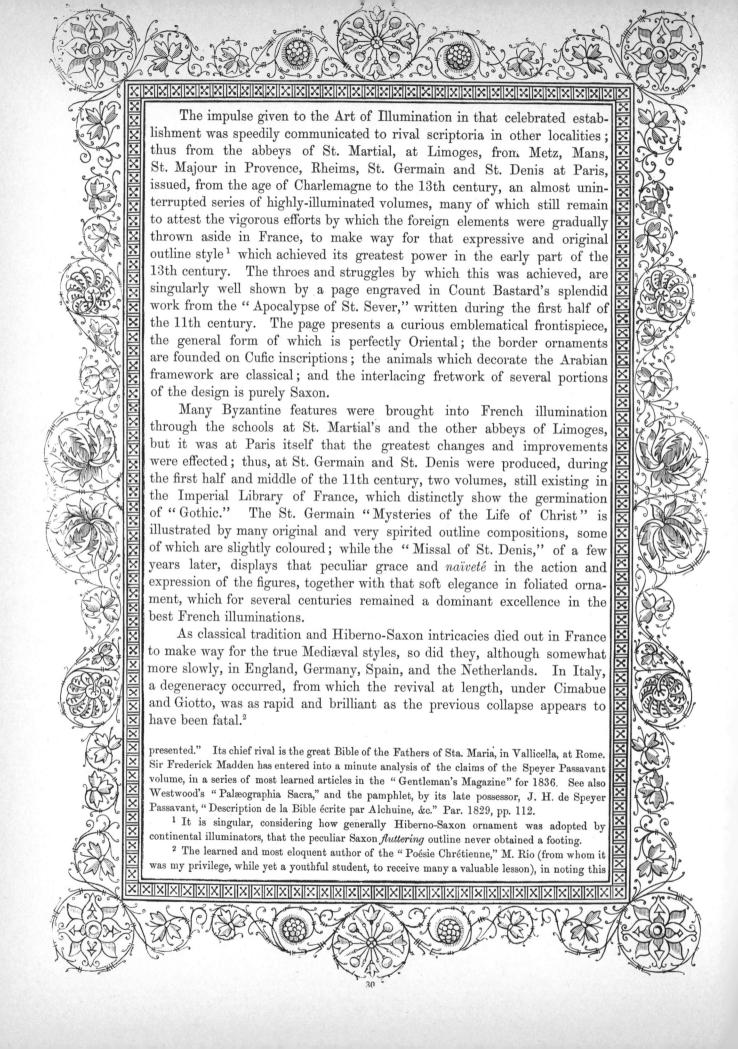

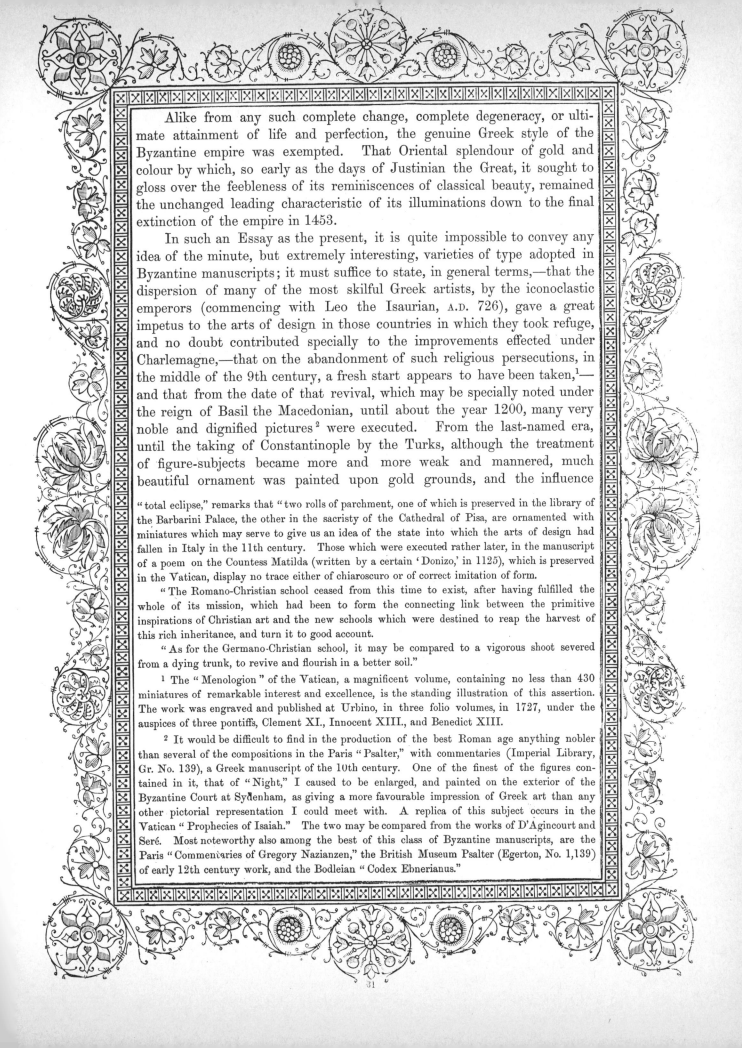

Alike from any such complete change, complete degeneracy, or ultimate attainment of life and perfection, the genuine Greek style of the Byzantine empire was exempted. That Oriental splendour of gold and colour by which, so early as the days of Justinian the Great, it sought to gloss over the feebleness of its reminiscences of classical beauty, remained the unchanged leading characteristic of its illuminations down to the final extinction of the empire in 1453.

In such an Essay as the present, it is quite impossible to convey any idea of the minute, but extremely interesting, varieties of type adopted in Byzantine manuscripts; it must suffice to state, in general terms,—that the dispersion of many of the most skilful Greek artists, by the iconoclastic emperors (commencing with Leo the Isaurian, A.D. 726), gave a great impetus to the arts of design in those countries in which they took refuge, and no doubt contributed specially to the improvements effected under Charlemagne,—that on the abandonment of such religious persecutions, in the middle of the 9th century, a fresh start appears to have been taken,[1]— and that from the date of that revival, which may be specially noted under the reign of Basil the Macedonian, until about the year 1200, many very noble and dignified pictures[2] were executed. From the last-named era, until the taking of Constantinople by the Turks, although the treatment of figure-subjects became more and more weak and mannered, much beautiful ornament was painted upon gold grounds, and the influence

"total eclipse," remarks that "two rolls of parchment, one of which is preserved in the library of the Barbarini Palace, the other in the sacristy of the Cathedral of Pisa, are ornamented with miniatures which may serve to give us an idea of the state into which the arts of design had fallen in Italy in the 11th century. Those which were executed rather later, in the manuscript of a poem on the Countess Matilda (written by a certain 'Donizo,' in 1125), which is preserved in the Vatican, display no trace either of chiaroscuro or of correct imitation of form.

"The Romano-Christian school ceased from this time to exist, after having fulfilled the whole of its mission, which had been to form the connecting link between the primitive inspirations of Christian art and the new schools which were destined to reap the harvest of this rich inheritance, and turn it to good account.

"As for the Germano-Christian school, it may be compared to a vigorous shoot severed from a dying trunk, to revive and flourish in a better soil."

[1] The "Menologion" of the Vatican, a magnificent volume, containing no less than 430 miniatures of remarkable interest and excellence, is the standing illustration of this assertion. The work was engraved and published at Urbino, in three folio volumes, in 1727, under the auspices of three pontiffs, Clement XI., Innocent XIII., and Benedict XIII.

[2] It would be difficult to find in the production of the best Roman age anything nobler than several of the compositions in the Paris "Psalter," with commentaries (Imperial Library, Gr. No. 139), a Greek manuscript of the 10th century. One of the finest of the figures contained in it, that of "Night," I caused to be enlarged, and painted on the exterior of the Byzantine Court at Sydenham, as giving a more favourable impression of Greek art than any other pictorial representation I could meet with. A replica of this subject occurs in the Vatican "Prophecies of Isaiah." The two may be compared from the works of D'Agincourt and Seré. Most noteworthy also among the best of this class of Byzantine manuscripts, are the Paris "Commentaries of Gregory Nazianzen," the British Museum Psalter (Egerton, No. 1,139) of early 12th century work, and the Bodleian "Codex Ebnerianus."

originally communicated to Arabian art from the Eastern Empire, was reflected back upon its later productions from the contemporary schools of Saracenic and Moorish decoration.[1] It is scarcely necessary to remark, that in all these inflexions of style the Russian, Syrian, and Armenian illuminators closely followed the example set them by the Byzantine scribes and painters.

Returning from the East to the extreme west of Europe, it is worthy of note how entirely the primitive Saxon styles, which wrought so important an influence upon the rest of Europe, were lost in the country from which they had been mainly promulgated. The successive social and political changes wrought by the ascendancy of the Danes, and ultimately of the Normans, put an almost total stop to Saxon illumination; and so complete was the abandonment of the Saxon character, that Ingulphus, in describing the fire which destroyed the noble library of his abbey at Croyland, in the year 1091, after dwelling on the splendour of the "chirographs written in the Roman character, adorned with golden crosses and most beautiful paintings," and especially "the privileges of the kings of Mercia, the most ancient and the best, in like manner beautifully executed with golden illuminations, but written in the Saxon character," goes on to state: "All our documents of this kind, greater and less, were about four hundred in number; and in one moment of a most dismal night, they were destroyed and lost to us by this lamentable misfortune. A few years before, I had taken from our archives a good many chirographs, written in the Saxon character, because we had duplicates, and in some cases triplicates, of them; and had given them to our Cantor, Master Fulmar, to be kept in the cloister, to help the juniors to learn the Saxon character, because that letter had for a long while been despised and neglected by reason of the Normans,[2] and was now known only to a few of the more aged; that so the younger ones, being instructed to read this character, might be more competent to use the documents of their monastery against their adversaries in their old age."

The Normans, a warlike but unlettered race, did but little for the first century after the Conquest, to restore the taste for learning which they and the Danes had displaced. While English progress in illumination was thus comparatively paralyzed, in France and Germany new styles, corresponding with those known in architecture as Romanesque, rapidly sprang into popularity. The plates in this work, 11th Century, Nos. 2 and 3,[3]

[1] Of this ornamental style the most remarkable specimens are the Vatican "Acts of the Apostles," and a beautiful volume in the library of the Duke of Hamilton. From the former, I have given some facsimiles in "The Geometrical Mosaics of the Middle Ages" (plate 20), in order to show the similarity of design between the gold ground mosaics of the Greeks and early Italians, and the embellishments of the illuminated manuscripts of the former.

[2] Ingulphus was at that very time indebted directly to the Conqueror, his early patron, for his abbacy.

[3] From the Harleian MS. No. 7183.

show the combination, with reminiscences of Carlovingian knotted ends to the initial letters, of foliated ornament, such as in the subsequent plates 12th Century, Nos. 3,[1] 4,[2] 5,[3] 6, 7, may be found developed, in Germany especially, into a fresh, luxuriant, and complete system. The complicated conventionality of foliage shown in these specimens, and greatly encouraged by the Emperor Frederick Barbarossa, A.D. 1152 to 1190, was never entirely abandoned by the Germans in their ornament; and at the end of the 13th and early part of the 14th centuries, when France and England were successfully imitating nature, the Teutonic races clung to a peculiarly crabbed style of crinkled foliation, which they reluctantly abandoned only in the 17th century.

With the accession of the Plantagenets, in 1154, and especially through the marriage of Henry II. with Eleanor of Guienne, French influence acquired a marked predominance in English illumination; and for about one hundred years from that date, the progress of style in England and France was parallel and almost identical. Gradually, in each, the Romanesque features disappeared, and by the middle of the 13th century, the fulness of mediæval illumination, as reflecting the perfection of Gothic architecture, was attained. The rapid growth of the Dominican and Franciscan orders during the first half of the century, and their eagerness to dispel the drowsiness into which the old well-to-do monastic establishments were fast slipping, gave a new life to all arts, including, of course, that of the transcription and illumination of the sources of learning, and, in those days, consequently, of power.

The present appears to be the most fitting place for a few notes, derived chiefly from the "Consuetudines" of the regulars,[4] on the general mediæval practice in relation to monastic libraries, of which England, France, Germany, and Italy possessed many during the 13th, 14th, and 15th centuries, rich, not only in sacred and patristic, but in profane literature as well.

The libraries of such establishments were placed by the abbot under the sole charge of the "armarian," an officer who was made responsible for the preservation of the volumes under his care: he was expected frequently to examine them, lest damp or insects should injure them; he was to cover them with wooden covers to preserve them, and carefully to mend and restore any damage which time or accident might cause; he was to make a note of any book borrowed from the library, with the name of the borrower; but this rule applied only to the less valuable portion of it, as the "great and precious books" could only be lent by the permission of

---

[1] No. 3, from Harleian, 2800. Considered by Sir Frederick Madden to have been written in the diocese of Treves, about 1190.

[2] Nos. 4, 6, 7, from Harleian, 3045. A German manuscript, written by Hrabinus de Cruch.

[3] No. 5, from the Royal Library B. M., No. 1, C. vii. Also German.

[4] See Martene Const. Canon. Reg. in "de Ant. Eccl. Ritibus," tom. iii. for full details.

the abbot himself. It was also the duty of the armarian to have all the books in his charge marked with their correct titles, and to keep a perfect list of the whole. Some of these catalogues are still in existence, and are curious and interesting, as showing the state of literature in the Middle Ages, as well as giving us the names of many authors whose works have never reached us. In perusing these catalogues, it is impossible not to be struck by the assiduous collection of classical authors, whose works sometimes equal, and at others actually preponderate over, the books of scholastic divinity. It was also the duty of the armarian, under the orders of his superior, to provide the transcribers of manuscripts with the writings which they were to copy, as well as with all the materials necessary for their labours; to make bargains as to payment, and to superintend the works during their progress. These books were not always destined for the library of the monastery in which they were transcribed, but were often eagerly bought by others, or by some generous layman, for the purpose of presenting to a monastic library; and their sale, particularly at an early period, added largely to the revenues of the establishment in which they were written or illuminated.

The different branches of the transcribing trade were occasionally united in the same person, but were more generally divided and practised separately, and by secular as well as by religious copyists. Of the former, there were at least three distinct branches—the illuminators, the notarii, and the librarii antiquarii. The last-mentioned were employed chiefly in restoring and repairing old and defaced manuscripts and their bindings. The public scribes were employed chiefly by monks and lawyers, sometimes working at their own houses; and at others, when any valuable work was to be copied, in that of their employer, where they were lodged and boarded during the time of their engagement.

A large room, as has been already stated, was in most monasteries set apart for such labours, and here the general transcribers pursued their avocation; but there were also, in addition, small rooms or cells, known also as scriptoria, which were occupied by such monks as were considered, from their piety and learning, to be entitled to the indulgence,[1] and used by them for their private devotions, as well as for the purpose of transcribing works for the use of the church or library. The scriptoria were frequently enriched by donations and bequests from those who knew the value of the

---

[1] This indulgence was, after all, not very luxurious, for as Mr. Maitland remarks ("Dark Ages," 2nd edition, p. 406): "Many a scribe has, I dare say, felt what Lewis, a monk of Wessobrun, in Bavaria, records as his own experience during his sedentary and protracted labours. In an inscription appended to a copy of Jerome's Commentary on Daniel, among other grounds on which he claims the sympathy and the prayers of the reader, he says,—

"'Dum scripsit friguit, et quod cum lumine solis
Scribere non potuit, perfecit lumine noctis.'"

For whilst he wrote he froze, and that which by daylight he could not
Bring to perfection, he worked at again by the aid of the moonlight.

works carried on in them, and large estates were often devoted to their support. The tithes of Wythessy and Impitor, two shillings and two-pence,—and some land in Ely, with two parts of the tithes of the lordship of Pampesward, were granted by Bishop Nigellus to the scriptorium of the monastery of Ely, the charter of which still exists in the church there. A Norman named Robert gave to the scriptorium of St. Alban's the tithes of Redburn, and two parts of the tithes of Hatfield; and that of St. Edmondesbury was endowed with two mills, by the same person.[1]

During the whole of the 12th and 13th centuries the pen played a more distinguished part than the brush in the art of illumination; since, not only was the former almost exclusively employed in outlining both foliage and figures, but the use of the latter was generally limited to filling up, and heightening with timid shadowing, the various parts defined by the former, and which were altogether dependent upon it for expression.[2] In fact, it appears as if the principal patterns in 13th century illumina-tion had been designed by stained-glass painters, the black outlines being equivalent in artistic result to the lead lines which, in the best specimens of grisaille and mosaic windows, keep the forms and colours distinct and perfect. This firm dark outlining was retained in England later than in France, and was combined in the former country with a more solid and somewhat less gay tone of colour than ever prevailed in the latter.

So late as the 15th century, this correspondence between stained glass work and illumination still obtained; thus, as Mr. Scharf remarks, in a note to his interesting paper on the King's College, Cambridge, windows, in the Transactions of the Archæological Institute for 1855, "The forty windows of the monastery of Horschau contained a series of subjects minutely corresponding to those of the Biblia Pauperum," &c.

The initial letters which in Romanesque illumination had expanded into very large proportions (plates 12th Century, Nos. 5 and 7), as a general rule,[3] diminished; but, in compensation, effloresced, as it were, into floreated terminations, which were at last not only carried down the side of the page, but even made to extend right across both the top and bottom of it. During the reigns of the three first Edwards in England, the tail, as it might be called, of the initial letter, running down the side of the page, gradually widened, until at length it grew into a band of orna-ment, occasionally panelled, and with small subjects introduced into the

[1] Ample information as to the libraries of the Middle Ages may be found by the English student in Fosbroke's "Encyclopædia of Antiquities," and "British Monachism," in Maitland's "Dark Ages," and (most agreeably and learnedly conveyed) in Merryweather's "Bibliomania in the Middle Ages." From these works and from Martene the preceding notes on the subject have been mainly condensed.

[2] See plates 12th Century, Nos. 3, 4, 5, 6, 7, and 13th, Nos. 2, 3, 4, 5, 6.

[3] In Italy the propensity for large letters was never relinquished. See plates 14th Cen-tury, Nos. 9, 13, 17, 19, 20, and 15th, Nos. 2, 7, 16, &c.

panels. In such cases, the initial letter occupying the angle formed by the side and top ornaments of the page, became subsidiary to the bracket-shaped bordering, which, in earlier examples, had been decidedly subsidiary to the initial letter. Thus plate 12th Century, No. 3, in Figs. 1, 2, 3, 4, 5, show progressive and transitional examples of the extension of the initial letter into the elongated bracket-shape. The succeeding plates 13th Century, Nos. 4 and 5, and the Frontispiece, furnish beautiful specimens of the floreated and panelled bracket ornaments, combined with the flourished and stretched-out initial letters. Plate 14th Century, No. 8, Fig. 1, shows the gradual encircling of the page with ornament derived from the initial letter; while plate 15th Century, No. 10, at length, displays the bordering completely surrounding the text or miniature. In this example the capital, although overwhelmed by the border, is still connected with it. In the following plate 15th Century, No. 11, in one instance the initial letter cuts on, but does not connect with, the bordering; and in another it is altogether detached from it. Lastly, in plates 15th Century, Nos. 14 and 15, we meet with the bordering surrounding the text or miniature completely, and irrespective of the lettering of the manuscript.

From the 12th century onwards, important illuminated manuscripts exist to the present day in such profusion as to deter me from individualizing in this necessarily brief essay. I shall rather dwell upon general characteristics of style, and upon the influence of the leading patrons of the art, in its palmiest days, in England, France, Germany, and the Netherlands. In these countries the infinite activity of the mendicant friars kept up a steady demand for manuscripts of all kinds: thus Richard de Bury, bishop of Durham, the greatest bibliophile of his age, and the tutor when prince, and friend while sovereign, of Edward III., relates, that in all his book-hunting travels: " Whenever we happened to turn aside to the towns and places where the aforesaid paupers had convents, we were not slack in visiting their chests and other repositories of books; for there, amidst the deepest poverty, we found the most exalted riches treasured up; there, in their satchels and baskets, we discovered not only the crumbs that fell from the master's table for the little dogs, but, indeed, the shew-bread without leaven, — the bread of angels, containing in itself all that is delectable."

These mendicant friars were looked upon with great jealousy by the clergy, who attributed to them the decrease in the number of students in the universities. Fitz Ralph, archbishop of Armagh and chaplain to Richard de Bury, accuses them of doing " grete damage to learning:" curiously enough, his accusation, contained in an oration denouncing them, bears testimony to their love of books and to their industry in collecting them. " For these orders of beggers, for endeles wynnynges that thei geteth by beggyng of the foreside pryvyleges of schriftes and sepultures and othere, thei beth now so multiplyed in conventes and in persons. That many men tellith that in general studies unnethe, is it founde to sillynge a pfitable book of ye faculte of art, of dyvynyte, of lawe canon, of phisik, other of lawe civil, but alle bookes beth y bougt of freres, so that en ech convent of freres is a noble librarye and a grete, and so that ene sech frere that hath state in schole, siche as thei beth nowe, hath an hughe librarye. And also y sent of my sugettes to schole thre other foure persons, and hit is said me that some of them beth come home agen for thei myst nought finde to selle ovn goode Bible; nother othere couenable books." Richard de Bury's example gave a stimulus to those who succeeded him, both at Durham and elsewhere.

That illumination was excessively popular in England during the 14th century among the leading families, is proved by the numbers of coats of arms emblazoned in many of the most remarkable English manuscripts. Thus in the Salisbury Lectionary, in the Douce, in Queen Mary's, and in the Braybrooke Psalters, appear the ancient coats of some of the best blood in the country. A most interesting contemporary illustration of the precise terms upon which these noble patrons employed the best illuminators of the day, has been furnished me by a kind and learned antiquarian friend,[1] in the shape of an extract from the fabric rolls of "York Minster,"[2] of which the following is a translation :—

"August 26th, 1346. — There appeared Robert Brekeling, scribe, and swore that he would observe the contract made between him and Sir John Forbor, viz., that he the said Robert would write one Psalter with the Kalender for the work of the said Sir John for 5s. and 6d.; and in the same Psalter, in the same character, a *Placebo* and a *Dirige*, with a Hymnal and Collectary, for 4s. and 3d. And the said Robert will illuminate ('luminabit') all the Psalms with great gilded letters, laid in with colours; and all the large letters of the Hymnal and Collectary will he illuminate with gold and vermilion, except the great letters of double feasts, which shall be as the large gilt letters are in the Psalter. And all the letters at the commencement of the verses shall be illuminated with good azure and vermilion; and all the letters at the beginning of the *Nocturns* shall be great uncial (unciales) letters, containing V. lines, but the *Beatus Vir* and *Dixit Dominus* shall contain VI. or VII. lines; and for the aforesaid illumination and for colours he [John] will give 5s. 6d., and for gold he will give 18d., and 2s. for a cloak and fur trimming. Item in one wardrobe—one coverlet, one sheet, and one pillow."[3]

[1] W. H. Blaauw, Esq.

[2] Edited by James Raine, Jun., for the Surtees Society. 8vo. Durham, 1859.

[3] The same series of rolls contain many very interesting entries ; as for instance,—

"1393 A.D. Soluti—de 4l. 6s. 8d. sol. hoc anno fratri Willelmo Ellerker pro scriptura duorum gradalium pro choro. de 40s. solutis domino Ricardo de Styrton pro eluminacione dictorum duorum gradalium—de 22s. 7½d. solutis dicto Willelmo pro pergameno empto per ipsum Willelmum.

"A.D. 1395. Roberto Bukebinder pro ligatura unius magni gradalis pro choro ex conven-

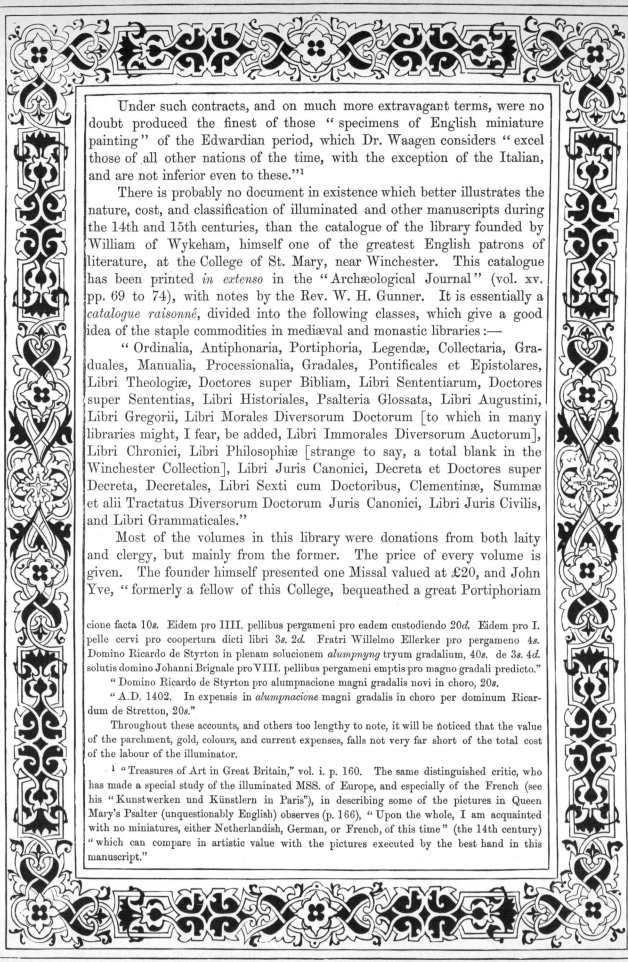

Under such contracts, and on much more extravagant terms, were no doubt produced the finest of those "specimens of English miniature painting" of the Edwardian period, which Dr. Waagen considers "excel those of all other nations of the time, with the exception of the Italian, and are not inferior even to these."[1]

There is probably no document in existence which better illustrates the nature, cost, and classification of illuminated and other manuscripts during the 14th and 15th centuries, than the catalogue of the library founded by William of Wykeham, himself one of the greatest English patrons of literature, at the College of St. Mary, near Winchester. This catalogue has been printed *in extenso* in the "Archæological Journal" (vol. xv. pp. 69 to 74), with notes by the Rev. W. H. Gunner. It is essentially a *catalogue raisonné*, divided into the following classes, which give a good idea of the staple commodities in mediæval and monastic libraries:—

"Ordinalia, Antiphonaria, Portiphoria, Legendæ, Collectaria, Graduales, Manualia, Processionalia, Gradales, Pontificales et Epistolares, Libri Theologiæ, Doctores super Bibliam, Libri Sententiarum, Doctores super Sententias, Libri Historiales, Psalteria Glossata, Libri Augustini, Libri Gregorii, Libri Morales Diversorum Doctorum [to which in many libraries might, I fear, be added, Libri Immorales Diversorum Auctorum], Libri Chronici, Libri Philosophiæ [strange to say, a total blank in the Winchester Collection], Libri Juris Canonici, Decreta et Doctores super Decreta, Decretales, Libri Sexti cum Doctoribus, Clementinæ, Summæ et alii Tractatus Diversorum Doctorum Juris Canonici, Libri Juris Civilis, and Libri Grammaticales."

Most of the volumes in this library were donations from both laity and clergy, but mainly from the former. The price of every volume is given. The founder himself presented one Missal valued at £20, and John Yve, "formerly a fellow of this College, bequeathed a great Portiphoriam

---

cione facta 10*s.* Eidem pro IIII. pellibus pergameni pro eadem custodiendo 20*d.* Eidem pro I. pelle cervi pro coopertura dicti libri 3*s.* 2*d.* Fratri Willelmo Ellerker pro pergameno 4*s.* Domino Ricardo de Styrton in plenam solucionem *alumpnyng* tryum gradalium, 40*s.* de 3*s.* 4*d.* solutis domino Johanni Brignale pro VIII. pellibus pergameni emptis pro magno gradali predicto."

"Domino Ricardo de Styrton pro alumpnacione magni gradalis novi in choro, 20*s.*

"A.D. 1402. In expensis in *alumpnacione* magni gradalis in choro per dominum Ricardum de Stretton, 20*s.*"

Throughout these accounts, and others too lengthy to note, it will be noticed that the value of the parchment, gold, colours, and current expenses, falls not very far short of the total cost of the labour of the illuminator.

[1] "Treasures of Art in Great Britain," vol. i. p. 160. The same distinguished critic, who has made a special study of the illuminated MSS. of Europe, and especially of the French (see his "Kunstwerken und Künstlern in Paris"), in describing some of the pictures in Queen Mary's Psalter (unquestionably English) observes (p. 166), "Upon the whole, I am acquainted with no miniatures, either Netherlandish, German, or French, of this time" (the 14th century) "which can compare in artistic value with the pictures executed by the best hand in this manuscript."

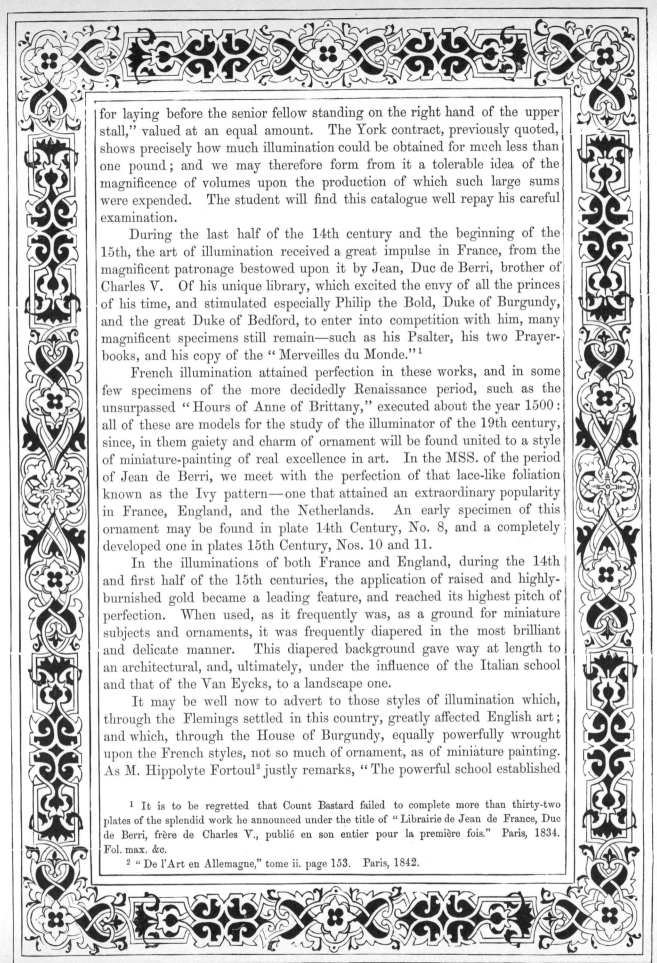

for laying before the senior fellow standing on the right hand of the upper stall," valued at an equal amount. The York contract, previously quoted, shows precisely how much illumination could be obtained for much less than one pound; and we may therefore form from it a tolerable idea of the magnificence of volumes upon the production of which such large sums were expended. The student will find this catalogue well repay his careful examination.

During the last half of the 14th century and the beginning of the 15th, the art of illumination received a great impulse in France, from the magnificent patronage bestowed upon it by Jean, Duc de Berri, brother of Charles V. Of his unique library, which excited the envy of all the princes of his time, and stimulated especially Philip the Bold, Duke of Burgundy, and the great Duke of Bedford, to enter into competition with him, many magnificent specimens still remain—such as his Psalter, his two Prayer-books, and his copy of the "Merveilles du Monde."[1]

French illumination attained perfection in these works, and in some few specimens of the more decidedly Renaissance period, such as the unsurpassed "Hours of Anne of Brittany," executed about the year 1500: all of these are models for the study of the illuminator of the 19th century, since, in them gaiety and charm of ornament will be found united to a style of miniature-painting of real excellence in art. In the MSS. of the period of Jean de Berri, we meet with the perfection of that lace-like foliation known as the Ivy pattern—one that attained an extraordinary popularity in France, England, and the Netherlands. An early specimen of this ornament may be found in plate 14th Century, No. 8, and a completely developed one in plates 15th Century, Nos. 10 and 11.

In the illuminations of both France and England, during the 14th and first half of the 15th centuries, the application of raised and highly-burnished gold became a leading feature, and reached its highest pitch of perfection. When used, as it frequently was, as a ground for miniature subjects and ornaments, it was frequently diapered in the most brilliant and delicate manner. This diapered background gave way at length to an architectural, and, ultimately, under the influence of the Italian school and that of the Van Eycks, to a landscape one.

It may be well now to advert to those styles of illumination which, through the Flemings settled in this country, greatly affected English art; and which, through the House of Burgundy, equally powerfully wrought upon the French styles, not so much of ornament, as of miniature painting. As M. Hippolyte Fortoul[2] justly remarks, "The powerful school established

[1] It is to be regretted that Count Bastard failed to complete more than thirty-two plates of the splendid work he announced under the title of "Librairie de Jean de France, Duc de Berri, frère de Charles V., publié en son entier pour la première fois." Paris, 1834. Fol. max. &c.

[2] "De l'Art en Allemagne," tome ii. page 153. Paris, 1842.

at Bruges by the Van Eycks, at the close of the 14th century, exercised an immense influence on all the schools of Europe, not excepting those of Italy;"—an influence which was, indeed, not altogether dissimilar from that brought to bear upon mannerism in Art by the Pre-Raffaelitism of the present day. The foundations of the Netherlandish school were sufficiently remote, but may be satisfactorily traced through existing miniatures and paintings. Herr Heinrich Otte, in his "Handbuch der Kirchlichen Kunst-Archäologie" (p. 187), gives a chronological list of the principal MSS. of Germanic production from the Carlovingian period to the commencement of the 13th century. Up to that period the Byzantine manner prevailed, mixed with a peculiar rudeness, such as may be recognized in the works of the great saint and bishop, Bernward of Hildesheim, whom Fiorillo and other writers look upon, with Willigis of Mainz, as the great animator of German art in the 11th century.[1] The conversion of this latter element into Gothic originality appears to have taken place during the 13th century, and a fine manuscript in the British Museum (B. R 2, b. 11), ascribed by Dr. Waagen to a period between 1240 and 1260, illustrates the transition.[2]

With the commencement of the 14th century appear the "Lay of the Minnesingers," one of the most peculiar of the Paris manuscripts, and others cited by Dr. Kugler, which carry on the evidence of progressive development until the power of expression obtained in painting by Meisters Wilhelm and Stephen of Cologne, is reflected in the contemporary miniatures.

Even did not the celebrated "Paris Breviary," and the British Museum "Bedford Missal," both executed in part by the three Van Eycks, Hubert, Jan, and Margaretha, for the great Regent of France, exist, the style of the panel-pictures painted by them would be quite sufficient to show that they must have been illuminators before they became world-renowned *oil-painters*. Through their conscientious study of nature, both in landscape and in portrait subjects, a complete change was wrought in the miniatures of all manuscripts produced after their influence had had time to penetrate into the scriptoria and ateliers of the contemporary artist-scribes. Had not the invention of printing rapidly supervened, there can be no doubt that even more extraordinary results than followed the general appreciation of their graces as illuminators would have been ensured. The later manuscripts of the German and Netherlandish schools of miniature-painting generally reflect the mixed cleverness and angularities of such masters as Rogier van der Weyde the elder, Lucas van Leyden, Martin Schongauer,

[1] See casts from his bronze doors and columns in the Crystal Palace, and his Three Gospels in the treasury of the Cathedral at Hildesheim. In Dr. F. H. Müller's " Beiträge zur teutschen Kunst und Geschichtskunde," very careful engravings of the plastic art of Bernward and Willigis may be compared with facsimiles of contemporary German illumination.

[2] The steps of the transition are also well indicated, and illustrated by reference to special MSS. in Kugler's "Kunstgeschichte," in his article on the "Nord., vornehml. Deutsche Malerei der Roman. Periode."

&c.; where, however, the manner of Hemling prevailed, spiritual beauty and refinement followed.

To dwell upon Spanish illuminated manuscripts would be comparatively profitless to the practical student; for all the peculiarities and excellences they would appear to have at any time possessed, may be found more perfectly developed at first in French, subsequently in Netherlandish, and ultimately in Italian volumes.[1] It remains, therefore, only to sketch, with a brevity altogether out of proportion to the great interest of the subject, the progress of the art in Italy.

If the delineation of naïve and graceful romantic incident, combined with elegant foliated ornament, reached perfection in the illuminations of the French school; if blazoning on gilded grounds was carried to its most gorgeous pitch in Oriental and Byzantine manuscripts; if intricate interlacements and minute elaboration may be regarded as the special characteristics of Hiberno-Saxon scribes; and if a noble tone of solid colour, combined with great humour and intense energy of expression, marked England's best productions,—it may be safely asserted, that it was reserved for the Italians to introduce into the embellishment of manuscripts those higher qualities of art, their peculiar aptitude for which so long gave them a pre-eminence among contemporaneous schools.

I therefore proceed to trace the names and styles of some few of the most celebrated among their illuminators; premising by a reminder to the student of the miserably low pitch to which art had been reduced in Italy during the 12th century. Even the most enthusiastic and patriotic writers agree in the all but total dearth of native talent. Greeks were employed to reproduce Byzantine mannerisms in pictures and mosaics, and to a slight extent no doubt as scribes. Illumination was scarcely known or recognized as an indigenous art; for Dante, even writing after the commencement of the 14th century, speaks of it as "quell' arte, che Alluminar è chiamata a Parisi."

Probably the earliest Italian manuscript showing signs of real art, is the "Ordo Officiorum Senensis Ecclesiæ," preserved in the library of the academy at Sienna, and illuminated with little subjects and friezes with animals, by a certain Oderico, a canon of the cathedral, in the year 1213.

The Padre della Valle[2] expressly cautions the student against con-

---

[1] The subject is one that I am unable to find has been treated with any great ability. The reader may, however, be referred to the following old Spanish works on the subject:— Andres Merino de Jesu-Cristo, "Escuela Palæographica, ó de leer Letras universas, antiguas y modernas, desde la entrada de los Godos en España" (Madrid, 1780, in fol. fig.);—Estev. de Terreros, "Palæographia Española, que contiene todos los modos conocidos, que ha habido de escribir en España, desde su principio y fundacion" (Madrid, Ibarra, 1758, in 4to. fig.); and Rodriguez-Christ., "Bibliotheca Universal de la Polygraphia Española" (Madrid, 1738, fol. fig.).

[2] "Lettere Sanese," tom. i. p. 278.

founding this Odericus with the Oderigi of Dante,[1] who died about the year 1300. The latter was unquestionably an artist of some merit, for Vasari[2] speaks of him as an " eccellente miniatore," whose works for the Papal library, although "in gran parte consumati dal tempo," he had himself seen and admired. Some drawings by the hand of this " valente uomo," as he is styled, Vasari speaks of possessing in his own collection.

Baldinucci makes out Oderigi to have been of the Florentine school on no other grounds than because Vasari describes him as " molto amico di Giotto in Roma;" and because Dante appears to have known him well. Lanzi,[3] however, more correctly classes him with the Bolognese school, from his teaching Franco Bolognese at Bologna, and on the strength of the direct testimony of one of the earliest commentators on Dante—Benvenuto da Imola. This same Franco worked much for Benedict IX., and far surpassed his master. Vasari especially commends the spirit with which he drew animals, and mentions a drawing in his own possession of a lion tearing a tree as of great merit. Thus Oderigi, the contemporary of Cimabue, and Franco, the pupil of Oderigi and contemporary of Giotto, appear to have been to the Art of Illumination what Cimabue and his pupil Giotto were to the Art of Painting,—the pupil in both cases infinitely excelling the master. To them succeeded, about the middle of the 14th century, a scarcely less celebrated pair—Don Jacopo Fiorentino, and Don Silvestro, both monks in the Camaldolese monastery, " degli Angeli," at Florence. The former, Baldinucci tells us, " improving, with infinite study, every moment not devoted to his monastic duties, acquired a style of writing greatly sought after for choral books." The latter, who was rather an artist than a scribe, enriched the productions of his friend with miniatures so beautiful, as to cause the books thus jointly produced to excite, at a later period, the special admiration of Lorenzo the Magnificent, and his son, the no less magnificent Leo X.[4] So proud were their brother monks of the skill of Frati Jacopo and Silvestro, that after their death they preserved their two right hands as honoured relics.

[1] The well-known passage in which Dante alludes to Oderigi occurs in the eleventh canto of the " Paradiso," and is as follows :—

" Oh, dissi lui, non se' tu Oderisi,
L' onor d' Agubbio, e l' onor di quell' arte
Che alluminar è chiamata a Parisi?
Frate, diss' egli, più ridon le carte
Che pennelegia Franco Bolognese:
L' onor è tutto or suo, e mio in parte.
Ben non sarei stato si cortese
Mentre ch' io vissi per lo gran disio
Dell' excellentia, ove mio cor intese.
Di tal superbia qui si paga il fio."

[2] Vita di Giotto.
[3] "Storia Pittorica," vol. xi. p. 13, ed. Pisa, 1815 ; and vol. v. pp. 8, 9, 10.
[4] Lanzi speaks of these choral books as " De' più considerabili che abbia l'Italia."

About a century later, the leading illuminators were Bartolomeo and Gherardo,—the former abbot of San Clemente, at Arrezzo, and the latter a Florentine painter and "miniatore," whom Vasari confounds with Attavante, a painter, engraver, and mosaicist. Of all the Italian artists who adopted the style of the illuminators, if they did not themselves illuminate, the most celebrated certainly are Fra Angelico da Fiesole[1] and Gentile da Fabriano. The majority of the works of both are little else than magnified miniatures of the highest merit.

The school of Siennese illumination was scarcely less distinguished than that of Florence. M. Rio dwells with enthusiasm on the books of the Kaleffi and Leoni, still preserved in the Archivio delle Riformazioni, and especially on those decorated by Nicolo di Sozzo, in 1334. The greatest master of the school, Simone Memmi, the intimate friend of Petrarch, was himself an illuminator of extraordinary excellence, as may be seen by the celebrated Virgil of the Ambrosian Library at Milan, which contains, amongst other beautiful miniatures by his hand, the fine portrait of Virgil, and a very remarkable allegorical figure of Poetry, quite equal in artistic merit to any of the artist's larger and better-known works in fresco or tempera.[2]

It is, however, in the library of the cathedral at Sienna, which retains many of the magnificent choir-books executed by Fra Benedetto da Matera, a Benedictine of Monte Cassino, and Fra Gabriele Mattei of Sienna, that the greatest triumphs of the school are still to be recognized. This series of volumes, although much reduced from its original extent by the abstractions made by Cardinal Burgos, who carried off a vast quantity to Spain, is still the finest belonging to any capitular establishment in Italy, and worthily represents the grandeur of Italian illumination in "cinque cento" days.

In various plates of this work, and more particularly in plates 14th Century, Nos. 2, 7, 9, 10, 12, 13, 17, 18, 19, 20, and 15th Century, Nos. 2, 8, and 16, specimens are engraved, which, although affording no illustration of the beauty of the *miniatures* by which such volumes were adorned, may still serve to convey a good idea of the scale of boldness and splendour upon which the initial letters and ornaments of Italian choral books were generally conceived and executed.

The series of similar volumes next in importance to those of Sienna, is attached to the choir of the church and monastic establishment of the Benedictines at Perugia, known as "San Tomaso de' Casinensi." Of these, nothing more need be said than that they are worthy of the stalls of the same choir, the design of which is attributed to Raffaelle, and the

[1] The Kensington Museum possesses two splendid leaves from a great "Chorale," which contain miniatures completely in the manner of Fra Angelico.

[2] The style, if not the hand, of Taddeo Bartolo, another of the great early masters of the Siennese school, may be distinctly traced in several existing miniatures.

execution to Stefano da Bergamo, and Fra Damiano, of the same town, the great "intarsiatore."

Formerly, as M. Rio observes,[1] " Ferrara could boast of possessing a series of miniatures, executed principally in the seclusion of its convents, from the time of the Benedictine monk Serrati, who in 1240 ornamented the books of the choir with figures of a most noble character,[2] till that of Fra Girolamo Fiorino, who, towards the beginning of the 15th century, devoted himself to the same occupation in the monastery of San Bartolomeo, and formed in his young disciple Cosmè a successor who was destined to surpass his master, and to carry this branch of art to a degree of perfection till then unknown. Even at the present day we may see, in the twenty-three volumes presented by the Bishop Bartolomeo della Rovere to the cathedral, and in the twenty-eight enormous volumes removed from the Certosa to the public library, how much reason the Ferrarese have to be proud of the possession of such treasures, and to place them by the side of the manuscripts of Tasso and Ariosto.

The " subjects generally treated by these mystical artists were marvellously adapted to their special vocation : they were the life of the holy Virgin, the principal festivals celebrated by the Church, or popular objects of devotion; in short, all the dogmas which were susceptible of this mode of representation, works of mercy, the different sacraments, the imposing ceremonies of religion, and, in general, all that was most poetical in liturgy or legend. In compositions of so exclusive a character, naturalism could only be introduced in subordination to the religious element."

While this was the case with the majority of illuminations executed under the auspices of the Church, in those of a secular nature, undertaken for the great princes and nobles, another set of characteristics prevailed. For the Gonzagas, Sforzas, D'Estes, Medici, Strozzi, Visconti, and other great families, the best artists were constantly employed in decorating both written and printed volumes, in which portraiture is freely introduced, and picturesque and historical subjects are represented with great vivacity and attention to costume and local truth. Thus in the truly exquisite " Grant of Lands," by Ludovico il Moro to his wife Beatrice D'Este, dated January 28th, 1494, and preserved in the British Museum, speaking portraits of both Ludovico and Beatrice are introduced, with their arms and beautiful arabesques.[3] Again, in the Hanrot " Sforziada,"

<hr>

[1] "Poetry of Christian Art," p. 140.

[2] " Ornò i libri corali di figure nobillissime."—Cittadella, " Catalogo dei Pittori e Scultori Ferraresi," vol. i. pp. 1—27.

[3] A small volume, which passed from the hands of the late Mr. Dennistoun into the collection of Lord Ashburnham, contains a series of arabesques and miniatures of the most interesting character, recalling in different pages, and in the highest perfection, the varied styles of Pietro Perugino, Pinturicchio, Lo Spagna, and others. The Duke of Hamilton's library is extraordinarily rich in Italian MSS.; his Grace's Dante with outline illustrations being of great importance.

the first page contains exquisite miniatures of three members of the princely family of the Sforzas, by the hand of the all-accomplished Girolamo dai Libri.[1] This artist, a truly celebrated Veronese and worthy fellow-townsman, with the almost equally able Fra Liberale, whose work in the manner of Giovanni Bellini excited the utmost envy on the part of the Siennese illuminators, was himself the son of a miniature painter, known as Francesco dai Libri, and bequeathed the name and art of his father to his own son,—thus maintaining the traditions of good design acquired in the great school of Padua, under Andrea Mantegna[2] and Squarcione, during three generations of illuminators. Girolamo was by far the most celebrated of the three. As a painter, his works possess distinguished merit, and there still remain good samples of his abilities in the churches of San Zeno and Sant' Anastasia, at Verona. He also derives some credit from the transcendent merits of his pupil Giulio Clovio. Vasari's description of the talents of Girolamo[3] gives so lively a picture of the style which reached its highest vogue at the end of the 15th, and during the first half of the 16th centuries in Italy, that I am tempted to translate it. "Girolamo," he says, "executed flowers so naturally and beautifully, and with so much care, as to appear real to the beholder. In like manner he imitated little cameos and other precious stones and jewels cut in intaglio, so that nothing like them, or so minute, was ever seen. Among his smallest figures, such as he represented on gems or cameos, some might be observed no larger than little ants, and yet in all of them might be made out every limb and muscle, in a manner which to be believed must needs be seen."

Mr. Ottley supposes that Giulio Clovio (born 1498, died 1578) worked previous to his receipt of the instruction of Girolamo in a drier manner, in which no evidence appears of that imitation of Michael Angelesque pose in his figures, which in his subsequent manner became so leading a characteristic of his style. It is in his earlier manner that Giulio is believed to have illuminated for Clement VII.[4] (1523—1534), while

[1] *See* Mr. Shaw's truly beautiful reproduction, in that gentleman's "Illuminated Ornaments," &c., of a portion of Arabesque border from this volume, containing a medallion portrait, Plate XXXV. A very beautiful Sforza MS. has lately been transferred from the possession of Mr. Henry Farrer to that of the Marquis D'Azeglio.

[2] That Andrea exercised a great influence upon miniature-painting may be recognized in the works of Girolamo: a grand leaf from a folio, on which is painted a seated allegorical figure of "Rome," in the possession of Mr. T. Whitehead, is so noble in every way, and so entirely in Andrea's manner, that it seems almost impossible to doubt its being by his hand. It may, however, possibly have been executed by his contemporary in the Mantuan school, "Giovanni dei Russi," who in 1455 illuminated the great Bible of the house of Este, for Borso, Duke of Modena.

[3] "Vita di Fra Giocondo e di Liberale, e d'altri Veronesi."

[4] The Celotti sale, which took place at Christie's on the 26th of May, 1825, and which included by far the most important collection of Italian illuminations ever brought to the hammer, contained no less than nineteen beautiful specimens extracted from the choral books of that pope.

for his successor, Paul III. (1534—1539), he worked abundantly, and gradually acquired that which is best known as his later manner, in which he continued to labour, according to Vasari, until 1578, at the great age of eighty years. Mr. Ottley, however, recognizes his hand in MSS. which must have been at least five years later—during the Pontificate of Gregory XIII.[1]

It is obviously impossible, in such an essay as the present, to dwell in detail upon the merits of so accomplished a master of his art. Fortunately we possess in this metropolis two fine specimens of his skill, both tolerably accessible—one in the Soane,[2] and the other in the British Museum.[3] A third, in the shape of an altar-card, attributed to him, is to be found in the Kensington Museum; and several fragments, formerly in Mr. Rogers's possession, have passed to Mr. Whitehead and to the British Museum. All of these exhibit a refinement of execution, combined with a brilliancy of colour and excellence of drawing, which has never been surpassed by any illuminator. Vasari gives a complete list and description of his principal works, and proves him to have been not less industrious than able.

A contemporary of Giulio's, whose name has been overpowered by the greater brilliancy of that of the Cellini of illumination, was a certain Apollonius of Capranica, or, as he signs himself, "Apollonius de Bonfratellis de Capranica, Capellæ et Sacristiæ Apostolicæ Miniator." Mr. Ottley most justly states,[4] " that it is impossible to speak in too high terms of the beauty of his borders, wherein he often introduces compartments with small figures, representing subjects of the New Testament, which are touched with infinite delicacy and spirit." His drawing, which is of a decidedly Michael-Angelesque character, is of less merit when the nude is represented on a larger scale. His harmony of colour is extraordinary, rather lower in tone than Giulio Clovio's, but equally glowing, and more powerful. Some beautiful specimens of his handicraft remain in the possession of Mr. T. M. Whitehead. The late Mr. Rogers possessed many fragments, the most precious of which have found their way into the National Collection. His work is usually dated, and the dates appear to range from 1558 to 1572. Apollonius having been official illuminator to the very institution from which Celotti derived his richest spoils, it may readily be imagined that his collection included an unprecedented series of beautiful examples of Buonfratelli's style.

Long after the invention of printing, the Apostolic Chamber retained

[1] *See* Baglioni, "Vite dei Pittori ed Architetti fioriti in Roma, dal 1572 sino al 1642,"—Vita di Giulio Clovio.

[2] Facsimiles of the exquisite pages of this volume are given in Mr. Noel Humphrey's work; they are perfect triumphs of chromo-lithographic skill, and their production by Mr. Owen Jones formed what Germans may hereafter call a "standpunkt" in the history of that art, of which this volume presents no unfavourable sample.

[3] Grenville Collection.

[4] In his catalogue of the sale of the Celotti collection.

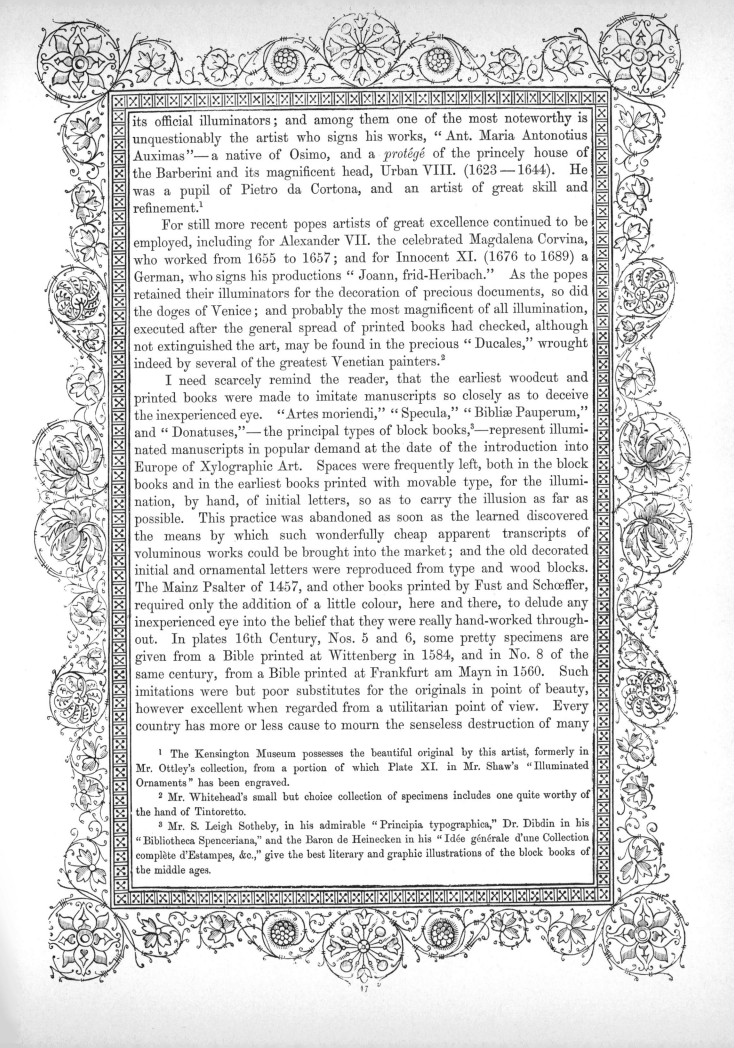

its official illuminators; and among them one of the most noteworthy is unquestionably the artist who signs his works, "Ant. Maria Antonotius Auximas"—a native of Osimo, and a *protégé* of the princely house of the Barberini and its magnificent head, Urban VIII. (1623 — 1644). He was a pupil of Pietro da Cortona, and an artist of great skill and refinement.[1]

For still more recent popes artists of great excellence continued to be employed, including for Alexander VII. the celebrated Magdalena Corvina, who worked from 1655 to 1657; and for Innocent XI. (1676 to 1689) a German, who signs his productions " Joann, frid-Heribach." As the popes retained their illuminators for the decoration of precious documents, so did the doges of Venice; and probably the most magnificent of all illumination, executed after the general spread of printed books had checked, although not extinguished the art, may be found in the precious "Ducales," wrought indeed by several of the greatest Venetian painters.[2]

I need scarcely remind the reader, that the earliest woodcut and printed books were made to imitate manuscripts so closely as to deceive the inexperienced eye. "Artes moriendi," "Specula," "Bibliæ Pauperum," and "Donatuses,"—the principal types of block books,[3]—represent illuminated manuscripts in popular demand at the date of the introduction into Europe of Xylographic Art. Spaces were frequently left, both in the block books and in the earliest books printed with movable type, for the illumination, by hand, of initial letters, so as to carry the illusion as far as possible. This practice was abandoned as soon as the learned discovered the means by which such wonderfully cheap apparent transcripts of voluminous works could be brought into the market; and the old decorated initial and ornamental letters were reproduced from type and wood blocks. The Mainz Psalter of 1457, and other books printed by Fust and Schœffer, required only the addition of a little colour, here and there, to delude any inexperienced eye into the belief that they were really hand-worked throughout. In plates 16th Century, Nos. 5 and 6, some pretty specimens are given from a Bible printed at Wittenberg in 1584, and in No. 8 of the same century, from a Bible printed at Frankfurt am Mayn in 1560. Such imitations were but poor substitutes for the originals in point of beauty, however excellent when regarded from a utilitarian point of view. Every country has more or less cause to mourn the senseless destruction of many

[1] The Kensington Museum possesses the beautiful original by this artist, formerly in Mr. Ottley's collection, from a portion of which Plate XI. in Mr. Shaw's "Illuminated Ornaments" has been engraved.

[2] Mr. Whitehead's small but choice collection of specimens includes one quite worthy of the hand of Tintoretto.

[3] Mr. S. Leigh Sotheby, in his admirable "Principia typographica," Dr. Dibdin in his "Bibliotheca Spenceriana," and the Baron de Heinecken in his "Idée générale d'une Collection complète d'Estampes, &c.," give the best literary and graphic illustrations of the block books of the middle ages.

noble old volumes which the printing-press never has, and now, alas! never can replace; but none more than England, in which cupidity and intolerance destroyed recklessly and ignorantly. Thus, after the dissolution of monastic establishments, persons were appointed to search out all missals, books of legends, and such "superstitious books," and to destroy or sell them for waste paper; reserving only their bindings, when, as was frequently the case, they were ornamented with massive gold and silver, curiously chased, and often further enriched with precious stones; and so industriously had these men done their work, destroying all books in which they considered popish tendencies to be shown by the illumination, the use of red letters, or of the Cross, or even by the—to them—mysterious diagrams of mathematical works,—that when, some years after, Leland was appointed to examine the monastic libraries, with a view to the preservation of what was valuable in them, he found that those who had preceded him had left little to reward his search. Bale, himself an advocate for the dissolution of monasteries, says: "Never had we bene offended for the losse of our lybraryes beyng so many in nombre and in so desolate places for the moste parte, yf the chief monuments and moste notable workes of our excellent wryters had bene reserved, yf there had bene in every shyre of Englande but one solemyne lybrary to the preservacyon of those noble workes, and preferrements of good learnynges in our posteryte it had bene yet somewhat. But to destroye all without consyderacyon is and wyll be unto Englande for ever a most horryble infamy amonge the grave senyours of other nations. A grete nombre of them wych purchased of those superstycyose mansyons reserved of those lybrarye bokes, some to serve their jaks, some to scoure theyr candelstyckes, and some to rubbe theyr bootes; some they solde to the grossers and sope sellers, and some they sent over see to the boke-bynders, not in small nombre but at tymes whole shippes ful. I know a merchant man, whyche shall at thys tyme be namelesse, that boughte the contents of two noble lybraryes for xl shyllyngs pryce, a shame it is to be spoken. Thys stuffe hathe he occupyed in the stide of greye paper for the space of more than these ten years, and yet hathe store ynough for as manye years to come. A prodyguose example is thys, and to be abhorred of all men who love theyr natyon as they shoulde do." Wherever the Reformation extended throughout Europe, a corresponding destruction of ancient illuminated manuscripts took place, and in localities where fanaticism failed to do its work of devastation, indifference proved a consuming agent of almost equal energy; and indeed there is no more forcible illustration of the untiring zeal and industry of the illuminators of old, than the fact, that, after all that has been done to stamp out the sparks still lingering in their embers, their works should still glow with such shining lights in all the great public libraries of Europe.

I now turn to the second portion of my theme.

PART II.

WHAT THE ART OF ILLUMINATING SHOULD BE IN THE PRESENT DAY.

ILLUMINATION, in whatever form practised, can never be properly regarded as any other than one of the genera into which the art of Poly-chromatic decoration may be subdivided. What was originally termed illumination, was simply the application of minium or red lead, as a colour or ink, to decorate, or draw marked attention to, any particular portion of a piece of writing, the general text of which was in black ink. The term was retained long after the original red lead was almost entirely superseded by the more brilliant cinnabar, or vermilion. As ornaments of all kinds were gradually superadded to the primitive distinctions, marked in manuscripts by the use of different-coloured inks, the term acquired a wider significance, and, from classical times to the present, has always been regarded as including the practice of every description of ornamental or ornamented writing.

Because such embellishments were, during the early and Middle Ages, and, in fact, until long after the invention of printing, almost invariably executed on vellum, there is no reason whatever why illumination should be applied to that material, or to paper, which has taken its place, only; wood, metal, slate, stone, canvas, plaster, all may be made to receive it. Again : because ancient illumination was almost entirely executed in colours, in the use of which water and some glutinous medium were the only " vehicles," there is no reason why modern illumination should not be worked in oil, turpentine, encaustic, fresco, tempera, varnish, and by every process in which decorative painting is ever wrought in these days. It is in such an extension that the most valuable functions of the art are likely to consist in all time to come. That utilitarian application which it, originally and for so many centuries, found in the production of beautiful books, copies of which could be elaborated by no other means than hand labour, has been, to a great extent, superseded by chromolithography and chromotypy. No doubt a wide field for useful, and even productive labour, is still left to the practical illuminator on paper and vellum, in designing and preparing exquisite originals for reproduction by those processes, as well as in the rich and tasteful blazoning of pedigrees, addresses, family records and memorials, and in the illustration for presentation, or for private libraries, of transcripts from favourite authors; but, at the same time, an equally elegant and useful application of the art would be to enrich ceilings, walls, cornices, string-courses, panels, labels round doors and windows, friezes, bands, chimney-pieces, and stained and painted furniture in churches, school-rooms, dwellings, and public buildings of all kinds, with beautiful and appropriate inscriptions, of graceful form and harmonious colouring. Such illumination would form, not only an agreeable, but an eminently useful decoration. How many texts and sentences, worthy, in every sense, of being "written in letters of gold," might not be thus brought prominently under the eyes of youth, manhood, and old age, for hope, admonition, and comfort. No more skill, energy, and taste are requisite for the production of this class of illumination than are essential for satisfactory work upon vellum and paper; and while in the one case the result of the labour may be made an incessant enjoyment for many, in the other, it is seldom more than a nine-days' wonder, shut up in a book or portfolio, and seen so seldom as scarcely to repay the amateur for the expense and trouble involved in its execution.

In the few remarks I am about to offer in respect to what the Art of Illumination really should be now, I propose to treat briefly, but specifically, of its application to each of the different substances on which it may be most satisfactorily worked; in the following series: vellum, paper, tracing-paper, canvas, plaster, stone, metal, wood. Dealing with design only in this section of my essay, I propose, in the following and concluding one, to adhere to the same order in noticing the best processes by which amateurs may carry out the class of work I would recommend to their notice.

To commence, therefore, with vellum: it is obvious that good copies of ancient illuminated manuscripts can be made on this material only, for there is a charm about the colour and texture of well-prepared calf-skin, which no paper can be made to possess. For the same reason, and on account of its extraordinary toughness and durability, it is especially suitable for pedigrees, addresses, and other documents which it may be considered desirable to preserve for future generations. To transcribe on vellum and decorate the writings of ancient and modern authors so as to form unique volumes, appears to me—nowadays, when God gives to every man and woman so much good hard work to do, if they will but do it—little else than a waste of human life. In days when few could read, and pictures drawn by hand were the only means within the reach of the priesthood, of bringing home to the minds of the ignorant populace the realities of Biblical history, and of stimulating the eye of faith by exhibiting to the material eye pictures of those sufferings and triumphs of saints and martyrs, on which the Church of Rome during the Middle Ages mainly based its assertions of supremacy, it was all very well to spend long lives of celibacy and monastic seclusion in such labours; but the same justification can never be pleaded again. I am quite ready to admit that the exceptional manufacture of these pretty picture-books may be not only agreeable, but even useful: it is the abuse, and not the occasional resort to the practice, I would venture to denounce. For instance, a mother could scarcely do a thing more likely to benefit her children, and to fix the lessons of love or piety she would desire to implant in their memories, than to illuminate for them little volumes, which, from their beauty or value, they might be inclined to treasure through life. Interesting her children in her work as it grew under her hand, how many precious associations in after-life might hang about these very books. Again: for young people, the mere act of transcription, independent of the amount of thought bestowed upon good words and pure thoughts, and the selection of ornament to appropriately illustrate them, would tend to an identification of the individual with the best and highest class of sentiments.

All that has been said with respect to illumination on vellum, applies, with equal force, to illumination on paper. There has to be borne in mind, however, the essential difference that exists between the relative durability of the two substances. Elaboration is decidedly a great element of beauty in illumination; and neatly-wrought elaboration cannot be executed without care, patience, and a considerable sacrifice of time: why, therefore, bestow that care, patience, and time upon a less permanent material, when one only a trifle more costly, but infinitely more lasting, is as easily procured? Work on paper, therefore, only as you would write exercises or do sums upon a slate; learn and practise upon paper, but reserve all more serious efforts for vellum only. No effect can be got upon the former material, which cannot, with a little more dexterity, be attained upon the latter.

As none of the other substances mentioned as those on which illumination may be executed, are available for making up into books, before proceeding to a consideration of the special conditions under which the art may be applied to them, I beg to offer the following recommendations with respect to design, as suitable for book-illustration generally.[1]

---

[1] Our good fortune in possessing at the present time, and in common use, a remarkably clear and easily intelligible set of alphabets, was thus admirably noted in a recent article in the *Times* newspaper of December 28th, 1859:—

"Happily for us, the written symbols employed by the Romans, which are now the chief medium of expression for all the languages of Europe, America, Australia, and the greater part of civilized Africa, reflect exactly the rough and stalwart energy which made Rome to Europe what we are to the world. They have bestowed on us an alphabet as practically effective, and as suited to the capabilities of human vision, as any that could have been devised. This alphabet of ours is like an Englishman's dress—plain and manageable; not very artistically arranged, it may be, nor remarkable for copiousness or flow of outline, but sufficiently elastic and capable of extension. Its symbols have certainly no graceful curves like the picturesque Persian; but, better than all flourishes, each letter has plain, unmistakable features of its own. The vowels, which are to the rest of the alphabet what the breath, or rather life itself, is to the body, are assigned their legitimate position, and are formed to be written continuously with the consonants. Lastly, though scanty in itself, it is abundantly equipped with capital letters, stops, italics, and every appliance for securing rapid legibility, so that the eye can take in the subject

Firstly :—Take care that your text be perfectly legible; for, however cramped and confused the contents of many of those volumes we most admire may now appear, it is to be remembered that they were all written in the handwriting most easily read by the students of the periods in which they were written. The old scribes never committed the solecism of which we are too often guilty, of bestowing infinite pains on writing that which, when written, not one in a hundred could, or can, decipher.

Secondly :—Fix the scale of your writing and ornament with reference to the size of your page, and adhere to it throughout the volume. This rule, which was rigidly observed in all the best periods of the art, is incessantly disregarded in the present day; and to such an extent, that not only does scale frequently differ, as we turn page after page, but the same page will frequently exhibit scroll-work, derived from some great choral folio, interwreathed with leafage borrowed from some pocket Missal or Book of Hours.

Thirdly :—If you adopt any historical style or particular period as a basis on which your text, miniatures, and ornamentation are to be constructed, maintain its leading features consistently, so as to avoid letting your work appear as though it had been begun in the 10th century, and only completed in the 16th; or, as I have once or twice seen, *vice versâ*. For however erratic changes of style may appear to be in Art, as they run one another down along the course of time, it will be invariably found that there exists a harmony between all contemporary features, which cannot be successfully disregarded; and this it is which has ever rendered eclecticism in art a problem,—not impossible, perhaps, to solve, but one which, as yet at least, has never met with a satisfactory practical solution.

Fourthly :—Sustain your energies evenly throughout your volume; for, remember, your critics will estimate your powers, not by your best page, but by a mean struck between your best and your worst. Book illumination is generally looked upon as microscopic work, demanding the greatest exactitude; and whatever merits any page may display, they will go for little, if that page is disfigured by a crooked line, or a single leaf insufficiently or incorrectly shadowed : and the greater the merit, the more notable the drawback.

Fifthly :—Rigidly avoid contrasting natural with conventional foliage. Adopt which you like, for by either beautiful effects may be produced; but mix them, and the charm of both is gone. Natural foliage may be successfully combined with any other varieties of conventional ornaments, excepting those based upon natural foliage.

Sixthly :—Take care that some at least of your dominant lines and borders are kept parallel to the rectangular sides of your pages; for unless

of a page at a glance. Oriental alphabets are the very reverse of all this. They are complex, cumbersome, unmanageable." Much the same might have been said of many of the mediæval ones.

your flowing and wayward ornaments are corrected by this soberer contrast, they will, however beautiful in themselves, have a straggling and untidy appearance in the volume. Where the lines of the text are strongly marked, as in black ink on a white ground, and the page is so far filled with text as to leave but little space for ornament, this rule may be, to a great extent, disregarded, for the lines of the text will themselves supply the requisite contrast to the flowing forms; but where the page is nearly filled with ornament, or when the text is faint only, as in gold lettering on a white ground, it becomes imperative.

Seventhly:—Be decided, but temperate, in your contrasts of colour. It would obviously exceed the limits of these notes, to attempt in them to enter upon the principles of the "harmony of colour;" they must be studied from treatises specially devoted to the subject. Such study must, however, be accompanied by constant experiment and practice; for it would be as foolish to expect a man to be a good performer upon any instrument, because he had learnt the theory of music, as it would be to suppose that he must necessarily paint in harmonious colouring, because he had studied the theory of balance in combination. To the experienced eye and hand, functions become intuitive, which, to the mere theorist, however profound, are toil and weariness of spirit.

Such are a few of the rules, by attention to which, the illuminators of old achieved some of their happiest effects, and which can never be safely disregarded by those who would emulate their efforts.

In taking up the class of substances on which illumination, as applied to general decoration, may be best executed, we meet, firstly, with one occupying a somewhat intermediate position,—viz., tracing-paper. I term its position intermediate, because it may be wrought upon in either oil or water-colour; and because, when so wrought upon, it may be either mounted on paper or card, and so made to contribute to book or picture enrichment; or attached to walls or other surfaces, brought forward in oil-colours, and be so enlisted in a general system of mural illumination. How this may best be done technically will be hereafter described; here I may notice only the use which may be made of this convenient material, by many not sufficiently advanced in design or drawing, to be able to invent or even copy correctly by free-hand, and yet desirous of embellishing some particular surface with decorative illumination. For instance, let it be desired to fill a panel of any given dimension with an illuminated inscription. Take a sheet of tracing-paper the exact size, double it up in both directions, and the creases will give the vertical and horizontal guide-lines for keeping the writing square and even: then set out the number of lines and spaces requisite for the inscription, fixing upon certain initial letters or alphabets for reproduction, from this work, or any other of a similar kind, and making the height of the lines correspond therewith. Then lay the tracing over, and trace with pen, pencil, or brush, each letter in succession, taking care to

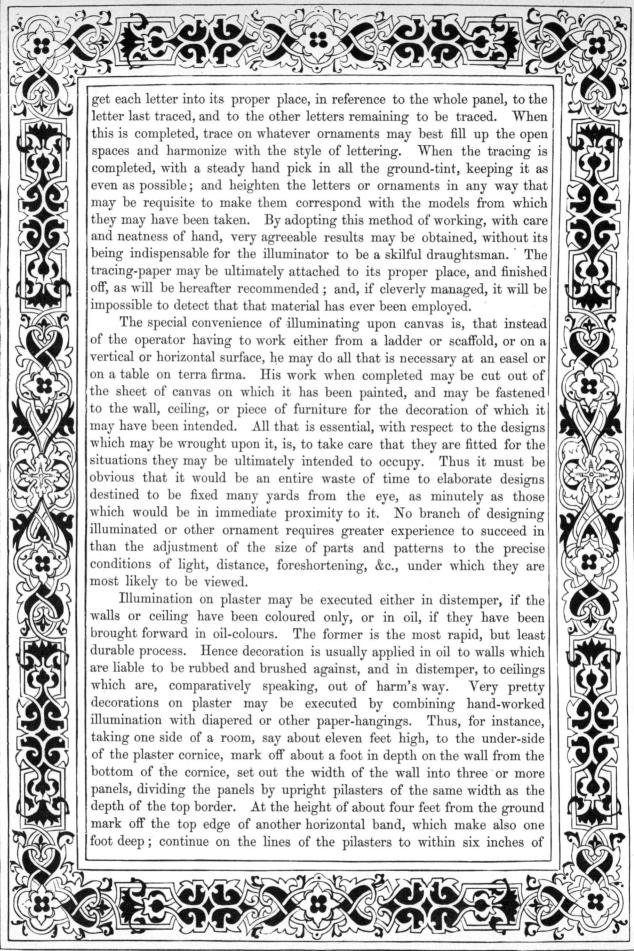

get each letter into its proper place, in reference to the whole panel, to the letter last traced, and to the other letters remaining to be traced. When this is completed, trace on whatever ornaments may best fill up the open spaces and harmonize with the style of lettering. When the tracing is completed, with a steady hand pick in all the ground-tint, keeping it as even as possible; and heighten the letters or ornaments in any way that may be requisite to make them correspond with the models from which they may have been taken. By adopting this method of working, with care and neatness of hand, very agreeable results may be obtained, without its being indispensable for the illuminator to be a skilful draughtsman. The tracing-paper may be ultimately attached to its proper place, and finished off, as will be hereafter recommended; and, if cleverly managed, it will be impossible to detect that that material has ever been employed.

The special convenience of illuminating upon canvas is, that instead of the operator having to work either from a ladder or scaffold, or on a vertical or horizontal surface, he may do all that is necessary at an easel or on a table on terra firma. His work when completed may be cut out of the sheet of canvas on which it has been painted, and may be fastened to the wall, ceiling, or piece of furniture for the decoration of which it may have been intended. All that is essential, with respect to the designs which may be wrought upon it, is, to take care that they are fitted for the situations they may be ultimately intended to occupy. Thus it must be obvious that it would be an entire waste of time to elaborate designs destined to be fixed many yards from the eye, as minutely as those which would be in immediate proximity to it. No branch of designing illuminated or other ornament requires greater experience to succeed in than the adjustment of the size of parts and patterns to the precise conditions of light, distance, foreshortening, &c., under which they are most likely to be viewed.

Illumination on plaster may be executed either in distemper, if the walls or ceiling have been coloured only, or in oil, if they have been brought forward in oil-colours. The former is the most rapid, but least durable process. Hence decoration is usually applied in oil to walls which are liable to be rubbed and brushed against, and in distemper, to ceilings which are, comparatively speaking, out of harm's way. Very pretty decorations on plaster may be executed by combining hand-worked illumination with diapered or other paper-hangings. Thus, for instance, taking one side of a room, say about eleven feet high, to the under-side of the plaster cornice, mark off about a foot in depth on the wall from the bottom of the cornice, set out the width of the wall into three or more panels, dividing the panels by upright pilasters of the same width as the depth of the top border. At the height of about four feet from the ground mark off the top edge of another horizontal band, which make also one foot deep; continue on the lines of the pilasters to within six inches of the top of the skirting, and draw in a horizontal border, six inches high, running all round upon the top edge of the skirting; then paint, in a plain colour, a margin, three or four inches wide, all round the panels formed by the bands and pilasters, and let the paper-hanger fill in the panels with any pretty diapered paper which may agree with the style and colour in which you may desire to work your illumination. The side of your room will then present two horizontal lines—one next the cornice, and one at about dado-height, suitable for the reception of illuminated inscriptions. In setting these out, care must be taken to bring a capital letter into a line with the centre of each pilaster, so that a foliated ornament, descending from the upper inscription, and ascending from the lower one, may meet and intertwine on the pilasters, forming panelled compartments for the introduction of subjects, if thought desirable.[1]

It is by no means necessary for the sides of these pilasters, or the bounding lines of the bands containing inscriptions, to be kept straight; they may be varied at pleasure, so long as they are kept symmetrical in corresponding parts, and uniformly filled up with foliation emanating from, or connected with, the illuminated letters. Agreeable results may be produced by variations of such arrangements as the one suggested. Frequently round doors, windows, fireplaces, &c., inscriptions may be executed with very good effect, either on label-scrolls or simple borders, and with greater or less brilliancy of colour, according to the circumstances of the case. Often simplicity and quiet have greater charms than glitter or brilliancy; thus black and red, on a light-coloured ground, the most primitive combination in the history of writing, is always sure to produce an agreeable impression: blue, crimson, or marone on gold, or *vice versâ*, are no less safe: black, white, and gold, counterchanged, can hardly go wrong. But it is scarcely necessary to dwell upon these details, as the plates in this volume furnish admirable tests by which the student may at once recognize the effects produced by almost any combination of form and colour he may feel desirous to introduce.

Few amateurs will be likely to attempt illuminations upon plaster ceilings, owing to the great difficulty they will experience in working over-head with a steady hand. They will generally do wisely—to execute the principal portions on paper, tracing-paper, or canvas,—to fasten them up, as will be hereafter directed,—and to confine the decoration actually painted on the ceiling, to a few panels, lines, or plain bands of colour, which may be readily executed by any clever house-painter or grainer, even if altogether ignorant of drawing and the art of design. The most beautiful illuminated ceiling of mediæval times, I believe to be that of the celebrated Jacques Cœur's house, at Bourges, in France. It is vaulted, and each compartment contains inscribed labels held by floating angels. The white draperies of

[1] For excellent examples, see plates 13th Century, Nos. 4 and 5, and 15th Century, No. 15.

the angels are relieved on a delicate blue ground only, so that the stronger contrast of the black writing on the white labels gives a marked predominance to the inscriptions; which, being arranged symmetrically, produce in combination agreeable geometrical figures.

Most of the preceding remarks apply equally to stone; but in reference to that material, there is one point to specially enforce,—namely, the advisability of not covering the whole of the surface with paint. There is about all stone a peculiar granulation, and in many varieties a slight silicious sparkle, which it is always well to preserve as far as possible. Illuminate, by all means, inscriptions, panels, friezes, &c., colour occasionally the hollows of mouldings, and gild salient members sufficiently to carry the colour about the monument, whether it may be a font, a pulpit, a tomb, a reredos, a staircase, a screen, or a doorway, and prevent the highly-illuminated portion from looking spotty and unsupported; but by no means apply paint all over. It is not necessary to produce a good effect; it destroys the surface and appearance of the stone, making it of no more worth than if it were plaster, and it clogs up all the fine arrises and angles of the moulded work or carving. Wherever stained glass is inserted in stonework, the application of illumination, or at any rate of coloured diaper-work of an analogous nature, is almost an imperative necessity, in order to balance the appearance of chill and poverty given to the stonework by its contrast with the brilliant translucent tints of the painted glass. In illuminating stonework, it seldom answers to attempt to apply decoration executed on paper or canvas; it should in all cases (excepting when it is at a great distance from the eye) be done upon the stone itself. The only exception is the one to which I shall allude in speaking of metal.

Slate, although from its portability and non-liability to change its shape under variations of temperature, a convenient material for filling panels, and forming slabs for attachment to walls, is not to be recommended to the amateur, owing to the difficulty he will experience in effecting a good and safe adhesion between his pigments and the surface of the slate. In what is called enamelled slate, an excellent attachment is secured by gradually and repeatedly raising the slate to a high temperature; but the process would be far too troublesome and expensive for practice by the great majority of amateurs.

Metal in thin sheets is liable only to the objection from which slate is free,—namely, that it is difficult to keep its surface from undulation in changes of temperature. In all other respects, both zinc, copper, lead, and iron, bind well with any oleaginous vehicle, and offer the great convenience that they may be cut out to any desired shape, and attached to any other kind of material by nails, screws, or even by strong cements, such as marine glue. Zinc is, perhaps, the best of all, as it cuts more readily than copper or iron, and keeps its shape better than lead; care should, however, be always taken to hang it from such points as shall allow it to freely contract and expand. If this is not attended to, its surface will never remain flat. It is a material particularly well adapted for cutting out into labels to surmount door and window arches, or to fill the arcading of churches and chapels, and to be illuminated with texts or other inscriptions. Very beautiful effects may be produced by combining illumination with the polished brass-work which is now so admirably manufactured by Messrs. Hardman, Hart, and others. Care should, however, be taken not to overdo any objects of this nature. Let the main lines of construction always remain unpainted, so that there may be no question as to the substance in which the article is made, and restrict the application of coloured ornament or lettering to panels, and, generally speaking, to the least salient forms. Of course, where it can be afforded, enamelling offers the most legitimate mode of illuminating metal-work; and ere long it is to be hoped that the beautiful series of processes by means of which so much durable beauty of colour was conferred on mediæval metal-work may be restored to their proper position in British Industry, and popularized as they should, and, I believe, might readily be.

To woodwork, illumination may be made a most fitting embellishment; and the application of a very little art will speedily be found to raise the varnished deal cabinet or bookcase far above the majority of our standard "institutions" in the way of heavy and expensive mahogany ones, in interest at least, if not in money value. Almost every article of furniture may thus be made, as it were, to speak and sympathize; for the return every decorated object makes to the decorator is always in direct proportion to the amount of life and thought he has put into his work. It is a common saying, that "what comes from the heart goes to the heart;" and in nothing does it hold good more than in the production of works of art of all kinds, including Illumination, which, through its specially dealing with written characters, has so direct an access to the intellect and affections.

In all appeals the decorative artist can make to the brain through the eye, he has open to him two distinct channels of communication in making out the scheme of his ornamentation,—the one by employing conventional forms,—and the other by introducing representations of natural objects. In the former, he usually eschews light, shade, and accidental effects altogether; and in the latter, he aims at reproducing the aspect of the object he depicts as nearly as possible as it appears to him. Both modes have found favour in the eyes of the great illuminators of old, and by the best they have been frequently and successfully blended.[1] Under the

[1] For striking illustrations of conventional ornament, see plates 6th Century, No. 2; 7th Century, Nos. 2 and 3; 8th Century, Nos. 2, 3, and 4; 9th Century, Nos. 2, 3, 4, 5, 6, and 7; 10th Century, Nos. 2 and 3; 11th Century, Nos. 2, 3, and 4; 12th Century, No. 3, and succeeding numbers, frequently following the natural system of growth in foliation pretty closely. For the mixed styles, most of the plates of the 13th, 14th, and 15th Centuries may be studied; while for the *natural* style, the 16th Century affords capital models in plates Nos. 3, 4, 10, and 11.

"conventional" series may be classed all productions dependent on either an Oriental or Hiberno-Saxon origin; among the "natural," the later, Netherlandish, Italian, and French illuminations may be grouped; and, in a mixed style, the majority of the best book-decorations of the mediæval period.

To be enabled to recognize intuitively how to blend or contrast, to adopt or avoid, these different modes of treatment of ornament, is given to but few, and is revealed to those few only, after years of study and of practice. Rules may assist,[1] but can never suffice to communicate the power; work of the most arduous kind, and persistent observation, can alone bestow it. Still, with good models upon which to base his variations, and goodwill, the amateur may do much, and will probably best succeed by recurring incessantly to Nature, and combining direct, or nearly direct, imitation of Nature with geometrical lines and masses of colour symmetrically disposed. To aid his footsteps in this direction, I know no more convenient councillor than Mr. Llewellyn Jewitt, whose historical introduction to his brother's "Manual of Illuminated and Missal Painting," published by Mr. Barnard of Oxford Street, contains some just remarks upon the subject.[2]

Having thus rapidly touched upon the series of materials upon which

---

[1] The best are contained in the writings of De Quincy, Owen Jones, Winkellman, Pugin, and Sir Charles Eastlake.

[2] *See* especially pages 24 to 28 inclusive, from which I transcribe a few elegant and suggestive passages.

"The student should keep," says Mr. Jewitt, "both in form and colour as near to Nature as possible. No fantastic design can be so elegant as one copied and studied from Nature. What, for instance, can be more beautiful or more appropriate for intertwining with rich scroll-work than the convolvulus, the maurandia, the woodbine, the tropeolum, or the passion-flower? These, painted upon a rich groundwork of diapered gold, or upon one of the beautiful grounds of the 15th century, composed of gold and blue or green, in fine waved or winding lines, crossing each other in every conceivable direction, form truly elegant studies, for almost all varieties of ornamentation. Whenever birds, insects, &c., are introduced, they should, as a general rule, be drawn true to nature; but they may, nevertheless, be turned and twisted into almost any position or shape. For instance, a lizard, with its beautiful emerald-green back, its yellow underparts, and rich brown mottlings, might be introduced with its long tail wrapped and twisted round the stem of a plant, and its little head, with brilliant eyes, shown just peeping out from under one of the beautiful flowers. The lady-bird, with its bright red wings, covered with small black spots, might also be well introduced, creeping upon a leaf or stem. Hairy caterpillars, ants, beetles, snails, glow-worms, and even spiders, form also beautiful additions to a design, and may be introduced in almost any form or shape. Butterflies and moths, in their endless and beautiful variety, with their wings of every conceivable colour and shade, and of the most exquisite forms, are truly amongst the most beautiful and appropriate objects which the student can have for his mind to dwell upon. But not only these,—for occasionally a squirrel might be introduced, perched upon the scroll-work; a cat, a goat, a dog, a monkey peeping out from behind a leaf; or indeed any animal, if artistically and naturally treated, may be introduced with really good effect. Flowers, fruits, shells, corn, &c., all add their beauties to a design; and, indeed, there is nothing in nature, no, not one object, but which may well be introduced into ornamental designing, and may be so translated and poeticised as to become appropriate to any subject."

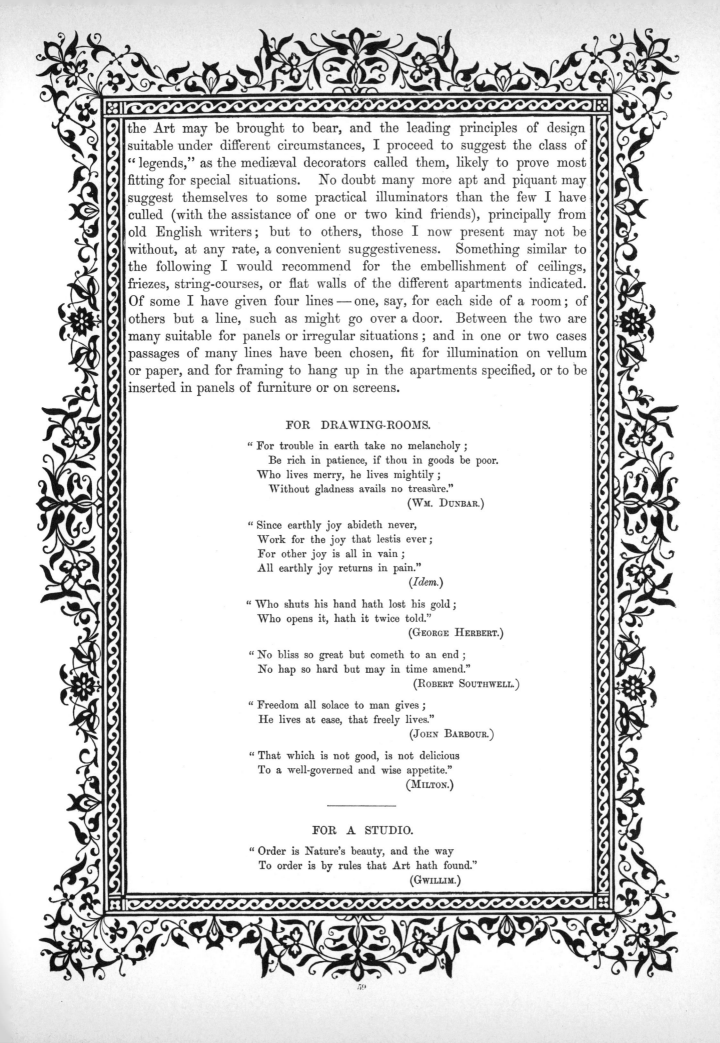

the Art may be brought to bear, and the leading principles of design suitable under different circumstances, I proceed to suggest the class of "legends," as the mediæval decorators called them, likely to prove most fitting for special situations. No doubt many more apt and piquant may suggest themselves to some practical illuminators than the few I have culled (with the assistance of one or two kind friends), principally from old English writers; but to others, those I now present may not be without, at any rate, a convenient suggestiveness. Something similar to the following I would recommend for the embellishment of ceilings, friezes, string-courses, or flat walls of the different apartments indicated. Of some I have given four lines — one, say, for each side of a room; of others but a line, such as might go over a door. Between the two are many suitable for panels or irregular situations; and in one or two cases passages of many lines have been chosen, fit for illumination on vellum or paper, and for framing to hang up in the apartments specified, or to be inserted in panels of furniture or on screens.

FOR DRAWING-ROOMS.

" For trouble in earth take no melancholy ;
    Be rich in patience, if thou in goods be poor.
Who lives merry, he lives mightily ;
    Without gladness avails no treasùre."
(WM. DUNBAR.)

" Since earthly joy abideth never,
    Work for the joy that lestis ever ;
For other joy is all in vain ;
    All earthly joy returns in pain."
(Idem.)

" Who shuts his hand hath lost his gold ;
    Who opens it, hath it twice told."
(GEORGE HERBERT.)

" No bliss so great but cometh to an end ;
    No hap so hard but may in time amend."
(ROBERT SOUTHWELL.)

" Freedom all solace to man gives ;
    He lives at ease, that freely lives."
(JOHN BARBOUR.)

" That which is not good, is not delicious
    To a well-governed and wise appetite."
(MILTON.)

FOR A STUDIO.

" Order is Nature's beauty, and the way
    To order is by rules that Art hath found."
(GWILLIM.)

FOR A FAMILY PORTRAIT-GALLERY OR HALL.

"Boast not the titles of your ancestors,
   Brave youths.: they're their possessions, none of yours.
When your own virtues equall'd have their names,
'Twill be but fair to lean upon their fames,
For they are strong supporters ; but till then
The greatest are but growing gentlemen."
                                        (BEN JONSON)

FOR BREAKFAST OR DINING-ROOMS.

"A good digestion turneth all to health."
                                        (WORDSWORTH.)

"If anything be set to a wrong taste,
   'Tis not the meat there, but the mouth's displeased.
Remove but that sick palate, all is well."
                                        (BEN JONSON.)

"Nature's with little pleased, enough's a feast ;
   A sober life but a small charge requires ;
But man, the author of his own unrest,
   The more he has, the more he still requires."

"To bread or drink, to flesh or fish,
   Yet welcome is the best dish."
                                        (JOHN HEYWOOD.)

"It is the fair acceptance, Sir, creates
The entertainment perfect, not the cates."
                                        (BEN JONSON, *Epigrams*, ci.)

"No simple word
That shall be utter'd at our mirthful board,
Shall make us sad next morning."
                                        (*Ibid.*)

"To spur beyond
Its wiser will the jaded appetite,
Is this for pleasure ? Learn a juster taste,
And know that temperance is true luxury."
                                        (ARMSTRONG, *Art of Preserving Health*, book ii.)

"What an excellent thing did God bestow on man,
   When He did give him a good stomach !"
                                        (BEAUMONT AND FLETCHER.)

"The stomach is the mainspring of our system. If it be not sufficiently wound up to
warm the heart and support the circulation, we can neither
            Think with precision,
            Sleep with tranquillity,
            Walk with vigour,
            Or sit down with comfort."
                                        (DR. KITCHENER.)

"The destiny of Nations has often depended upon the digestion of a Prime Minister."
(DR. KITCHENER.)

"Is't a time to talk
When we should be munching?"
(JUSTICE GREEDY, in MASSINGER'S *New Way to pay Old Debts*.)

"No roofs of gold o'er riotous tables shining,
Whole days and sums devoured with endless dining."
(CRASHAW'S *Religious House*.)

"Now good digestion wait on appetite,
And health on both."
(SHAKSPERE.)

"When you doubt, abstain."
(ZOROASTER.)

"Where there is no peace, there is no feast."
(CLARENDON.)

"Not meat, but cheerfulness, makes the feast."

"Who carves, is kind to two; who talks, to all."
(GEORGE HERBERT.)

FOR KITCHENS.

"A feast must be without a fault;
And if 'tis not all right, 'tis nought."
(KING'S *Art of Cookery*.)

"Good-nature will some failings overlook,
Forgive mischance, not errors of the cook."
(*Ibid.*)

FOR SUPPER-ROOMS.

"Oppress not nature sinking down to rest
With feasts too late, too solid, or too full."
(ARMSTRONG, *Art of Preserving Health*.)

"As men
Do walk a mile, women should talk an hour
After supper: 'tis their exercise."
(BEN JONSON, *Philaster*, act 2, sc. 4.)

FOR STILL-ROOMS.

"The nature of flowers Dame Physic doth show;
She teaches them all to be known to a few."
(TUSSER, *Five Hundred Points of good Husbandry*.)

"The knowledge of stilling is one pretty feat,
The waters be wholesome, the charges not great."
(*Id. ibid.*)

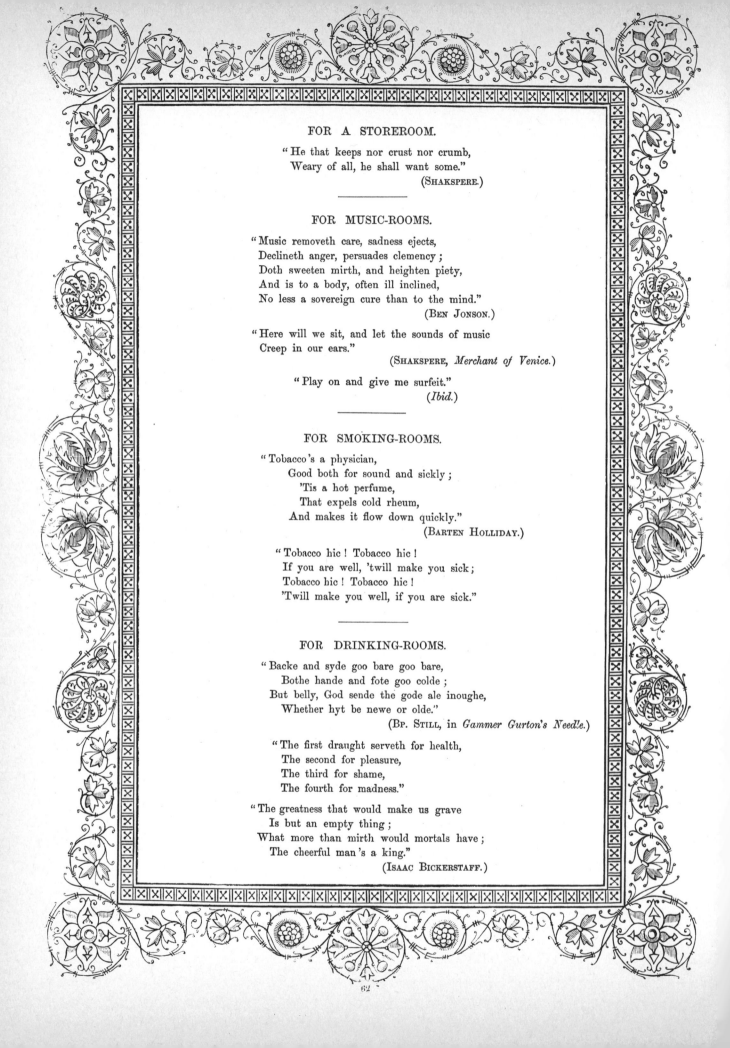

FOR A STOREROOM.

"He that keeps nor crust nor crumb,
    Weary of all, he shall want some."

(SHAKSPERE.)

FOR MUSIC-ROOMS.

"Music removeth care, sadness ejects,
    Declineth anger, persuades clemency;
    Doth sweeten mirth, and heighten piety,
    And is to a body, often ill inclined,
    No less a sovereign cure than to the mind."

(BEN JONSON.)

"Here will we sit, and let the sounds of music
    Creep in our ears."

(SHAKSPERE, Merchant of Venice.)

"Play on and give me surfeit."

(Ibid.)

FOR SMOKING-ROOMS.

"Tobacco's a physician,
    Good both for sound and sickly;
    'Tis a hot perfume,
    That expels cold rheum,
    And makes it flow down quickly."

(BARTEN HOLLIDAY.)

"Tobacco hic! Tobacco hic!
    If you are well, 'twill make you sick;
    Tobacco hic! Tobacco hic!
    'Twill make you well, if you are sick."

FOR DRINKING-ROOMS.

"Backe and syde goo bare goo bare,
    Bothe hande and fote goo colde;
    But belly, God sende the gode ale inoughe,
    Whether hyt be newe or olde."

(BP. STILL, in Gammer Gurton's Needle.)

"The first draught serveth for health,
    The second for pleasure,
    The third for shame,
    The fourth for madness."

"The greatness that would make us grave
    Is but an empty thing;
    What more than mirth would mortals have;
    The cheerful man's a king."

(ISAAC BICKERSTAFF.)

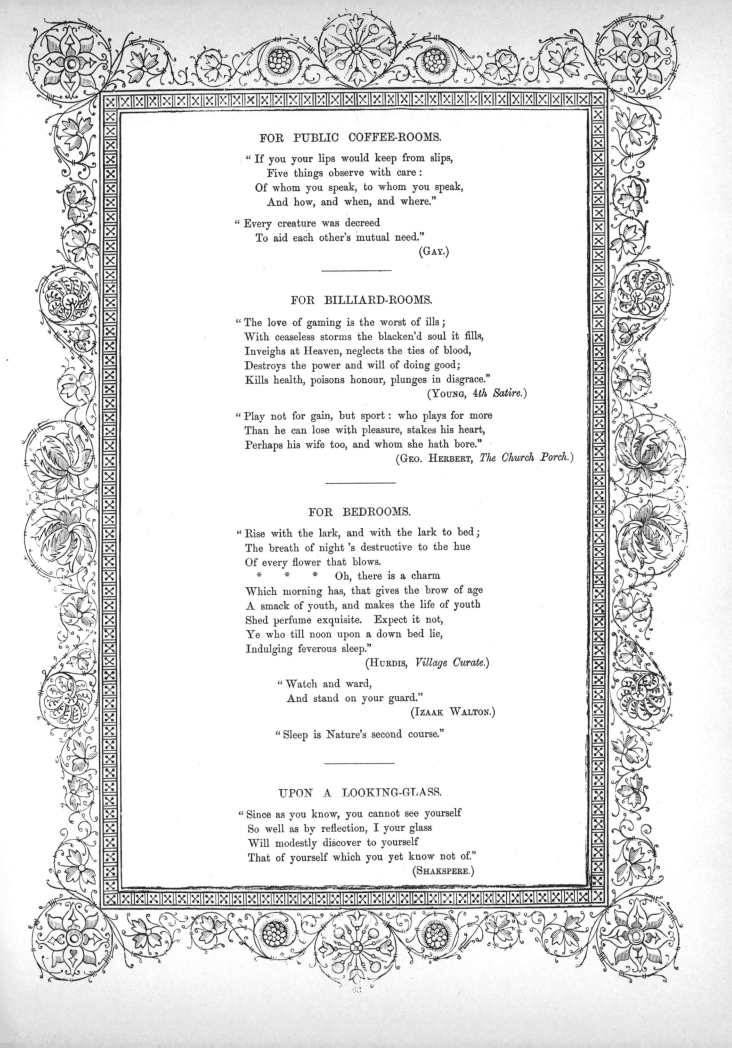

FOR PUBLIC COFFEE-ROOMS.

" If you your lips would keep from slips,
    Five things observe with care :
Of whom you speak, to whom you speak,
    And how, and when, and where."

" Every creature was decreed
    To aid each other's mutual need."
                           (GAY.)

FOR BILLIARD-ROOMS.

" The love of gaming is the worst of ills;
With ceaseless storms the blacken'd soul it fills,
Inveighs at Heaven, neglects the ties of blood,
Destroys the power and will of doing good;
Kills health, poisons honour, plunges in disgrace."
                    (YOUNG, *4th Satire.*)

" Play not for gain, but sport : who plays for more
Than he can lose with pleasure, stakes his heart,
Perhaps his wife too, and whom she hath bore."
        (GEO. HERBERT, *The Church Porch.*)

FOR BEDROOMS.

" Rise with the lark, and with the lark to bed ;
The breath of night 's destructive to the hue
Of every flower that blows.
    *   *   *   Oh, there is a charm
Which morning has, that gives the brow of age
A smack of youth, and makes the life of youth
Shed perfume exquisite. Expect it not,
Ye who till noon upon a down bed lie,
Indulging feverous sleep."
            (HURDIS, *Village Curate.*)

  " Watch and ward,
    And stand on your guard."
              (IZAAK WALTON.)

" Sleep is Nature's second course."

UPON A LOOKING-GLASS.

" Since as you know, you cannot see yourself
So well as by reflection, I your glass
Will modestly discover to yourself
That of yourself which you yet know not of."
                  (SHAKSPERE.)

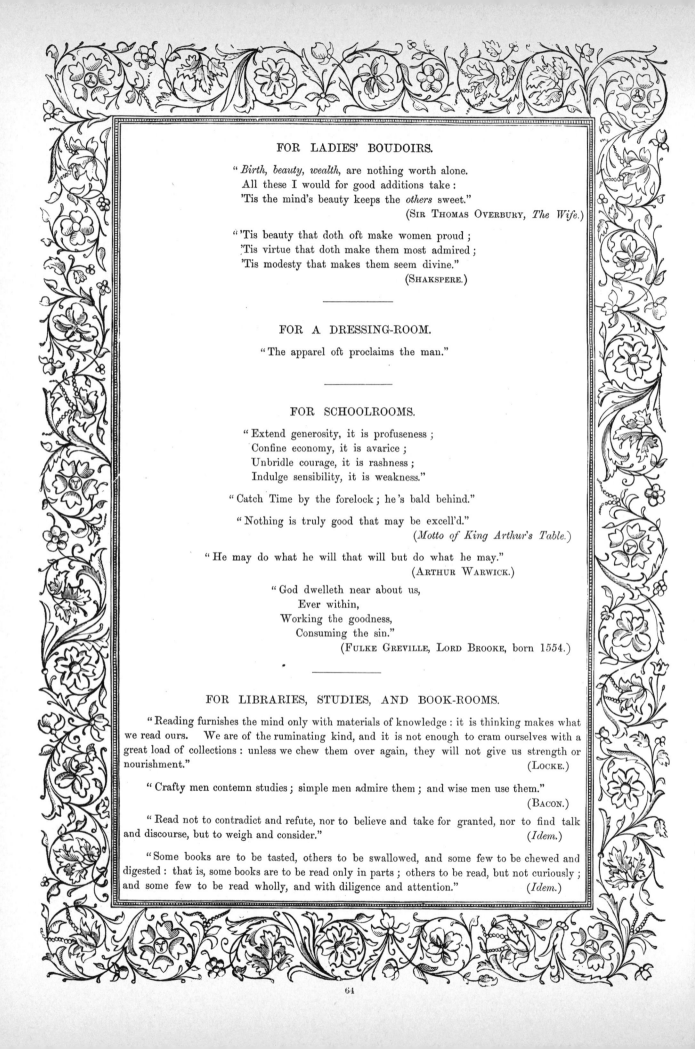

FOR LADIES' BOUDOIRS.

" *Birth, beauty, wealth,* are nothing worth alone.
All these I would for good additions take :
'Tis the mind's beauty keeps the *others* sweet."

(SIR THOMAS OVERBURY, *The Wife.*)

" 'Tis beauty that doth oft make women proud ;
'Tis virtue that doth make them most admired ;
'Tis modesty that makes them seem divine."

(SHAKSPERE.)

FOR A DRESSING-ROOM.

"The apparel oft proclaims the man."

FOR SCHOOLROOMS.

" Extend generosity, it is profuseness ;
Confine economy, it is avarice ;
Unbridle courage, it is rashness ;
Indulge sensibility, it is weakness."

" Catch Time by the forelock ; he's bald behind."

" Nothing is truly good that may be excell'd."

(*Motto of King Arthur's Table.*)

" He may do what he will that will but do what he may."

(ARTHUR WARWICK.)

" God dwelleth near about us,
Ever within,
Working the goodness,
Consuming the sin."

(FULKE GREVILLE, LORD BROOKE, born 1554.)

FOR LIBRARIES, STUDIES, AND BOOK-ROOMS.

" Reading furnishes the mind only with materials of knowledge : it is thinking makes what we read ours.   We are of the ruminating kind, and it is not enough to cram ourselves with a great load of collections : unless we chew them over again, they will not give us strength or nourishment."   (LOCKE.)

" Crafty men contemn studies ; simple men admire them ; and wise men use them."

(BACON.)

" Read not to contradict and refute, nor to believe and take for granted, nor to find talk and discourse, but to weigh and consider."   (*Idem.*)

" Some books are to be tasted, others to be swallowed, and some few to be chewed and digested : that is, some books are to be read only in parts ; others to be read, but not curiously ; and some few to be read wholly, and with diligence and attention."   (*Idem.*)

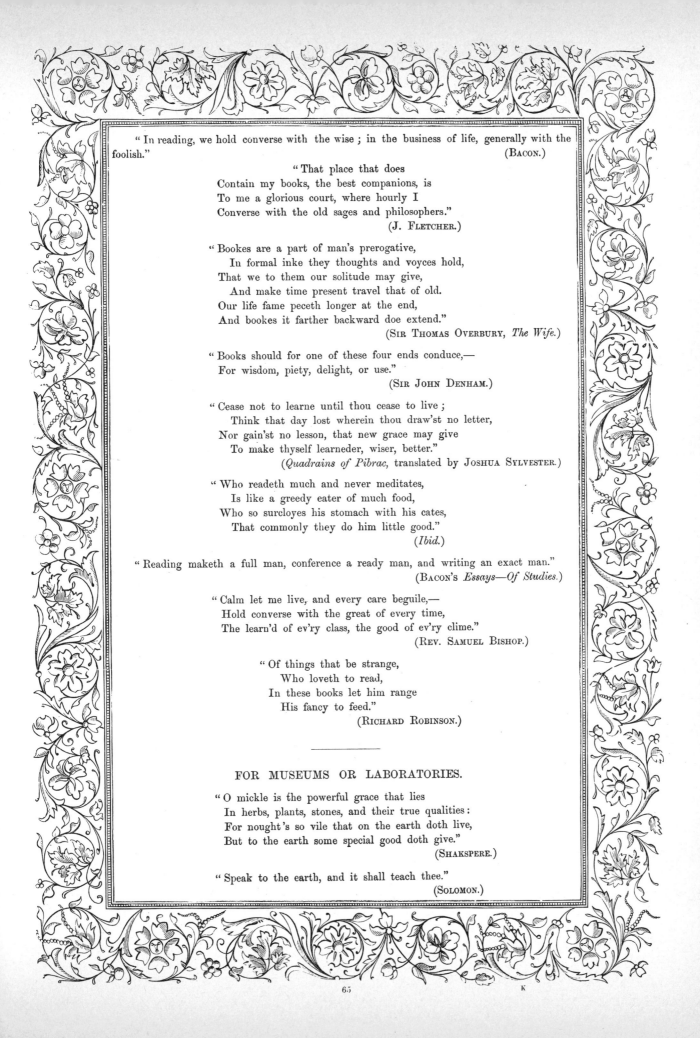

"In reading, we hold converse with the wise ; in the business of life, generally with the foolish."
(BACON.)

"That place that does
Contain my books, the best companions, is
To me a glorious court, where hourly I
Converse with the old sages and philosophers."
(J. FLETCHER.)

"Bookes are a part of man's prerogative,
In formal inke they thoughts and voyces hold,
That we to them our solitude may give,
And make time present travel that of old.
Our life fame peceth longer at the end,
And bookes it farther backward doe extend."
(SIR THOMAS OVERBURY, *The Wife*.)

"Books should for one of these four ends conduce,—
For wisdom, piety, delight, or use."
(SIR JOHN DENHAM.)

"Cease not to learne until thou cease to live ;
Think that day lost wherein thou draw'st no letter,
Nor gain'st no lesson, that new grace may give
To make thyself learneder, wiser, better."
(*Quadrains of Pibrac*, translated by JOSHUA SYLVESTER.)

"Who readeth much and never meditates,
Is like a greedy eater of much food,
Who so surcloyes his stomach with his cates,
That commonly they do him little good."
(*Ibid.*)

"Reading maketh a full man, conference a ready man, and writing an exact man."
(BACON'S *Essays—Of Studies*.)

"Calm let me live, and every care beguile,—
Hold converse with the great of every time,
The learn'd of ev'ry class, the good of ev'ry clime."
(REV. SAMUEL BISHOP.)

"Of things that be strange,
Who loveth to read,
In these books let him range
His fancy to feed."
(RICHARD ROBINSON.)

———

FOR MUSEUMS OR LABORATORIES.

"O mickle is the powerful grace that lies
In herbs, plants, stones, and their true qualities :
For nought's so vile that on the earth doth live,
But to the earth some special good doth give."
(SHAKSPERE.)

"Speak to the earth, and it shall teach thee."
(SOLOMON.)

FOR A SURGICAL MUSEUM.

"There is no theam more plentifull to scan,
Than is the glorious, goodly frame of Man."

(JOSHUA SYLVESTER's *Du Bartas*, 6th day.)

FOR JUSTICE-ROOMS.

"'Tis not enough that thou do no man wrong,—
Thou even in others must suppress the same,
Righting the weake against th' unrighteous strong,
Whether it touch his life, his goods, his name."

(*Quadrains of Pibrac*, trans. by JOSHUA SYLVESTER.)

"Upon the Law thy Judgments alwayes ground,
And not on man: For that 's affection-less.
But man in Passions strangely doth abound;
Th' one all like God: Th' other too-like to beasts."

(*Id. eod.*)

FOR CASINOS OR SUMMER-HOUSES.

"Abusèd mortals, did you know
Where joy, heart's ease, and comfort grow,
You'd scorn proud towers,
And seek them in these bowers;
Where winds, perhaps, sometimes our woods may shake,
But blustering care can never tempest make."

(SIR HENRY WOTTON.)

"We trample grasse, and prize the flowers of May;
Yet grasse is greene when flowers doe fade away."

(ROBERT SOUTHWELL.)

"Blest who no false glare requiring,
Nature's rural sweets admiring,
Can, from grosser joys retiring,
Seek the simple and serene."

(ISAAC BICKERSTAFF.)

FOR A COUNTING-HOUSE.

"*Omnia Somnia.*"

"Gae, silly worm, drudge, trudge, and travell,
So thou maist gain
Some honour or some golden gravell:
But Death the while to fill his number,
With sudden call
Takes thee from all,
To prove thy daies but dream and slumber."

(JOSHUA SYLVESTER, *Mottoes.*)

FOR OFFICES OR WORKSHOPS.

" Have more than thou showest ;
    Speak less than thou knowest ;
    Lend more than thou owest ;
    Learn more than thou trowest."
(SHAKSPERE.)

" A spending hand that alway poureth out,
    Had need to have a bringer-in as fast ;
And on the stone that still doth turn about
    There groweth no moss : these proverbs yet do last."
(SIR T. WYATT.)

" How many might in time have wise been made,
    Before their time, had they not thought them so ?
What artist e'er was master of his trade
    Yer he began his prenticeship to know ?

" To some one act apply thy whole affection,
    And in the craft of others seldom mell ;
But in thine own strive to attain perfection,
    For 'tis no little honour to excell."
(Quadrains of Pibrac, translated by JOSHUA SYLVESTER.)

" If youth knew what age would crave,
    Youth would then both get and save."

" Flee, flee, the idle brain ;
    Flee, flee from doing naught ;
For never was their idle brain,
    But bred an idle thought."

" Get to live ; then live and use it, else it is not true that thou hast gotten."
(G. HERBERT.)

" To him that is willing, ways are not wanting."

FOR SHOPS.

" Whoso trusteth ere he know,
    Doth hurt himself and please his foe."
(SIR THOMAS WYATT.)

" Think much of a trifle,
    Though small it appear ;
Small sands make the mountain,
    And moments the year."

FOR A BELL-TURRET.

" We take no note of time
    But from its loss ; to give it then a tongue
Is wise in man."
(YOUNG's Night Thoughts.)

FOR A BATHING-HOUSE.

"Do not fear to put thy feet
Naked in the river sweet ;
Think nor leach, or newt, or toad
Will bite thy foot, where thou hast trod."
(BEAUMONT AND FLETCHER, *Faithful Shepherdess.*)

With those still more admirable "legends" which may be selected from the Bible I do not meddle. In it golden words of comfort and admonition lie strewn so thickly, that error cannot be made by a selector. It may not be amiss, also, for the illuminator to remember, that not unfrequently "a verse may find him whom a sermon flies."

I cannot quit this portion of my theme without one word of summary, in the way of advice, to the designer of illumination, on whatever material applied. Briefly, then, let him eschew quaintness, and aim at beauty ; let him not shrink from beauty in old times because it was masked in quaintness ; but with a discriminating eye let him learn to winnow the chaff from the wheat, and, scattering the one to the winds, let him garner up the other in the storehouse of his memory, and for the sustenance of his artistic life ; and let him rest assured that the most original designers, in all ages, have been usually those who have gathered most widely and profoundly from the failures, successes, and experiences of their predecessors.

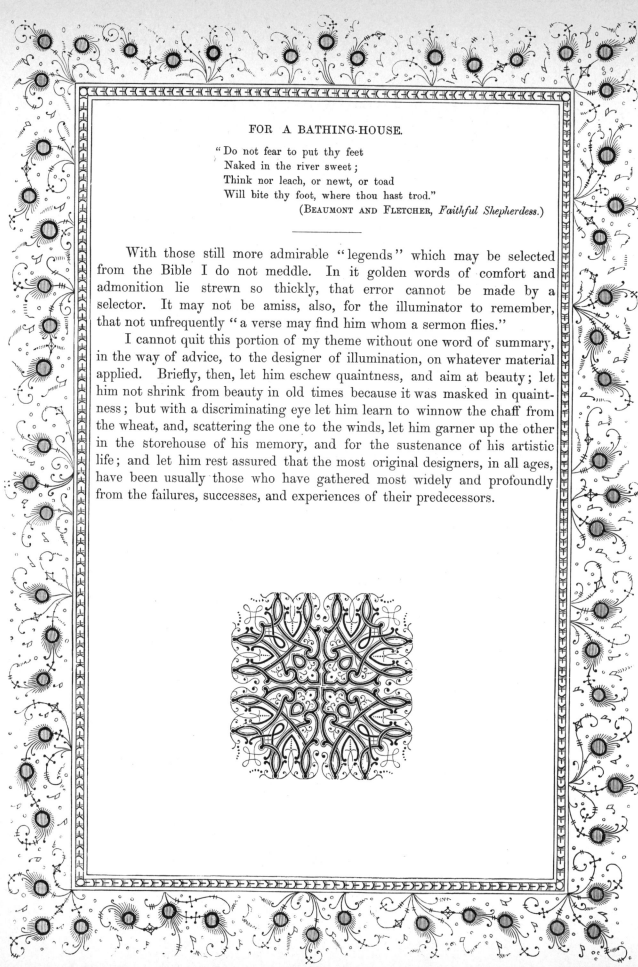

PART III.

HOW THE ART OF ILLUMINATING MAY BE PRACTISED.

———

ON analysis it will be found that this section of my Essay resolves itself into three divisions, embracing respectively, 1stly, the ancient processes; 2ndly, the modern processes; and, 3rdly, the possible processes, not yet introduced into common use. Of the last, I do not purpose speaking in the present work. Notices of the first of these might of course have been incorporated with the historical section of this Essay; but, upon reflection, I considered it would be most useful to the student to introduce them, in a collected form, in this place; and for the following reasons:— 1stly, In order that they might not interrupt the thread of the narrative; and, 2ndly, because I considered it desirable to put the ancient and modern processes in direct contrast, so that the amateur might be the better enabled to reject what is obsolete in the former, and to revive any which might appear to promise greater technical excellence or facility than he might be enabled to obtain through the employment of the latter.

I commence, therefore, with *the Ancient processes*.

Sir Charles Eastlake, who has profoundly studied the history and theory of the subject, has justly remarked[1] the intimate relation which, in the classical ages, existed between the physician and the painter,—the former discovering, supplying, and frequently preparing, the materials used by the latter. This ancient connection was not broken during those ages when almost all knowledge and practice of either medicine or art were limited to the walls of the cloister. The zealous fathers not only worked themselves to the best of their ability, but delighted in training up their younger brethren to perpetuate the credit and revenue derived from their skill, knowledge, and labour, by the monasteries to which they were attached. "Nor was it merely by oral instruction that technical secrets were communicated: the traditional and practical knowledge of the monks was condensed in short manuscript formulæ, sometimes on the subject of the arts alone, but oftener mixed up with chemical and medicinal receipts. These collections, still more heterogeneous in their

———

[1] "Materials for a History of Oil-painting," by Charles Lock Eastlake: London, 1847.

contents as they received fresh additions from other hands, were afterwards published by secular physicians, under the title of 'Secreta.' The earliest of such manuals serve to show the nature of the researches which were undertaken in the convent for the practical benefit of the arts. Various motives might induce the monks to devote themselves with zeal to such pursuits. It has been seen that their chemical studies were analogous; that their knowledge of the materials fittest for technical purposes, derived as it was from experiments which they had abundant leisure to make, was likely to be of the best kind. Painting was holy in their eyes; and, although the excellence of the work depended on the artist, it was for them to insure its durability. By a singular combination of circumstances, the employers of the artist, the purchasers of pictures (for such the fraternities were in the majority of cases), were often the manufacturers of the painter's materials. Here, then, was another plain and powerful reason for furnishing the best-prepared colours and vehicles. The cost of the finer pigments was, in almost every case, charged to the employer; but economy could be combined with excellence of quality, when the manufacture was undertaken by the inmates of the convent."

All that is asserted in this passage with respect to painting, holds equally good with regard to the materials requisite for the practice of the Art of Illumination; and the same treatises which are illustrative of art generally, almost invariably include specific instructions with regard to the particular branch of it I am now endeavouring to illustrate.

Fortunately, the series of these "Secreta" both commences from a remote date, and is tolerably complete from that to a quite recent period. Scattered allusions to the processes of art and industry may be met with in the writings of several authors of the Alexandrian Neo-Platonic school in the early ages of the Church, from whom the Byzantine Greeks, no doubt, learnt much; but the most ancient collection on the subject is to be met with in the treatise of Heraclius, or Eraclius, "de Artibus Romanorum."[1] It would appear not to have been written earlier than the 7th or later than the 10th century,[2] its art being, as Mr. Robert Hendrie, the learned translator and editor of the essay of Theophilus, of whom mention will presently be made, observes, "of the school of Pliny, increased, it is true, by Byzantine invention, but yet essentially Roman."[3] The next collection, in point of age, is that published by Muratori,[4] and well known as the "Lucca Manuscript," ascribed by Mabillon to the age of Charlemagne, and

[1] The most copious text of Heraclius is contained in the Le Bègue collection of writers on art, brought together by Master John Le Bègue, of Paris, in the 15th century.

[2] Sir Charles Eastlake does not place Heraclius so early as Raspe and Mr. Hendrie do. I incline to agree with the last-named critics.

[3] The text of Heraclius is given not from the Le Bègue manuscript, but from one less perfect, formerly at Cambridge, but now in the British Museum, Egerton 840 A, in Raspe's work—"A Critical Essay on Oil-painting." London, 1781.

[4] Muratori, "Antiq. Ital. Medii Ævi," p. 269.

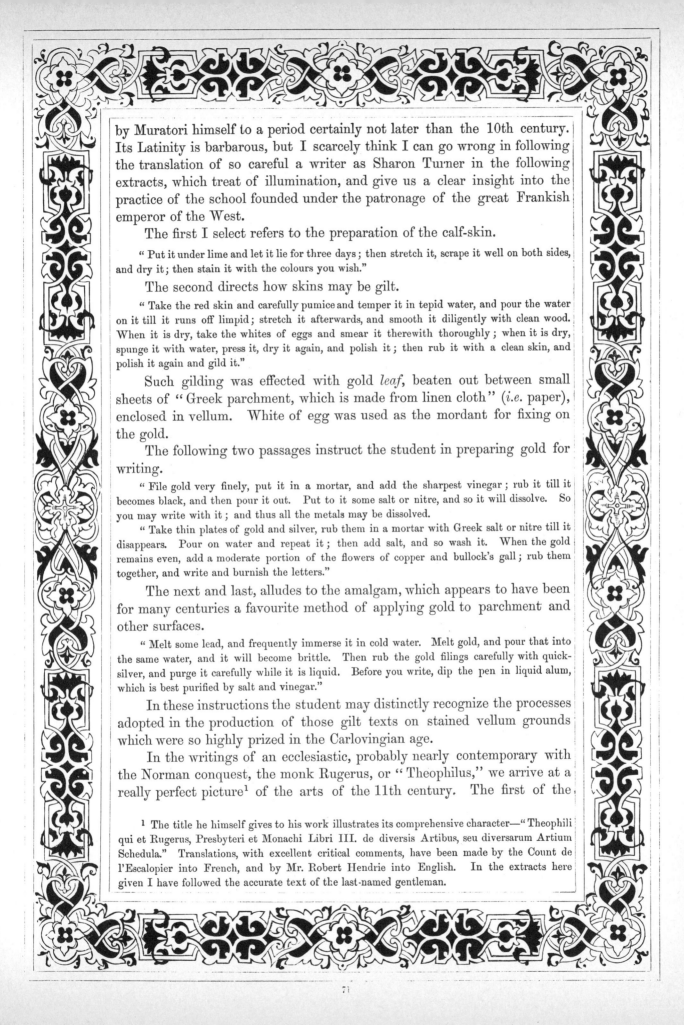

by Muratori himself to a period certainly not later than the 10th century. Its Latinity is barbarous, but I scarcely think I can go wrong in following the translation of so careful a writer as Sharon Turner in the following extracts, which treat of illumination, and give us a clear insight into the practice of the school founded under the patronage of the great Frankish emperor of the West.

The first I select refers to the preparation of the calf-skin.

"Put it under lime and let it lie for three days; then stretch it, scrape it well on both sides, and dry it; then stain it with the colours you wish."

The second directs how skins may be gilt.

"Take the red skin and carefully pumice and temper it in tepid water, and pour the water on it till it runs off limpid; stretch it afterwards, and smooth it diligently with clean wood. When it is dry, take the whites of eggs and smear it therewith thoroughly; when it is dry, spunge it with water, press it, dry it again, and polish it; then rub it with a clean skin, and polish it again and gild it."

Such gilding was effected with gold *leaf*, beaten out between small sheets of "Greek parchment, which is made from linen cloth" (*i.e.* paper), enclosed in vellum. White of egg was used as the mordant for fixing on the gold.

The following two passages instruct the student in preparing gold for writing.

"File gold very finely, put it in a mortar, and add the sharpest vinegar; rub it till it becomes black, and then pour it out. Put to it some salt or nitre, and so it will dissolve. So you may write with it; and thus all the metals may be dissolved.

"Take thin plates of gold and silver, rub them in a mortar with Greek salt or nitre till it disappears. Pour on water and repeat it; then add salt, and so wash it. When the gold remains even, add a moderate portion of the flowers of copper and bullock's gall; rub them together, and write and burnish the letters."

The next and last, alludes to the amalgam, which appears to have been for many centuries a favourite method of applying gold to parchment and other surfaces.

"Melt some lead, and frequently immerse it in cold water. Melt gold, and pour that into the same water, and it will become brittle. Then rub the gold filings carefully with quick-silver, and purge it carefully while it is liquid. Before you write, dip the pen in liquid alum, which is best purified by salt and vinegar."

In these instructions the student may distinctly recognize the processes adopted in the production of those gilt texts on stained vellum grounds which were so highly prized in the Carlovingian age.

In the writings of an ecclesiastic, probably nearly contemporary with the Norman conquest, the monk Rugerus, or "Theophilus," we arrive at a really perfect picture[1] of the arts of the 11th century. The first of the

[1] The title he himself gives to his work illustrates its comprehensive character—"Theophili qui et Rugerus, Presbyteri et Monachi Libri III. de diversis Artibus, seu diversarum Artium Schedula." Translations, with excellent critical comments, have been made by the Count de l'Escalopier into French, and by Mr. Robert Hendrie into English. In the extracts here given I have followed the accurate text of the last-named gentleman.

three books into which his "Schedule of different Arts" is divided, is dedicated entirely to painting. It contains forty chapters, of which thirty refer to the preparation and application of pigments generally, both for oil, tempera, and fresco painting, and ten to the various processes connected with illumination. Of these, the following are the most important.

CHAPTER XXX.

OF GRINDING GOLD FOR BOOKS, AND OF CASTING THE MILL.

WHEN you have traced out figures or letters in books, take pure gold and file it very finely in a clean cup or small basin, and wash it with a pencil in the shell of a tortoise, or a shell which is taken out of the water. Have then a mill with its pestle, both cast from metal of copper and tin mixed together, so that three parts may be of pure copper, and the fourth of pure tin, free from lead. With this composition the mill is cast in the form of a small mortar, and its pestle round about an iron in the form of a knot, so that the iron may protrude of the thickness of a finger, and in length a little more than half a foot, the third part of which iron is fixed in wood carefully turned, in length about one yard, and pierced very straightly; in the lower part of which, however, of the length of four fingers from the end, must be a revolving wheel, either of wood or of lead, and in the middle of the upper part is fixed a leather strap, by which it can be pulled, and, in revolving, be drawn back. Then this mill is placed in a hollow, upon a bench fitted for it, between two small wooden pillars firmly fixed into the same bench, upon which another piece of wood is to be inserted, which can be taken out and replaced, in the middle of which, at the lower part, is a hole in which the pestle of the mill will revolve. These things thus disposed, the gold, carefully cleansed, is put into the mill, a little water added, and the pestle placed, and the upper piece of wood fitted, the strap is drawn and is permitted to revolve, again pulled, and again it revolves, and this must so be done for two or three hours. Then the upper wood is taken off, and the pestle washed in the same water with a pencil. Afterwards the mill is taken up, and the gold, with the water, is stirred to the bottom with the pencil, and is left a little, until the grosser part subsides; the water is presently poured into a very clean basin, and whatever gold comes away with the water is ground. Replacing the water and the pestle, and wood above being placed, again it is milled in the same way as before, until it altogether comes away with the water. In the like manner are ground silver, brass, and copper. But gold is ground most carefully, and must be lightly milled; and you must often inspect it, because it is softer than the other metals, that it may not adhere to the mill or the pestle, and become heaped together. If through negligence this should happen, that which is conglomerate is scraped together and taken out, and what is left is milled until finished. Which being done, pouring out the upper water with the impurities from the basin, wash the gold carefully in a clean shell; then pouring the water from it, agitate it with the pencil, and when you have had it in your hand for one hour, pour it into another shell, and keep that very fine part which has come away with the waters. Then again, water being placed with it, warm it and stir it over the fire, and, as before, pour away the fine particles with the water, and you may act thus until you shall have purified it entirely. After this wash with water the same refined part, and in the same manner a second and a third time, and whatever gold you gather mix with the former. In the same way you will wash silver, brass, and copper. Afterwards take the bladder of a fish which is called *huso* (sturgeon), and washing it three times in tepid water, leave it to soften a night, and on the morrow warm it on the fire, so that it does not boil up until you prove with your finger if it adhere, and when it does adhere strongly, the glue is good.

CHAPTER XXXI.

HOW GOLD AND SILVER ARE LAID IN BOOKS.

Afterwards take pure minium (red lead), and add to it a third part of cinnabar (vermilion), grinding it upon a stone with water. Which being carefully ground, beat up the clear of the white of an egg, in summer with water, in winter without water ; and when it is clear, put the minium into a horn and pour the clear upon it, and stir it a little with a piece of wood put into it, and with a pencil fill up all places with it upon which you wish to lay gold. Then place a little pot with glue over the fire, and when it is liquefied, pour it into the shell of gold and wash it with it. When you have poured which into another shell, in which the purifying is kept, again pour in warm glue, and holding it in the palm of your left hand, stir it carefully with the pencil, and lay it on where you wish, thick or thin, so, however, that there be little glue, because, should it exceed, it blackens the gold and does not receive a polish ; but after it has dried, polish it with a tooth or bloodstone carefully filed and polished, upon a smooth and shining horn tablet. But should it happen, through negligence of the glue not being well cooked, that the gold pulverizes in rubbing, or rises on account of too great thickness, have near you some old clear of egg, beat up without water, and directly with a pencil paint slightly and quickly over the gold ; when it is dry, again rub it with the tooth or stone. Lay in this manner silver, brass, and copper in their place and polish them.

The raised gold was not always produced by the mixture of red lead and white of egg recommended by Theophilus. It was, especially in Italy, frequently made of a composition of "gesso," or plaster, and in the 15th century was often punctured all over by way of ornament. It may be occasionally met with stamped over in patterns, with intaglio punches. This "gesso raising," though very brilliant, possessed little tenacity, and in many examples it has scaled off, while the more ancient "raising" prescribed by Theophilus has adhered perfectly.

CHAPTER XXXII.

HOW A PICTURE IS ORNAMENTED IN BOOKS WITH TIN AND SAFFRON.

But if you have neither of these (gold, silver, brass, or copper), and yet wish to decorate your work in some manner, take tin pure and finely scraped, mill it and wash it like gold, and apply it with the same glue, upon letters or other places which you wish to ornament with gold or silver ; and when you have polished it with a tooth, take saffron, with which silk is coloured, moistening it with clear of egg without water, and when it has stood a night, on the following day cover with a pencil the places which you wish to gild, the rest holding the place of silver. Then make fine traits round letters and leaves, and flourishes from minium, with a pen, also the stuffs of dresses and other ornaments.

CHAPTER XXXIII.

OF EVERY SORT OF GLUE FOR A PICTURE OF GOLD.

If you have not a bladder (of the sturgeon), cut up thick parchment or vellum in the same manner,—wash and cook it. Prepare also the skin of an eel carefully scraped, cut up and washed in the same manner. Prepare thus also the bones of the head of the wolf-fish washed and dried, carefully washed in water three times. To whichever of these you have prepared, add a third part of very transparent gum, simmer it a little, and you can keep it as long as you wish.

CHAPTER XXXIV.

HOW COLOURS ARE TEMPERED FOR BOOKS.

These things thus accomplished, make a mixture of the clearest gum and water as above, and temper all colours except green, and ceruse, and minium, and carmine. Salt green is worth nothing for books. You will temper Spanish green with pure wine, and if you wish to make shadows, add a little sap of iris, or cabbage, or leek. You will temper minium, and ceruse, and carmine, with clear of egg. Compose all preparations of colours for a book as above, if you want them for painting figures. All colours are laid on twice in books, at first very thinly, then more thickly ; but twice for letters.

The next extract I give is of great interest in the technical history of illumination, on three accounts: firstly, because it guides the student to recognize in madder the purple stain and colour, so highly prized in the early periods of the art; secondly, because it shows him the manner in which fugitive vegetable tints were protected from the decomposing influence of the atmosphere by an albuminous varnish; and thirdly, because it illustrates the ordinary modern processes of under painting, and glazing with transparent colour. The "folium" of the Greek illuminators was procured from plants growing abundantly near Athens, while that of the Hiberno-Saxon scribes was obtained from the "norma" or "gorma" of the Celts. Mr. Hendrie, in his learned notes to Theophilus, has traced successive recipes for the preparation of "folium," in which the identity of the base giving the colouring matter is clearly established. It is curious that the collections of "Secreta" should give as the only countries supplying the materials for making "folium," those two in which the use of the bright purple stain ascends to the very earliest of their decorated manuscripts. The following is the description given by Theophilus:—

CHAPTER XXXV.

OF THE KINDS AND THE TEMPERING OF FOLIUM.

There are three kinds of folium, one red, another purple, a third blue, which you will thus temper. Take ashes, and sift them through a cloth, and, sprinkling them with cold water, make rolls of them in form of loaves, and placing them in the fire, leave them until they quite glow. After they have first burnt for a very long time, and have afterwards cooled, place a portion of them in a vessel of clay, pouring urine upon them and stirring with wood. When it has deposed in a clear manner, pour it upon the red folium, and, grinding it slightly upon a stone, add to it a fourth part of quick lime, and when it shall be ground and sufficiently moistened, strain it through a cloth, and paint with a pencil where you wish, thinly; afterwards more thickly. And if you wish to imitate a robe in a page of a book, with purple folium; with the same tempering, without the mixture of lime, paint first with a pen, in the same page, flourishes or circles, and in them birds or beasts, or leaves; and when it is dry, paint red folium over all, thinly, then more thickly, and a third time if necessary; and afterwards paint over it some old clear of egg. Paint over also with glaire of egg, draperies, and all things which you have painted with folium and carmine. You can likewise preserve the burned ashes which remain for a long time, dry.

I conclude[1] the series of receipts extracted from Theophilus by one

[1] I cannot take leave of this good old monk, the influence exercised by whose writings during the whole of the Middle Ages, is proved by the numerous transcripts of them executed at different periods, still preserved in most of the chief European libraries, without giving him credit for a pure and liberal philanthropy worthy of imitation in all ages. Nothing can be more dignified and noble than the words in which he concludes the introduction to his work. After reciting the various arts he has endeavoured to illustrate, and the sufferings and labour through which the knowledge he desires to convey to others had been acquired by himself, he winds up by saying :—

"When you shall have re-read this often, and have committed it to your tenacious memory, you shall thus recompense me for this care of instruction, that, as often as you shall successfully have made use of my work, you pray for me for the pity of omnipotent God, who knows that I have written these things which are here arranged, neither through love of human approbation, nor through desire of temporal reward, nor have I stolen anything precious or rare through envious jealousy, nor have I kept back anything reserved for myself alone; but, in augmentation

not further bearing upon the Art of Illumination, than as proving the nature of the ink which has generally retained its colour so wonderfully in the ancient manuscripts.

CHAPTER XL.

OF INK.

To make ink, cut for yourself wood of the thorn-trees in April or May, before they produce flowers or leaves, and collecting them in small bundles, allow them to lie in the shade for two, three, or four weeks, until they are somewhat dry. Then have wooden mallets, with which you beat these thorns upon another piece of hard wood, until you peel off the bark everywhere, put which immediately into a barrelful of water. When you have filled two, or three, or four, or five barrels with bark and water, allow them so to stand for eight days, until the waters imbibe all the sap of the bark. Afterwards put this water into a very clean pan, or into a cauldron, and fire being placed under it, boil it; from time to time, also, throw into the pan some of this bark, so that whatever sap may remain in it may be boiled out. When you have cooked it a little, throw it out, and again put in more; which done, boil down the remaining water unto a third part, and then, pouring it out of this pan, put it into one smaller, and cook it until it grows black and begins to thicken, add one third part of pure wine, and putting it into two or three new pots, cook it until you see a sort of skin show itself on the surface; then taking these pots from the fire, place them in the sun until the black ink purifies itself from the red dregs. Afterwards take small bags of parchment carefully sewn, and bladders, and pouring in the pure ink, suspend them in the sun until all is quite dry; and when dry, take from it as much as you wish, and temper it with wine over the fire, and, adding a little vitriol, write. But, if it should happen through negligence that your ink be not black enough, take a fragment of the thickness of a finger, and putting it into the fire, allow it to glow, and throw it directly into the ink.

The next collection of Secreta, in point of importance and probable antiquity, is the " Mappæ Clavicula," or " little key to drawing," a manu-script treatise on the preparation of pigments, and on various processes of the decorative arts practised during the Middle Ages, in the possession of Sir Thomas Phillipps, of Middle Hill.[1] The proprietor of the volume, Mr. Hendrie, Sir Charles Eastlake, and (last, not least) Mr. Albert Way, agree in considering it highly probable that it may be an English collec-tion, probably of about the reign of Henry II. Like the " Schedula" of Theophilus, it presents a very miscellaneous series of recipes, and tends to prove, what is very generally believed by the learned, that the " Masters of Arts" of old were frequently skilled, not in special departments of production, such as the modern division-of-labour system has created, but in multifarious avocations, such as we should not now readily recognize as likely to be practised by any single individual.

These collections remarkably illustrate the class of knowledge likely to have been possessed by such apparently versatile geniuses as St. Dunstan, St. Eloi, Bernward of Hildesheim, Tutilo the monk of St. Gall, and many others. The author of the " Mappæ Clavicula," in a few lines of poetical introduction to his teachings, defines the first necessity for painters to be, a

of the honour and glory of His name, I have consulted the progress and hastened to aid the necessities of many men."

[1] It will be found given in extenso in the 32nd vol. of " The Archæologia," pp. 183—244, with an elaborate letter from its possessor.

knowledge of the manufacture of colours, then a command over the various modes of mixing them, then dexterity in using and heightening them in different kinds of work; and, ultimately, he commends to their attention a variety of information for the advancement of art generally, derived from the writings of many learned men.—"Sicut liber iste docebit." Thus under two hundred and nine heads, but with some tautology, he proceeds to treat, as Sir Thomas Phillipps observes, not only of the composition of colours, but "of a variety of other subjects, in a concise and simple manner, and generally very intelligibly; as for instance, architecture, mensuration of altitudes, the art of war, &c." Among the recipes, in addition to those referring to pigments, are many relating to illuminating. The following, for instance, is curious as defining clearly what were the best and most important tints for illumination :—

Of different Colours.

"These colours are clear and full-bodied for parchment :—Azorium (azure), Vermiculum (vermilion), Sanguis Draconis (dragon's blood), Carum (yellow ochre), Minium (red lead), Folium (madder purple), Auripigmentum (orpiment), Viride Græcum (acetate of copper), Gravetum Indicum (indigo), Brunum (brown), Crocus (yellow), Minium Rubeum vel Album (red or white lead), Nigrum Optimum ex carbone vitis (the best black made from carbonized vine twigs); all these colours are mixed with white of egg."

The mixture of colours appears to have been reduced to a perfect system, each hue having others specially adapted and used, for heightening and lowering the pure tint; thus the author gives directions which are likely to be scarcely less useful to the illuminator of the present day than they were to those of old.

Of Mixtures.

"If, therefore, you should desire to know the natures and mixtures of these [the above-given] colours, and which are antagonistic to each other, lend your ear diligently.

"Mix azure with white lead, lower with indigo, heighten with white lead. Pure vermilion you may lower with brown or with dragon's blood, and heighten with orpiment. Mix vermilion with white lead, and make the colour which is called *Rosa*, lower it with vermilion, heighten it with white lead. Item, you may make a colour with dragon's blood and orpiment, which you may lower with brown, and heighten with orpiment. Yellow ochre you may lower with brown, and heighten with red lead (query, with white). Item, you may make Rosam [1] of yellow ochre and white lead, deepen with yellow ochre, heighten with white lead. Reddish purple (folium) may be lowered with brown, and heightened with white lead. Item, mix folium with white lead, lower with folium, and heighten with white lead. Orpiment may be lowered with vermilion, but cannot be heightened, because it stains all other colours."

Of Tempering.

"Greek green you will temper with acid, deepen with black, and heighten with white, made from stag's horn (ivory black). Mix green with white lead, deepen with pure green, and heighten with white lead. Greenish blue, deepen with green, heighten with white lead. Yellow, deepen with vermilion, heighten with white lead. Indigo, deepen with black, heighten with azure. Item, mix indigo with white, deepen with azure, heighten with white lead. Brown, deepen with black, heighten with red lead. Item, make of brown and white lead a drab (Rosam),

---

[1] There is some confusion about this word, for it is used to denote mixtures which would produce real rose-colour, light warm yellow, and a perfect drab.

lower with brown, heighten with white lead. Item, mix yellow with white lead, lower with yellow, heighten with white lead. Lower red lead with brown, heighten with white lead. Item, red lead with brown, deepen with black, heighten with red lead. Item, you may make flesh-colour of red lead and white, lower with vermilion, heighten with white lead."

Which Colours are Antagonistic.

" If you wish to know in what manner colours are antagonistic, this is it. Orpiment (sulphuret of arsenic) does not agree with purple (folio), nor with green (acetate of copper), nor with red lead, nor white lead. Green does not agree with purple.[1]

" If you wish to make grounds, make a fine rose-colour of vermilion and white. Item, make a ground of purple mixed with chalk. Item, make a ground of green mixed with vinegar. Item, make a ground of the same green, and when it shall have become dry, cover it with size ('caule').

" If you wish to write in gold, take powder of gold and moisten it with size, made from the very same parchment on which you have to write; and with the gold and size near to the fire; and, when the writing shall be dry, burnish with a very smooth stone, or with the tooth of a wild boar. Item, if then you should wish to make a robe or a picture, you may apply gold to the parchment, as I have above directed, and shade with ink or with indigo, and heighten with orpiment."

The above are the principal passages in the " Mappæ Clavicula," which supply deficiencies in most other books of Secreta; and I have translated them at length, both on account of the accuracy with which I have found the directions followed in ancient illuminated manuscripts, and because I believed that a knowledge of this ancient scale of colours might greatly facilitate accurate copying from old examples. I need scarcely say, that as the art of painting improved in Italy and the Netherlands, the illuminator's palette became enriched with several new and very brilliant colours;—such as the ultramarines and carmines (exceedingly scarce in early manuscripts) which make the books produced at Rome and in Northern Italy, during the 16th and 17th centuries, glow with a vivacity never previously attained. Every improvement made in one country was, however, speedily communicated through these very art-treatises to other countries, and thus we find lakes and carmines freely used in England during the 15th century.[2] Ultramarine, indeed, forms the special subject of an essay by a Norman, comprised among the Le Bègue MSS. (already referred to), under the following title, which proves its novelty in Western Europe, at the beginning of the 15th century :—

" Anno 1411, Johannes de . . . . (illegible) Normannus de *Azurro novo*, lapidis lazulli ultramarini."

The next collection of Secreta in importance, and probably in date to the " Mappæ Clavicula," is that of a Frenchman, Peter de St. Audemar. " With this treatise," observes Sir Charles Eastlake, " may be classed a similar one in the British Museum, written in the 14th century," but treating of a somewhat earlier practice in art. The identity of the colours

[1] That is, the mineral green with the vegetable madder.
[2] A beautiful example may be found in Dan Lydgate's legends of St. Edmund and St. Fremund, MS. Harleian, 2278.

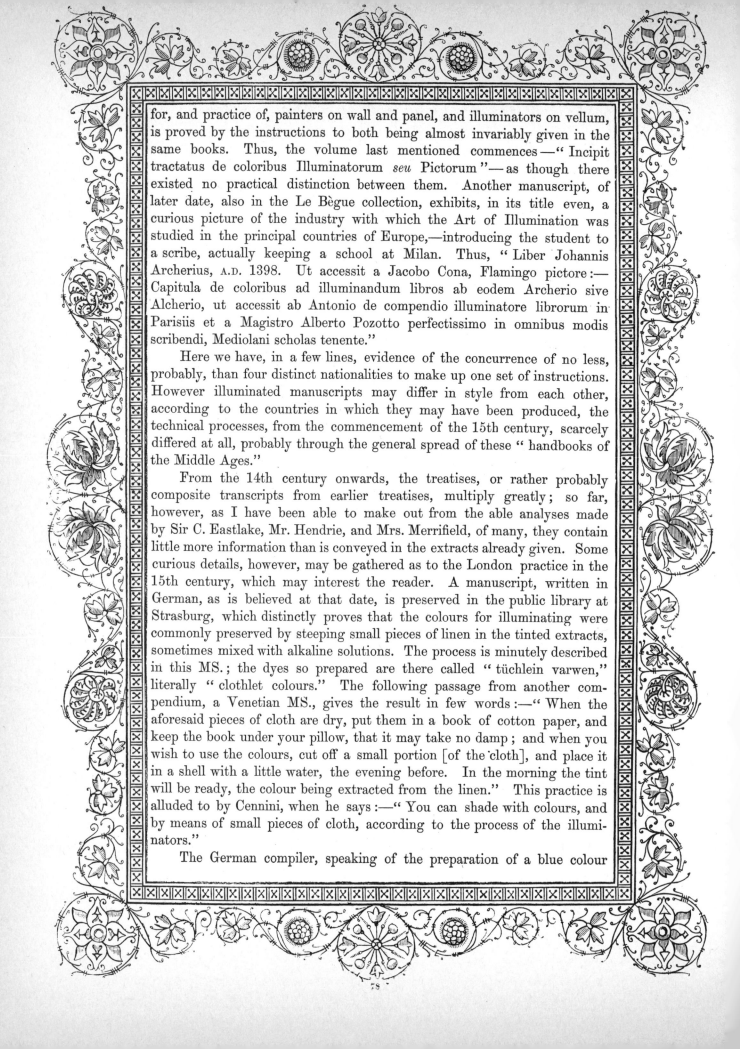

for, and practice of, painters on wall and panel, and illuminators on vellum, is proved by the instructions to both being almost invariably given in the same books. Thus, the volume last mentioned commences—" Incipit tractatus de coloribus Illuminatorum *seu* Pictorum "—as though there existed no practical distinction between them. Another manuscript, of later date, also in the Le Bègue collection, exhibits, in its title even, a curious picture of the industry with which the Art of Illumination was studied in the principal countries of Europe,—introducing the student to a scribe, actually keeping a school at Milan. Thus, " Liber Johannis Archerius, A.D. 1398. Ut accessit a Jacobo Cona, Flamingo pictore :— Capitula de coloribus ad illuminandum libros ab eodem Archerio sive Alcherio, ut accessit ab Antonio de compendio illuminatore librorum in Parisiis et a Magistro Alberto Pozotto perfectissimo in omnibus modis scribendi, Mediolani scholas tenente."

Here we have, in a few lines, evidence of the concurrence of no less, probably, than four distinct nationalities to make up one set of instructions. However illuminated manuscripts may differ in style from each other, according to the countries in which they may have been produced, the technical processes, from the commencement of the 15th century, scarcely differed at all, probably through the general spread of these " handbooks of the Middle Ages."

From the 14th century onwards, the treatises, or rather probably composite transcripts from earlier treatises, multiply greatly; so far, however, as I have been able to make out from the able analyses made by Sir C. Eastlake, Mr. Hendrie, and Mrs. Merrifield, of many, they contain little more information than is conveyed in the extracts already given. Some curious details, however, may be gathered as to the London practice in the 15th century, which may interest the reader. A manuscript, written in German, as is believed at that date, is preserved in the public library at Strasburg, which distinctly proves that the colours for illuminating were commonly preserved by steeping small pieces of linen in the tinted extracts, sometimes mixed with alkaline solutions. The process is minutely described in this MS.; the dyes so prepared are there called " tüchlein varwen," literally " clothlet colours." The following passage from another compendium, a Venetian MS., gives the result in few words :—" When the aforesaid pieces of cloth are dry, put them in a book of cotton paper, and keep the book under your pillow, that it may take no damp ; and when you wish to use the colours, cut off a small portion [of the cloth], and place it in a shell with a little water, the evening before. In the morning the tint will be ready, the colour being extracted from the linen." This practice is alluded to by Cennini, when he says :—" You can shade with colours, and by means of small pieces of cloth, according to the process of the illuminators."

The German compiler, speaking of the preparation of a blue colour

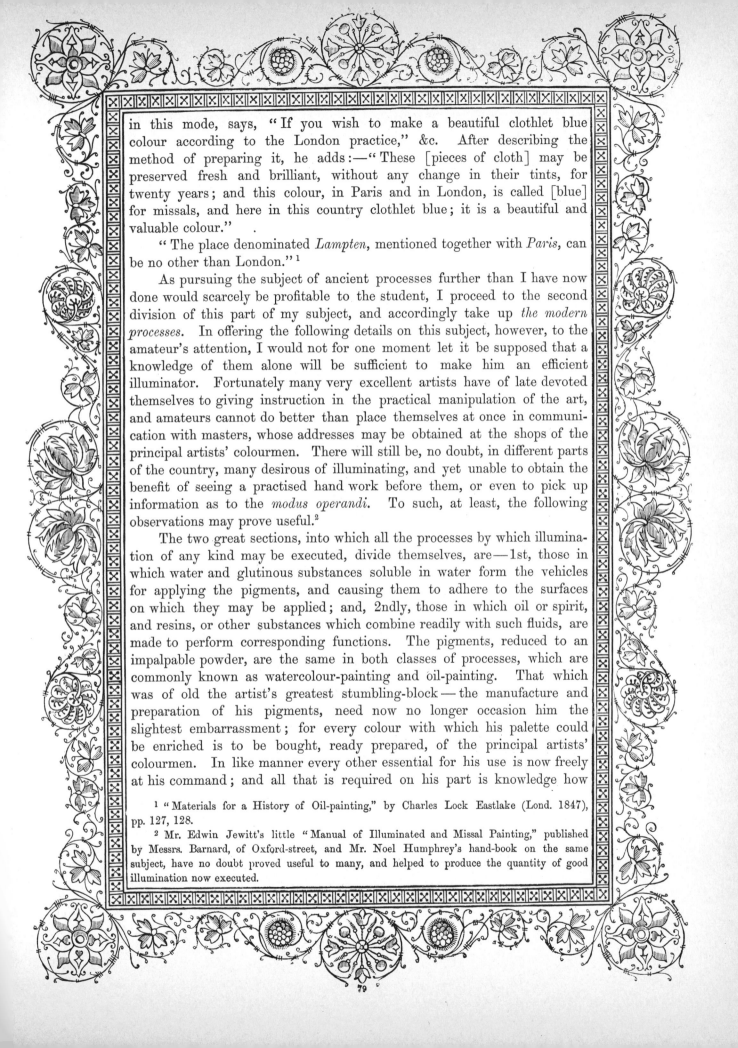

in this mode, says, " If you wish to make a beautiful clothlet blue colour according to the London practice," &c. After describing the method of preparing it, he adds :—" These [pieces of cloth] may be preserved fresh and brilliant, without any change in their tints, for twenty years; and this colour, in Paris and in London, is called [blue] for missals, and here in this country clothlet blue; it is a beautiful and valuable colour."   .

" The place denominated *Lampten*, mentioned together with *Paris*, can be no other than London." [1]

As pursuing the subject of ancient processes further than I have now done would scarcely be profitable to the student, I proceed to the second division of this part of my subject, and accordingly take up *the modern processes*. In offering the following details on this subject, however, to the amateur's attention, I would not for one moment let it be supposed that a knowledge of them alone will be sufficient to make him an efficient illuminator. Fortunately many very excellent artists have of late devoted themselves to giving instruction in the practical manipulation of the art, and amateurs cannot do better than place themselves at once in communication with masters, whose addresses may be obtained at the shops of the principal artists' colourmen. There will still be, no doubt, in different parts of the country, many desirous of illuminating, and yet unable to obtain the benefit of seeing a practised hand work before them, or even to pick up information as to the *modus operandi*. To such, at least, the following observations may prove useful.[2]

The two great sections, into which all the processes by which illumination of any kind may be executed, divide themselves, are—1st, those in which water and glutinous substances soluble in water form the vehicles for applying the pigments, and causing them to adhere to the surfaces on which they may be applied; and, 2ndly, those in which oil or spirit, and resins, or other substances which combine readily with such fluids, are made to perform corresponding functions. The pigments, reduced to an impalpable powder, are the same in both classes of processes, which are commonly known as watercolour-painting and oil-painting. That which was of old the artist's greatest stumbling-block — the manufacture and preparation of his pigments, need now no longer occasion him the slightest embarrassment; for every colour with which his palette could be enriched is to be bought, ready prepared, of the principal artists' colourmen. In like manner every other essential for his use is now freely at his command; and all that is required on his part is knowledge how

[1] " Materials for a History of Oil-painting," by Charles Lock Eastlake (Lond. 1847), pp. 127, 128.

[2] Mr. Edwin Jewitt's little " Manual of Illuminated and Missal Painting," published by Messrs. Barnard, of Oxford-street, and Mr. Noel Humphrey's hand-book on the same subject, have no doubt proved useful to many, and helped to produce the quantity of good illumination now executed.

to employ the materials which others most dexterously and carefully place at his disposal.

In commencing the collection of that information which I am now endeavouring to communicate, I felt it my duty to enter into correspondence with all those manufacturers whose products I had at different times personally tested ; and I accordingly addressed myself to the following, whose materials, with insignificant exceptions, I have invariably found satisfactory, both in nature and quality.

R. ACKERMAN, 191, Regent-street, W.

L. BARBE, 60, Quadrant, Regent-street, W.

J. BARNARD, 339, Oxford-street, W.

Messrs. BRODIE & MIDDLETON, 79, Long-acre, W.C.

H. MILLER, 56, Long-acre, W.C.

J. NEWMAN, 24, Soho-square, W.

Messrs. REEVES & SONS, 113, Cheapside, E.C.

Messrs. ROBERSON, 99, Long-acre, W.C.

Messrs. ROWNEY & Co., 51, Rathbone-place, W.

Messrs. SHERBORNE & TILLYER, 321, Oxford-street, W.

Messrs. WINSOR & NEWTON, 38, Rathbone-place, W.

From each of the above-mentioned firms I have obtained valuable information, and from several, excellent samples of their products. I am glad, therefore, to take the present opportunity of expressing my obligations to them. From Messrs. Winsor & Newton, especially, I have received the kindest and most intelligent co-operation; and I am happy to be the channel of making public the results of a series of experiments, on the combinations of colours and the use of various materials for illuminating purposes, suggested by me, and made with great tact and judgment by Mr. W. H. Winsor. Messrs. Winsor & Newton and Mr. Barnard have, up to the present time, done most to smooth away the difficulties which beset the illuminator. Messrs. Newman, Messrs. Rowney & Co., Messrs. Reeves & Sons, and Mr. Barbe, have also recently contributed valuable improvements or special adaptations.[1]

The colours best suited for illuminating I believe to be as follows :—

B	Lemon Yellow	....	
A	Gamboge	....	
A	Cadmium Yellow	....	Yellow.
D	Mars Yellow	....	

---

[1] For illumination in water-colour on paper, cardboard, or vellum, Messrs. Winsor & Newton, Rowney, Barnard, Newman, and others, fit up boxes with special selections of all requisite materials ; including all that can be wanted for the application and burnishing of gold and other metals. Messrs. Miller's " Glass Mediums, Nos. 1 and 2," and Newman's " Preparation for sizing albumenized papers," are exceedingly useful for mixing with illuminating colours ; giving great hardness and body to them, and preventing them from " washing up," in working over with glazing and other tints. I have found Mr. Barbe's powder body-colours give remarkably solid tints, with great freedom in working.

B	Rose Madder .... ⎫	
A	Crimson Lake.............. ⎪	
C	Carmine .... ⎬ Red.	
C	Orange Vermilion .... ⎪	
A	Vermilion .... ⎭	
A	Cobalt .... ⎫	
A	French Blue .... ⎬ Blue.	
D	Smalt .... ⎭	
D	Mars Orange .... ⎫ Orange.	
B	Burnt Sienna .... ⎭	
C	Burnt Carmine .... ⎫ Purple.	
D	Indian Purple............. ⎭	
A	Emerald Green .... ⎫ Green.	
C	Green Oxide of Chromium ⎭	
B	Vandyke Brown.............. Brown.	
A	Lampblack .... Black.	
A	Chinese White .... White.	

These colours are selected from the list of water-colours made at the present day (upwards of eighty), and will, I think, be found to be all that can well be required for illuminating. The whole number is by no means indispensable, and I have therefore marked by different letters of the alphabet,—1st, A, those without which it would be useless to commence work; 2ndly, B, those which should first be added; 3rdly, C, those which are required for very great brilliancy in certain effects; and, 4thly, D, those which may be regarded as luxuries in the art. The C are really important; the D are much less so. Messrs. Winsor & Newton have arranged them into four different lists, which are placed in boxes (complete with colours and materials for working in water-colours), of the respective retail values of £1. 1s., £1. 11s. 6d., £2. 2s., and £3. 3s. Boxes corresponding with, or slightly varying from these, in selection of colours and materials, may be obtained from other artists' colourmen.

I now proceed to notice these colours *seriatim*, in reference to their tints, both when used alone and when mixed with other colours.

YELLOWS.

Lemon Yellow.—A vivid high-toned yellow, semi-opaque, is extremely telling upon gold. Mixed with cadmium yellow it furnishes a range of brilliant warm yellows. It mixes well with gamboge, orange vermilion, cobalt, emerald green, and oxide of chromium, and with any of these produces clean and useful tints.

Gamboge.—A bright transparent yellow of light tone; works freely, and is very useful for glazing purposes. In combination with lemon yellow it affords a range of clean tints. When mixed with a little Mars yellow it produces a clear, warm, transparent tone of colour.

Cadmium Yellow.—A rich glowing yellow, powerful in tint, and semi-transparent. This is a most effective colour for illuminating. When judiciously toned with white, it furnishes a series of useful shades. Mixed with lemon yellow it produces a range of clean vivid tints. It does not, however, make good greens—they are dingy. Mixed with carmine, or glazed with it, it gives a series of strong luminous shades.

Mars Yellow.—A semi-transparent warm yellow, of slightly russet tone, but clean and bright in tint. Useful where a quiet yellow is required; mixes well with gamboge; does not make good greens.

REDS.

Rose Madder.—A light transparent pink colour of extremely pure tone. It is delicate in tint, but very effective, on account of its purity. Mixed with cobalt, it affords clean, warm, and cold purples. The addition of a little carmine materially heightens the tone of this colour, though at the same time it somewhat impairs its purity.

Crimson Lake.—A rich crimson colour, clean and transparent; washes and mixes well. More generally useful than carmine, though wanting the intense depth and brilliancy of the latter colour.

Carmine.—A deep-toned luminous crimson, much stronger than crimson lake. Is clean and transparent. The brilliancy of this powerful colour can be increased, by using it over a ground of gamboge.

Orange Vermilion.—A high-toned opaque red, of pure and brilliant hue, standing in relation to ordinary vermilion as carmine to crimson lake. It is extremely effective, and answers admirably where vivid opaque red is required; it works, washes, and mixes well. Its admixture with cadmium results in a fine range of warm luminous tints. When mixed with lemon yellow, it furnishes a series of extremely clean and pure tints; when toned with white, the shades are clear and effective. This is a most useful colour.

Vermilion.—A dense, deep-toned red, powerful in colour, and opaque. It is not so pure in tone as orange vermilion, and is of most service when used alone; it can, however, be thinned with white and with yellows.

BLUES.

Cobalt Blue.—A light-toned blue, clean and pure in tint, and semi-transparent. This is the lightest blue used in illuminating, and by the addition of white can be "paled" to any extent, the tints keeping clear and good. Mixed with lemon yellow, it makes a clean useful green. Its admixture with gamboge is not so satisfactory, and the green produced by its combination with Mars yellow is dirty and useless. With rose madder it produces middling, warm and cold purples (*i. e.* marones, and lilacs or violets); with crimson lake, strong and effective ones; with carmine, ditto. A series of quiet neutral tints can be produced by its admixture with orange vermilion. The tints in question are clean and good, and might occasionally be useful.

French Blue.—A deep rich blue, nearly transparent; is the best substitute for genuine ultramarine. The greens it makes with lemon yellow, gamboge, cadmium, and Mars yellow, are not very effective or useful. The violets and marones it forms with rose madder are granulous and unsatisfactory; with carmine they are somewhat better; but those formed with crimson lake are very good.

Smalt.—A brilliant, full-toned blue; deep in tone, and nearly transparent; luminous and very effective when used alone. It is granulous, and does not wash or mix well. The greens it makes are not particularly useful.

ORANGES.

Mars Orange.—A brilliant orange of very pure tone, transparent and lighter in colour than burnt sienna; and is not so coarse or staring. An effective and useful colour.

Burnt Sienna.—A deep rich orange, transparent and effective; works well and mixes freely.

PURPLES.

Indian Purple.—A rich deep-toned violet, or cold purple colour; most effective when used alone. Can be lightened with French blue or cobalt, and the tints will be found useful.

Burnt Carmine.—A rich deep-toned marone or warm purple colour; transparent and brilliant; luminous and effective when used alone; mixed with orange vermilion, it produces a strong rich colour, and a quiet fleshy one when mixed with cadmium yellow.

GREENS.

Emerald Green.—An extremely vivid and high-toned green, opaque. No combination of blue and yellow will match this colour, which is indispensable in illuminating. It can be "paled" with white, and the tints thus produced are pure and clean. The tints afforded by its admixture with lemon-yellow are also clear and effective.

Green Oxide of Chromium.—A very rich deep green, opaque, but effective. The tone of this green renders it extremely useful in illuminating; mixed with emerald green, it furnishes a series of rich semi-transparent tints. Mixed with lemon-yellow, it gives quiet, useful shades of green; and when this combination is brightened with emerald green, the shades are luminous and effective.

BROWN.

Vandyke Brown.—A deep, rich, transparent brown, luminous and clear in tint; works, washes, and mixes well. The best of all the browns for illuminating.

BLACK.

Lampblack.—The most dense and deep of all the blacks, free from any shade of brown or grey.

WHITE.

Chinese White.—A preparation of oxide of zinc, permanent, and the white best adapted for illuminating. It is not only useful *per se*, but is indispensable for toning or reducing other colours.

In making the list of the colours just described, I have assumed as a *sine quâ non* that the colours used in illuminating should be permanent. All those enumerated are so (in water-colours), with the exception of carmine and crimson lake; and these, though theoretically not permanent, are yet found in practice to be *very* lasting, especially when not too much exposed to the light. It is a curious fact, that crimson lake, though a weaker colour than carmine, is yet more permanent, in consequence of its different base, and that it will better stand exposure to light.

I here take the opportunity of warning amateurs, allured by their evident brilliancy, against the use, in illumination, of the following five colours, viz.—pure scarlet, red lead, chrome yellow, deep chrome, and orange chrome. None of these are permanent; the first-named being fugitive, and the others in time turning black; but this is the less to be regretted, as there are permanent colours answering equally well for illumination. Of course, these are less fugitive in books, which are generally protected from the action of light and air, than they would be in pictures.

The preceding remarks on pigments apply, with no difference worth noting, to colours prepared either for oil or for water-colour; which may therefore be laid on, by varying the vehicle for their proper application, to the surfaces of any of those materials which have been specified, in the Second Part of this Essay, as available for different kinds of illumination. I now proceed to notice the special processes requisite in each case, commencing with those which may be best employed for vellum. This substance consists of sheep-skin, carefully cleansed and scraped, and repeatedly washed in diluted sulphuric acid. The surface is rubbed down with fine pumice-stone to a smooth face, and in that condition it is fit for working upon. It is sold, prepared for use, at all the principal shops. If it has not been previously strained, or if many tints are likely to be floated over the surface, it will be well to strain it down upon a strainer or board before attempting to draw upon it. This may be done by damping the vellum, and then either gluing or nailing its edges down. When dry, it will be found to lie perfectly flat and smooth. It may be well, then, to wash it over with a dilute preparation of ox gall, to overcome any possible greasiness, and prepare it to receive colour freely. Mr. Barnard, and, I believe, other artists' colourmen, supply vellum mounted in block-books, similar to those made up of drawing-paper for sketching on; and by providing himself with one of those, the amateur may avoid the trouble of having to mount his own vellum.

As it is by no means easy to remove pencil-marks from vellum (and indeed it is never wise to attempt it, for the black-lead unites with the animal fat, which can never be entirely got out of the material, and rubs under the action of Indian-rubber or bread into a greasy smudge), it is always well to set out the design in the first instance upon drawing-paper. The best mode for good work is to complete the outline on drawing-paper, and then to trace it carefully with a hard pencil on a piece of tracing-paper, about one inch larger each way than the entire surface of the vellum; then cut out, the exact size of the vellum, a piece of tracing or tissue paper, rubbed evenly over with powdered red chalk.[1] Lay the tracing down (pencilled side upwards) in its right place upon the vellum, and fasten down one edge with pins, gum, or mouth-glue. Then slip the transfer-paper, with the chalked side downwards, between the vellum and the tracing until it exactly covers the former—touching the back of the transfer-paper with two or three drops of gum on its margin. Then lay the tracing over, and fasten down another of its edges. The gum drops will prevent the transfer-paper slipping away from the tracing-paper, when the drawing-board or strainer is placed upon a sloping desk or easel. Taking care to keep a piece of stout card or pasteboard under the hand, go over all the lines of the tracing with a blunted etching-point, or a very hard pencil cut sharp. This having been done, on removing both the tracing- and the transfer-paper, it will be found that a clear red outline has been conveyed to the surface of the vellum. At this stage of the work, as nothing dirties more readily than this material, it will be well to fasten over the surface a clean sheet of paper with a flap cut in it, by raising up and folding back portions of which, the artist may get to the part of the surface upon which he may desire to work without exposing any of the rest. As the effect of

[1] This had better be bought ready prepared, since some experience is requisite in so applying the red chalk as to prevent its depositing under the weight of the hand, and yet coming off sufficiently in the line traced by the point.

the writing on the page gives as it were the key-note for the general effect of the illuminated ornaments, it will be well to complete the former before proceeding to the latter.[1]

If the lines of the writing fixed upon are fine and delicate, they will look best, and work most freely with Indian ink; but if they are bold and solid, involving some extent of black surface, they will present a better appearance if wrought in lampblack; the principal difference between the two being that Indian ink is finer, and, if good, always retains a slight gloss, while lampblack gives a fuller tint, and dries off quite mat, or with a dead surface, corresponding with that of most other body-colour tints used in illuminating. Great care must be taken to keep the writing evenly spaced, upright, and perfectly neat, as it is almost impossible to erase without spoiling the vellum, and as no beauty of ornament will redeem an untidy text. If a portion of the writing is to be in red, it should be in pure vermilion; and if in gold, it should be highly burnished, as will be hereafter directed. The writing being satisfactorily completed, the artist may proceed to lay in his ground tints, generally mixing them with more or less white to give them body and solidity. Colours prepared with water are best adapted for illumination on vellum; and those known as *moist* colours are to be preferred for this work, as they give out a greater volume of colour, and possess more tenacity or power of adhering to the surface of the material on which they are used than the dry colours. Of moist colours there are two descriptions, viz., solid and liquid; and of these I give the preference to the former, as some colours, such as lemon yellow and smalt, will not keep well in tubes; added to which, there is waste in using them in this form where only small quantities are required, as the colour cannot be replaced in the tube when once squeezed out. The tube colours possess, however, the valuable property of being always clean when a bit of pure colour is required. The solid moist colours are apt to get dirtied in rapid working, and occasionally mislead the eye which is not quick at detecting a lowered tint. Mr. Barbe's body-colours, which are of very good quality, are prepared in powder, combined with a glutinous substance, on moistening which with water, the tints are fit for application. Messrs. Winsor & Newton's body-colours are also very excellent. Flatness of tint is best secured by using the first colour well mixed with body, and put on boldly; this forms the brightest tint; then shade with pure transparent colour, and finish off with the high lights.

Very useful models have been prepared by Mr. Barnard, for teaching amateurs the different modes of shading, &c. They consist of outline plates (the first series containing the Beatitudes from the Gospel of St. Matthew) partially coloured by hand. The beginner will find it a very useful exercise

[1] The experienced illuminator will generally do his writing before he gets in the outline of his ornament, and he will frequently dispense with the transferring process altogether; but it would be by no means safe for a beginner to do so.

to complete a few of these before trying his hand upon more original works upon vellum. The greatest care must be taken to have every implement perfectly clean. Experience alone can teach the artist the value of what are called glazing or transparent colours, such as the lakes, carmine, madders, gamboge, &c. Some tints may be used either as glazing colours or as body-tints, according to their preparation, and according to the degree of thickness with which they are applied. As a general principle, all shades should be painted in transparent colour, all lights in opaque. Reflected lights may often be best given by scumbling thin body-colour over transparent shade. In order to prepare the tints for these operations, it may be well to use a little of Newman's or Miller's preparations with them. The less tints are retouched after the first application, the more clear and brilliant they are likely to remain. Above all things never let the paint-brush go near the mouth, and never attempt to correct or retouch a tint while it is in process of drying, as doing so will infallibly make it look streaky and muddy. In all these processes of manipulation, however, practice, good example, and good tuition, must teach what the minutest directions would fail to satisfactorily convey. The principal colours having been applied, the next difficulty will be to heighten them with gold and silver.

The principal metallic preparations used in illumination may be enumerated as follows:—gold leaf, gold paper, shell gold, saucer gold, gold paint, silver leaf, shell silver, and shell aluminium. Of these, the leaves, paper, and paint, are of English, and the shells and saucers of French manufacture. Occasionally gold and silver powder and German-metal leaf are employed, though too rarely to make them important enough to claim general notice.

The first-mentioned preparation of gold—gold-leaf—is the pure metal beaten into very thin leaves, generally $3\frac{1}{8}$ inches, $3\frac{1}{4}$ inches, or $3\frac{3}{8}$ inches square; but for illuminating purposes it should be still smaller—say $2\frac{1}{2}$ inches square, as it is easier to handle than a larger size. For the same reason it is better to have the leaf doubly as thick as it is usually beaten. Gold leaf is sold in "books," each of which contains twenty-five gold "leaves," and, for ordinary and general purposes, it is by far the best and most useful metallic preparation; but the difficulty of handling and laying it on deters amateurs from employing it, and it is difficult in writing to furnish a practical description of the *modus operandi*. The following is the usual mode:—

"Carefully open the book of gold, and if in so doing you disturb the leaf, gently blow it down flat again. If a whole leaf be required, take a rounded 'tip,' and quietly so place it on the leaf that the top of the tip be close to the edge of the leaf. In so doing, the sides of the tip will be brought down upon the side edges of the leaf, which then can be securely taken up and placed where required. If a small piece of gold leaf only be wanted, cautiously take up a leaf from the book by passing a 'gilder's knife'

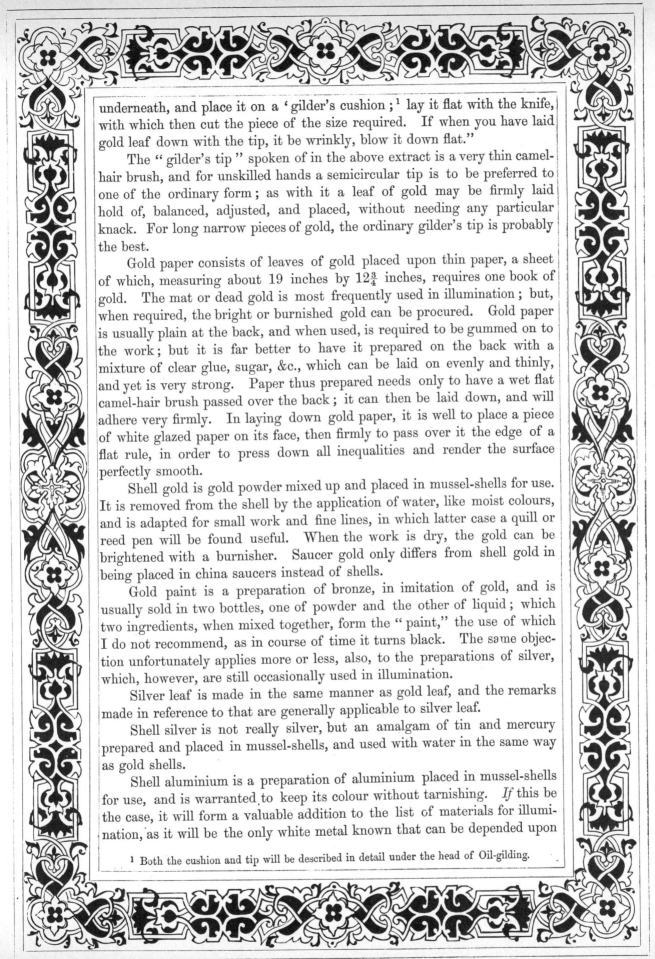

underneath, and place it on a 'gilder's cushion;[1] lay it flat with the knife, with which then cut the piece of the size required. If when you have laid gold leaf down with the tip, it be wrinkly, blow it down flat."

The "gilder's tip" spoken of in the above extract is a very thin camel-hair brush, and for unskilled hands a semicircular tip is to be preferred to one of the ordinary form; as with it a leaf of gold may be firmly laid hold of, balanced, adjusted, and placed, without needing any particular knack. For long narrow pieces of gold, the ordinary gilder's tip is probably the best.

Gold paper consists of leaves of gold placed upon thin paper, a sheet of which, measuring about 19 inches by $12\frac{3}{4}$ inches, requires one book of gold. The mat or dead gold is most frequently used in illumination; but, when required, the bright or burnished gold can be procured. Gold paper is usually plain at the back, and when used, is required to be gummed on to the work; but it is far better to have it prepared on the back with a mixture of clear glue, sugar, &c., which can be laid on evenly and thinly, and yet is very strong. Paper thus prepared needs only to have a wet flat camel-hair brush passed over the back; it can then be laid down, and will adhere very firmly. In laying down gold paper, it is well to place a piece of white glazed paper on its face, then firmly to pass over it the edge of a flat rule, in order to press down all inequalities and render the surface perfectly smooth.

Shell gold is gold powder mixed up and placed in mussel-shells for use. It is removed from the shell by the application of water, like moist colours, and is adapted for small work and fine lines, in which latter case a quill or reed pen will be found useful. When the work is dry, the gold can be brightened with a burnisher. Saucer gold only differs from shell gold in being placed in china saucers instead of shells.

Gold paint is a preparation of bronze, in imitation of gold, and is usually sold in two bottles, one of powder and the other of liquid; which two ingredients, when mixed together, form the "paint," the use of which I do not recommend, as in course of time it turns black. The same objection unfortunately applies more or less, also, to the preparations of silver, which, however, are still occasionally used in illumination.

Silver leaf is made in the same manner as gold leaf, and the remarks made in reference to that are generally applicable to silver leaf.

Shell silver is not really silver, but an amalgam of tin and mercury prepared and placed in mussel-shells, and used with water in the same way as gold shells.

Shell aluminium is a preparation of aluminium placed in mussel-shells for use, and is warranted to keep its colour without tarnishing. If this be the case, it will form a valuable addition to the list of materials for illumi-nation, as it will be the only white metal known that can be depended upon

[1] Both the cushion and tip will be described in detail under the head of Oil-gilding.

for not tarnishing. The preparation is at present a new one, but bids fair to be very serviceable.

Water-mat gold size is a preparation for laying down gold leaf, *i. e.*, causing it to adhere to a given surface. The mode of using it is as follows: —Take a small brush saturated with water, and thoroughly charge it with the size. With the brush so charged, trace out the required form or pattern, and upon this lay the gold leaf, pressing it lightly down with cotton-wool. When all is dry, gently rub off the superfluous gold with cotton-wool.

"Burnish gold size" is a preparation for laying down the gold leaf that is intended afterwards to be burnished (*i. e.*, polished with a tooth or agate burnisher). That prepared by Messrs. Winsor and Newton may be used as follows:—Place the bottle in warm water to dissolve its contents, which, however, must not be allowed to get hot, but merely be made liquid. Stir up the preparation with a hogs-hair brush, which then thoroughly charge with the mixture; with it trace out the pattern required to be burnished, then let the work dry. When quite dry, let the surface of the pattern be wetted with clean cold water, and on it (while damp) place the gold leaf. Let all get perfectly dry, and then burnish as required. When a very bright surface is wanted, two coats of the size should be used; the second being put on after the first is dry.

The "raising preparation" made by the same firm, is adapted for raising the surface of the work, so as to obtain relief, and is particularly required for imitating rich MSS. of the 14th and 15th centuries. It is used as follows:—Place the bottle in hot water, and when its contents are dissolved, stir it well up with a small hogs-hair brush, then fully charge it, draw out the form intended to be raised, and deposit the "raising" on the surface. If the height thus attained be not sufficient, wait till the preparation is dry, and go over it again, and so on until you gain the height you require, when it must be allowed to become quite hard; then go over it with the water-mat gold size, and while this is wet put on the gold; press gently down with cotton-wool, and when dry brush off the superfluous gold with cotton-wool; when putting on the "raising," take care to keep the surface level, unless it may be required to be hollowed or indented.

Mr. Barnard has also prepared a gold size and raising preparation, adapted for laying gold on vellum or paper, which answers well both for mat and burnish gilding. The mode of using it is as follows:—Wash a little of the gold size off with a brush dipped in water, using it thinly for the flat parts of your design, and in greater body for that portion of the drawing which you wish to appear raised; after allowing it to remain for a few minutes, till nearly dry, apply the gold, and press it down with a piece of cotton-wool. It must now remain untouched for about an hour, when the superfluous gold may be removed by means of the wool, and in case of defect, the gold size and gold must be again applied. Preparations of a somewhat similar nature are sold by Messrs. Rowney, Newman, and other artists' colourmen.[1]

Very pretty effects may be obtained by partial burnishing of the gold in patterns, and dotting it over with the point of the sharp burnisher in indentations, arranged in geometrical forms. The best manuscripts of the Edwardian period were often highly wrought after this fashion.

When finished, it is scarcely necessary to recommend that the vellum sheet should be either put carefully away until enough of others corresponding with it are done to make up a volume, or should be glazed so as to protect its surface. One dirty or greasy finger laid upon it, and the effect of much beautiful work, which may have taken weeks to elaborate, is fatally marred.

All the above instructions apply as well for working on paper or cardboard as on vellum. The amateur who has once succeeded on vellum, is not likely to take again to the humbler practice of working on the less noble materials, which, however, will always be exceedingly useful for practising and sketching upon. I have occasionally seen printed volumes gracefully illustrated by hand with borders, such as surround these pages, and with elegant inventions, in the form of head and tail pieces, insertions, &c., applicable to the subject of the volume. Many of the works of old English authors are peculiarly suited for this class of embellishment. How beautiful might not a Walton's "Angler" or a Bunyan's "Pilgrim's Progress" be made if appropriately enriched in this style.

Tracing-paper, and the facilities it offers to those little gifted with talents for drawing, I have already noticed. It remains, however, to observe, that it possesses an additional practical convenience in being ready for taking colour, either with oil, water, or varnish, as vehicles, without the previous application of any special preparation. Hence it may be fastened up when completed, either by pasting as ordinary paper, by gluing, if for attachment to wood, or by paying over the back with boiled oil and copal varnish, or with white lead ground in oil with some litharge, and then pressing down until it may be made to lie perfectly flat and adhere to any surface previously painted in oil-colour. Being very thin, its edges will scarcely show at all, even if applied to the middle of a flat panel; but, to make sure, it is always well to run a line with a full brush of thick colour, either in oil or distemper, over the edge, extending for one half of its width upon the tracing-paper, and for the other half upon the surface to which it may have been applied.

[1] The amateur may of course prepare mordants of different degrees of tenacity and body for his own use, by the employment, and various combinations, of leather and parchment size, isinglass, red lead, gum arabic, sugar, honey, glycerine, borax, bol ammoniac, glaire, and similar substances; but his time will be more profitably spent in improving himself in design than it could be (nowadays) in experimenting on the "materia technica" of art.

Of the remaining materials on which illumination for the decoration, not of books but of apartments, may be readily executed, canvas, stone, metal, and wood, are generally wrought upon by the ordinary processes of oil-painting; while plaster, especially in the form of ceilings, is more frequently treated by means of distemper-painting. I propose, therefore, to give, firstly, some general directions as to setting out work, &c., applicable to both methods; secondly, a notice of the processes generally required for oil-colour illumination; thirdly, a brief description of the mode of working in distemper; and fourthly, to wind up with some instructions as to the application of varnish which may be employed to heighten and preserve illumination executed by either of the above methods.

The operation of setting out lines upon walls or other surfaces is by no means easy. It involves care and judgment, a quick eye, and a very steady hand. It is the indispensable preliminary before ornamental-work or illumination can be executed, as it can alone correctly give the forms of panels, borders, &c., for which cartoons may have to be prepared. Lines may be either drawn with pencil, or prepared charcoal or chalk, or else struck by means of a chalked string. For lines which are vertical, a weight called a plumb-bob must be attached to one end of the string. The best shape for this is that of half an egg, as the flat side will then lie close to the wall. Two persons are required in setting out these lines,— one working above and the other below. The one at the top marks the points at the distance each line is required to be from others. The string being chalked either black or white,—according as the line has to show upon a light or dark ground,—he holds it to one of the points, and lets fall the weighted end, which, when quite steady, the person who is below strains tight, and raising the string between his finger and thumb in the middle, lets it fall back sharply on the wall. The result, if carefully executed, is a perfectly straight and vertical line. The horizontal lines require to be drawn with a straight-edge or ruler, and may be either set out at a true right angle to the vertical lines geometrically by the intersection of arcs of circles, or by a large square, or may be defined, irrespectively of mathematical correctness, by measuring up or down from a ceiling or floor line. The distances apart are as before measured out, but in long lines must be marked as many times as the length of the straight-edge may require. This being set at each end to the points marked, the line is drawn along it. Circles and curved lines may be struck from their proper centres with large wooden compasses, one leg carrying a pencil. Drawing lines with the brush requires great practice. A straight-edge is placed upon the chalk lines, with the edge next the line slightly raised, and the brush, well filled with colour, drawn along it, just touching the wall, the pressure being never increased, and the brush refilled whenever it is near failing; but great care must be taken that it be not too full, as in that case it will be apt to blotch the line, or drop the colour upon the lower portions of the wall. Drawing lines in colour overhead upon a ceiling is even more difficult, and is beyond the capabilities of most amateurs.

The patterns of ornament are executed either by means of stencils cut in oiled paper, according to the method which will be next described, or else by pounces, which are the full-sized drawings pricked along all the lines with a needle upon a flat cushion; powdered charcoal, tied up in a cotton bag, is then dabbed upon the paper which has been set up on the wall, or else the back is rubbed over with drawing-charcoal and brushed well with a flat brush, like a stone brush. In both cases the result is that the dust passes on to the walls through the pricked holes, and forms are thus sufficiently indicated to the painter.

Stencilling is a process by which colour is applied through interstices cut in a prepared paper, by dabbing with a brush. The design to be stencilled is drawn upon paper which has been soaked with linseed oil and well dried. The pattern is then cut out with a sharp knife upon a sheet of glass, care being taken to leave such connections as will keep the stencil together. The next tint is then to be laid on in the same manner, and so on till the darkest tint is done, each tint being allowed to dry before a second is applied.

I do not purpose dwelling in detail on the preparation, or "bringing forward," as it is called, of surfaces to receive oil-colour; since, for such mechanical work, it will be always well to employ a good house-painter. I may observe, however, that the first operation, where the surface is absorbent, is to stop the suction, either by a plentiful application of boiled oil alone, boiled oil and red lead, or size. Several successive coats of paint should then be applied, and in order to obtain smoothness, the surface of each should be well rubbed down. The last coat should be mixed with turpentine, and no oil, in order to kill the gloss, or, as it is termed, to "flat" the surface. For most decoration and illumination, the work should be brought forward in white, as, by shining partially through most of the pigments ultimately applied, it will greatly add to their brilliancy. Zinc white will stand much better than white lead. Messrs. Roberson, of Long Acre, prepare an excellent wax medium, which dries with a perfectly dead encaustic surface, and answers admirably for mural-painting of all kinds. I caused it to be employed for all the decoration executed under my direction at the Sydenham Crystal Palace. Miller's glass medium will also be found very useful to artists and amateurs. In laying on all ground tints, great care should be taken to keep them flat; and the less, as a general rule, tints are mixed, worked over and over, and messed about, the brighter they will be. The principal colours having dried, the setting out of the lettering, &c., may be proceeded with; the following directions being duly attended to.

The Setting-out of Letters.[1]

In regard to the proportion of Roman capital letters, it may be taken as a general rule, that the whole of the letters, with the exception of S, J, I, F, M, and N, are formed in squares. The top and bottom of the letters should project the width of the thick line. The letters I and J are formed in a vertical parallelogram, half the width of the square; the letters M and N in a horizontal parallelogram, one third larger than the square. The letters A, B, E, F, H, X, and Y, are either divided, or have projections from the middle. This rule may be varied, and the division placed nearer the top than the base of the square. Capitals in the same word should have a space equal to half a square between them; at the beginning of a word, a whole square, and between the divisions of a sentence two squares should be left.

This is the general rule for the proportions of the letters; but they may be made longer or wider, as may be deemed expedient.

The small letters are half the size of the capitals; the long lines of the letters b, d, f, h, k, and l, are the same height as the capitals; the tails of j, p, q, and y, descending in like proportion. The letter s is founded on the form of two circles at a tangent to each other. These rules are applicable to sloping as well as to upright letters. In *italic* letters it is usual to make the capitals three times the height of the smaller letters, and the long strokes of the small letters nearly equal to the capitals.

The letters having been duly set out, and painted on the walls, the amateur must next either himself encounter, or employ some experienced hand to overcome, the technical difficulties of successfully gilding those portions of his work he may desire to remain in gold. The following directions may assist him; but he is not likely to succeed until practice shall have given him considerable dexterity and confidence :—

Gilding for Walls, &c.

The implements with which the gilder should provide himself are not numerous, nor are they expensive, as they consist merely of a cushion of particular form, a knife for cutting the gold-leaf, a tip for transferring it, and a cotton ball or pad for pressing it down; these and a few brushes are all the requisites, with the addition of an agate burnisher when burnish gilding is desired.

The cushion is a species of palette made of wood, about nine by six inches, having on the upper surface a covering of leather stuffed with wool, and on the under side a loose band, through which the thumb being passed, the cushion is kept firmly resting on the left hand. To prevent the gold flying off (for being extremely light this very readily takes place), a margin of parchment is fixed on the edge of the cushion, rising about three inches,

[1] This information is principally derived from Nathaniel Whittock's "Decorative Painter's and Glazier's Guide."

and enclosing it on three sides. The knife very much resembles a palette-knife, the blade is about four inches long and half an inch wide, perfectly straight, and cutting on one edge only.

The "tip" is the brush with which the gold-leaf is applied. It is formed by placing a line of badger-hair between two thin pieces of cardboard, and is generally about three inches wide. The "dabber" is merely a pinch of cotton-wool, lightly tied up in a piece of very soft rag, or, what is better, the thin silk called Persian. It is often used without covering, but is then very apt to take up the uncovered gold-size, and so to soil the leaf already laid down. Camel-hair brushes are useful for intricate parts, and for cleaning off the superfluous gold a long-haired brush, called a "softener," is requisite.

There should be also at hand a small stone and muller (these are also made in glass, which are cleaner) for grinding up the oil and gold-size.

The operator, having stocked himself with the above tools, may now proceed to lay the gold-leaf upon the work he desires to gild. There are two methods of doing this, known in the trade as "Oil-gilding" and "Water-gilding;" and so called from the composition of the size which serves as a vehicle for making the gold-leaf adhere to the work.

The following is the usual process in oil-gilding :—This method costs less and will wear much better than water-gilding, which will be presently described ; but has not its delicate appearance and finish, nor can it be burnished or brightened up. Though the oil gold-size can always be purchased of good quality, it may be well to describe the fat oil of which it is principally composed.

Linseed oil, in any quantity, is exposed during the summer in the open air, but as much away from dust as possible, for about two months, during which time it must be often stirred, and it will become as thick as treacle. It is a good practice to pour into the pot a quantity of water, so that the oil may be lifted from the bottom of it, as all the impurities of the oil sink into the water, and do not again mix when it is stirred. When of the consistency above mentioned, the oil is separated from the water, and being put into a bottle, is subjected to heat till it becomes fluid again, when all remaining impurities will sink, and the oil, being carefully poured off from the sediment, forms what is termed "fat oil." The gilder commences by priming the work, should it not have been painted, using for the purpose a small portion of yellow ochre and vermilion, mixed with drying oil. When this is quite dry, a coat of the oil gold-size, compounded with the fat oil just described, japanner's gold-size, and yellow ochre, is laid on, and when this is perfectly dry, a second should be given, or even a third. A superior finish is produced by going over the work, before using the size, with Dutch rushes or fish-skin, which gives a finer surface to it. After the last coat of size is applied, the work must be left for about a day, to set, taking care to keep it from dust ; and the proper state for receiving the gold-leaf is known by touching the size with the finger, when it should be just "tacky," that is adhesive, without leaving the ground on which it has been laid.

The gilder then, taking on his left hand his cushion, transfers to it the gold-leaves from the books in which they are purchased. This is not very easy to a beginner, as the gold cannot be touched except by the knife. Gilders manage it by breathing under the leaf in the direction it is desired to send it, and flatten it on the cushion by the same gentle blowing or breathing. It is now cut to the required shape, and applied to the sized surfaces by means of the tip, which, if drawn across the hair or face each time it is used, will slightly adhere to the gold. The whole leaves are sometimes transferred from the books to the work at once ; and when there is much flat space, it facilitates the process. As the leaves are laid on the size, they are pressed gently down with the cotton ball, or in sunken parts with camel-hair brushes ; and when perfectly dry, the loose leaf is removed by gently brushing over the work with the softener, when, if there should be found any places ungilt, such spots are touched with japanners' gold-size, and the leaf applied as before. The process of oil-gilding is then complete.

Water or burnish-gilding differs from the former in the use of parchment instead of oil size, and has received its name from being moistened with water in rendering the size adhesive, and also from its fitness for burnishing. Its superior beauty, however, is balanced by its being less durable than oil-gilding, and, unlike the latter, unfit to be exposed to damp air; it is therefore only used for indoor work or ornamentation. The parchment size is made by boiling down slips of parchment or cuttings of glovers' leather, till a strong jelly be formed, the proportions being one pound of cuttings to six quarts of water, which must be boiled till it shrinks to two quarts. While hot, the liquid should be strained through flannel; and when cold, the jelly required will be fit for use.

The work to be gilded will require several coats of composition : the first, or priming coat, is made of size thinned with water, and a little whiting; with this the work is brushed over, using a thicker mixture when there are defects which need to be stopped. Successive coats are then laid on to the number of seven or eight, and the last, being moistened with water, is worked over and smoothed on the plain parts with Dutch rushes. After this is completed, a coating is laid on, composed of bol ammoniac 1 pound, black lead 2 ounces, ground up on the stone with 2 ounces of olive oil. This is one out of many receipts; all, however, are diluted for use with parchment size warmed up with two-thirds water, and forming what is called water gold-size. Two coats of this should be laid on; the part about to be burnished should then be again rubbed with a soft cloth till quite even, and care taken that each coat be perfectly dry before the subsequent one be laid on. The work is now moistened in successive portions with a camel-hair brush and water, and while moist covered with gold-leaf in precisely the same manner as described in the directions for oil-gilding, great caution being observed in order to avoid wetting the leaf already laid down, as a discoloration would be the result. The work is now left for about four-and-twenty hours, when the parts which are to be burnished may be tried in two or three places. Care should be taken not to let the work get too dry, as in that case it would require more burnishing, and yet not give a good result. This state is known by its polishing slowly, and if it be too wet it will peel off; but should the places where the trials are made all polish quickly and evenly, the work may then be finished; for which purpose agates cut in proper forms and set into handles, are sold at the artists' colour-shops.[1]

<hr>

[1] Japanners' gilding is a branch of oil-gilding, the size or ground being made with 1 pound of linseed oil, to which, while boiling, is added gradually 4 ounces of gum animi in powder, the whole being stirred until the gum is completely dissolved, and kept boiling till the mixture is of a thick consistence, in which state it should be strained through a thick flannel, and stored in a wide-mouthed stoppered bottle. Vermilion is ground up with the size before it is applied, to render it opaque; and if it does not leave the brush freely, it should be thinned with oil of turpentine.

The gold powder may be either real gold, or what is called Dutch metal, or imitation gold. Gold powder is produced by grinding the leaf gold with pure honey on the stone till it is perfectly reduced to powder, and afterwards dissolving the mixture in water till the honey is completely removed, and for this several waters are necessary; the water is then poured off, and the powder dried. If this gold be mixed up with weak gum-water and spread upon cockle shells, it is then called shell gold, which is used in drawings only.

The Dutch gold powder is made by reducing the Dutch leaf gold by exactly the same process; and if well protected by varnishing, its appearance is little inferior to the genuine metal. There is another method of procuring gold powder, which is by precipitating grain gold into powder by means of aqua regia, which is made by dissolving four parts of pure spirit of nitre and one part of sal ammoniac in powder. This process was (as has been already stated) well known to the mediæval illuminators. In 4 ounces of this compound, ½ an ounce of grain gold is dissolved under the action of a slight heat; a solution of green vitriol, consisting of copperas 1 dram, water 1 ounce, being gradually added. When the precipitation has ceased, the gold powder must be carefully washed and dried, and will be found to be more brilliant than that made from leaf gold. The use of japanners' gold-size is very similar to oil-gilding, and is equally simple. If the material to be gilded is brought to a smooth and clean face, the size may be laid on at once without other preparation; using great care, however, not to touch any part but what you wish to gild, as the gold will adhere wherever there is size. Priming with a mixture of chalk and size is sometimes used for a first coat, but not by the best japanners, as the work is liable to chip off; no material should therefore be japanned which cannot be made smooth. For hard or close-grained wood, metal, leather, or paper, one or two coats of varnish will answer all requirements; very great care being observed that each coat of varnish be perfectly dry and hard before it is again touched. It is a good practice to allow the work to stand a day or two between the applications; then the japanners' gold-size may be added, and touching with the finger as before described will indicate the proper state for applying the gold, whether in leaf or powder. Either may be employed; but in the case of colours being intermixed and subsequently varnished, the powder is usually adopted; it is easily laid on by means of a camel-hair brush, the work being set aside to get thoroughly dry, when the superfluous metal is removed with a soft brush. In case more size should have been prepared than is needed, the remainder, if water be poured over it, will keep for future use.

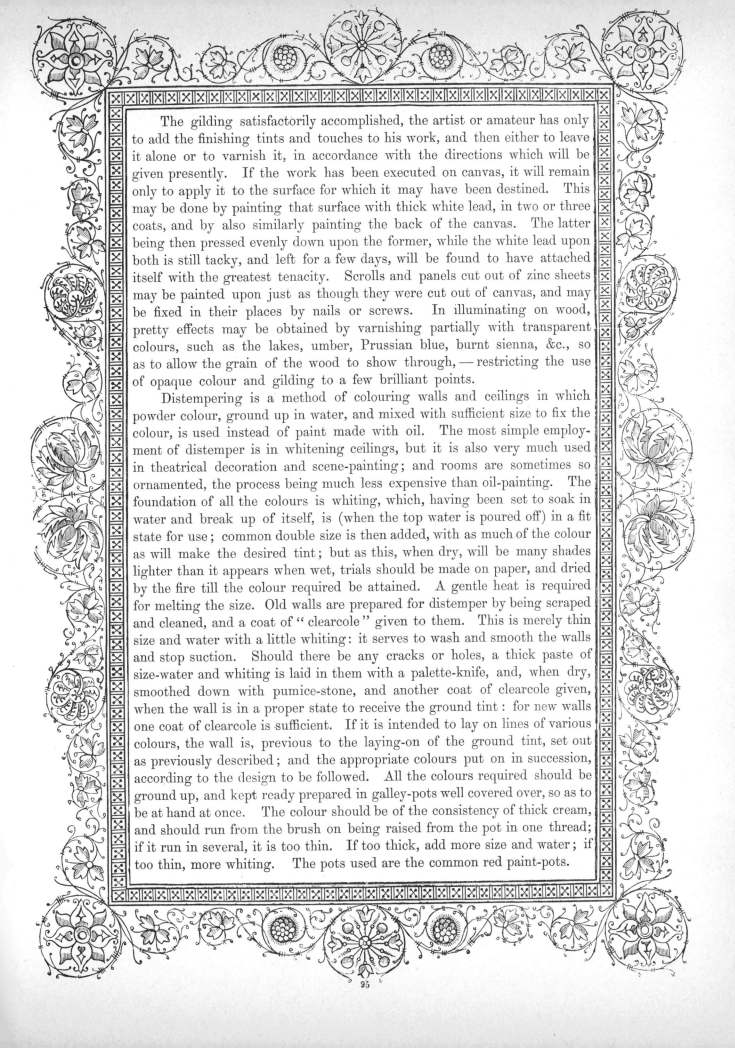

The gilding satisfactorily accomplished, the artist or amateur has only to add the finishing tints and touches to his work, and then either to leave it alone or to varnish it, in accordance with the directions which will be given presently. If the work has been executed on canvas, it will remain only to apply it to the surface for which it may have been destined. This may be done by painting that surface with thick white lead, in two or three coats, and by also similarly painting the back of the canvas. The latter being then pressed evenly down upon the former, while the white lead upon both is still tacky, and left for a few days, will be found to have attached itself with the greatest tenacity. Scrolls and panels cut out of zinc sheets may be painted upon just as though they were cut out of canvas, and may be fixed in their places by nails or screws. In illuminating on wood, pretty effects may be obtained by varnishing partially with transparent colours, such as the lakes, umber, Prussian blue, burnt sienna, &c., so as to allow the grain of the wood to show through, — restricting the use of opaque colour and gilding to a few brilliant points.

Distempering is a method of colouring walls and ceilings in which powder colour, ground up in water, and mixed with sufficient size to fix the colour, is used instead of paint made with oil. The most simple employment of distemper is in whitening ceilings, but it is also very much used in theatrical decoration and scene-painting; and rooms are sometimes so ornamented, the process being much less expensive than oil-painting. The foundation of all the colours is whiting, which, having been set to soak in water and break up of itself, is (when the top water is poured off) in a fit state for use; common double size is then added, with as much of the colour as will make the desired tint; but as this, when dry, will be many shades lighter than it appears when wet, trials should be made on paper, and dried by the fire till the colour required be attained. A gentle heat is required for melting the size. Old walls are prepared for distemper by being scraped and cleaned, and a coat of "clearcole" given to them. This is merely thin size and water with a little whiting: it serves to wash and smooth the walls and stop suction. Should there be any cracks or holes, a thick paste of size-water and whiting is laid in them with a palette-knife, and, when dry, smoothed down with pumice-stone, and another coat of clearcole given, when the wall is in a proper state to receive the ground tint: for new walls one coat of clearcole is sufficient. If it is intended to lay on lines of various colours, the wall is, previous to the laying-on of the ground tint, set out as previously described; and the appropriate colours put on in succession, according to the design to be followed. All the colours required should be ground up, and kept ready prepared in galley-pots well covered over, so as to be at hand at once. The colour should be of the consistency of thick cream, and should run from the brush on being raised from the pot in one thread; if it run in several, it is too thin. If too thick, add more size and water; if too thin, more whiting. The pots used are the common red paint-pots.

VARNISHING.

Varnish is a solution of resin in oil or spirits of wine. [1]

Surfaces which are to be varnished should be of the greatest smoothness and polish which it is possible to attain. Dark colours are best calculated for varnishing; the lighter colours, such as sky-blue, apple-green, rose-colour, delicate yellow, &c., will not bear varnishing so well, and in spite of the greatest care are liable to get dirty.

The best preparation for stopping suction in absorbent surfaces, and so rendering them fit to take varnish, is made of isinglass or parchment size; for the darker colours it may be made of common clear glue. Four or five coats will be necessary for the brighter colours; two or three will be sufficient for the darker ones. Great care must be taken not to wash up water or distemper colours in laying on the first coat, nor to lay on a second coat before the first is perfectly dry; nor must the varnishing be proceeded with before the last coat of size is thoroughly dry. Varnish may be applied on surfaces brought forward in oil without any special preparation, provided the oil has become thoroughly dry and hard.

This process serves both to enhance and preserve the beauty of the colours, and in some degree to counteract the destructive influence of the atmosphere and of insects.

Varnishes suitable for the work in hand, such as clear copal spirit varnish, oil copal varnish, white hard varnish, &c., may be procured from any one who supplies drawing materials. The varnishing itself requires some little care. It should be performed in a place perfectly free from dust, in a bold manner with large brushes, steadily, rapidly, and uniformly, not returning too frequently to the same spot, more especially when using spirit varnish, which loses its fluidity much sooner than oil varnish. Whichever varnish is used, it should be very thin: if spirit varnish, the room must be of a moderate temperature; for if too cold, the varnishing is apt to be rough, white, and unequal; if too hot, it is liable to have air-bladders, and to crumble and spoil. Oil varnishing may be done in a room of warmer temperature. A second coat of varnish must on no account be laid on before the first coat is quite dry. If the work is to be polished, the spirit varnish must be applied from five to eight times, oil varnish three or four; but if the work is not to be polished, then four coats of the former and two of the latter will generally be found sufficient.

When thoroughly dry, the face of the varnish may be polished with pumice-stone, tripoly, water, and sweet oil. If it be an oil varnish, procure some of the finest pulverized pumice-stone, and mix it with water to about the consistence of cream; with a piece of linen rag dipped in this mixture rub the work till all inequalities disappear, and the surface is as smooth as glass; then dry it with a cloth, and polish once more with tripoly and sweet oil; then dry it with a piece of soft linen, rub it with starch reduced to a fine powder, and finish with a clean soft linen cloth, until the varnish assumes a dazzling appearance. If it is a spirit varnish, omit the pumice-stone, and begin with the tripoly and water; after this use the tripoly and sweet oil, and finish as before described for the oil varnish.

The difference is so striking between the polished and unpolished surfaces, as to amply repay the additional trouble required in the polishing. The polishing powders must be kept in thoroughly clean vessels, a single grain of sand being sufficient to spoil the polish.

---

[1] The superiority of the Chinese and Japanese varnishing is chiefly owing to the excellence of a particular species of resin found in China and Japan. The varnishes made with oil are longer drying than those made with spirits of wine, but are of greater durability. The spirits of wine should be highly rectified: if oil is used, it should be linseed. It is safer to purchase the varnish ready prepared than to attempt the making of it, as the solution of resin, particularly in oil, is somewhat dangerous.

M. DIGBY WYATT.

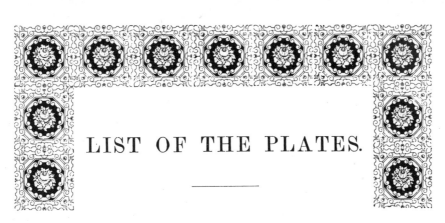

LIST OF THE PLATES.

The Frontispiece is adapted from Add. MS. 17,341, and Reg. I. D. I. of the British Museum.

VI. CENTURY, No. 1.

The manuscript (Bodleian, No. 93) from which this interesting and early alphabet has been taken, is one formerly in Lord Hatton's possession. It is preserved in the Bodleian Library with other manuscripts formerly belonging to the same proprietor. Although possessing no great claims to notice as a work of art, since it contains no miniatures, this precious copy of the Gospels may well take precedence of all others in this country, with the exception of the companion set preserved in the library of Corpus Christi, Cambridge; since Wanley, one of the most industrious and cautious students of palæography, has not hesitated to regard them as the identical copies once preserved at St. Augustine's Monastery, in Kent, and valued through long ages as having been the property of the great missionary. To such a supposition the character of the text, and many very ancient inscriptions contained in the work, give at least plausibility. Be this as it may, however, there can be no question that Mr. Westwood is perfectly justified in placing it, as he has done, in a recent article in the "Archæological Journal" (together with the Cottonian MS. Vespasian A 1, from which our Plates, "7th Century, Nos. 1 and 2," have been taken), in that very rare class, of which about six authentic specimens only are known; and which he regards as having issued from a Scriptorium founded in this country by the immediate followers of St. Augustine. From that source emanated, he considers, "some of the most beautiful manuscripts, written in the purest uncial or rustic capitals, but decorated with initials in the Anglo-Saxon or Irish style." Were it not for such a combination, it would be exceedingly difficult to recognize the possibility that several manuscripts, which we may nationally be most proud to claim, could have been written and illuminated in this country.

VI. CENTURY, No. 2.

All the beautiful specimens shown on this Plate have been taken from the Golden Greek Canons of Eusebius, in the British Museum (Add. MSS., No. 5,111), one of the most important relics of the decoration of the school of Justinian the Great which time has spared to us. (*See* page 10.) From its breadth of style and bold treatment of colour, this MS. furnishes an excellent model for illuminators or decorators to study, reproduce, and improve upon.

VII. CENTURY, No. 1.

The Cottonian manuscript (Vesp. A 1) supplies the material for this Plate. It contains the Roman Psalter, with an Anglo-Saxon interlineal translation. I have drawn attention to the peculiar class to which this manuscript belongs at page 19.

VII. CENTURY, No. 2.

This Plate gives various details from the same source which furnished those for the preceding one. The principal specimen, Fig. 9, is a portion of a triumphal arch (recto 31), beneath which David is represented seated, and playing on the lyre. He is surrounded by attendants rejoicing, and blowing horns and trumpets. The execution of this subject, which is the most important illumination in the volume, is quite antique in character; the colours being applied with a free brush in a style altogether differing from the fine pen-work, not only of the rest of the volume, but even of the archway which forms the framing to the subject. Small figures recur in various headings, but they are all drawn in a more minute, laboured, and ignorant style than those of the illumination of King David. Gold, silver, and the beautiful purple stain abound throughout the volume, which is written in classical majuscule letters throughout. The Hibernian features of surrounding the initial letters and ornaments with red dots, and using a spiral, the eye of which expands into a triple whorl, abound throughout.

VII. CENTURY, No. 3.

The Figures 8 and 12 of this Plate are also from the Cottonian Vesp. A 1. All the rest have been selected from, probably, the most interesting manuscript in existence. It is preserved in the same series (the Cottonian) under the title of Nero, D IV. and is best known as St. Cuthbert's Gospels. This manuscript, having been alluded to at page 16, need not be now further dwelt on.

VII. CENTURY, No. 4.

All from the Durham Book. Nero, D IV.

VIII. CENTURY, No. 1,

Presents us with a complete alphabet, and various ornamental initials made up from manuscripts, executed on the Continent at a period immediately anterior to the age of Charlemagne.

VIII. CENTURY, No. 2.

Count Bastard, in his magnificent work, has given an important collection of examples of the early Spanish, or Visigothic characters, from a book of the Sacraments of the Church, preserved in the Imperial Library of Paris; and from his facsimiles the materials for this plate have been selected.

VIII. CENTURY, No. 3.

The same source (Count Bastard's work) supplies us with the subjects engraved on this and on the following seven Plates. Those on the Plate now under notice, and on that which succeeds it, were taken by Count Bastard from a treatise on Medicine, in the National Library of France, under the No. 626. It includes the works of Oribasius, Alexander of Tralles, and Dioscorides, and was formerly preserved in the chapter-house of Notre Dame, at Chartres.

VIII. CENTURY, No. 4.

These letters scarcely yet display the elegance or magnificence of the true Caroline character which we reach in

VIII. CENTURY, No. 5.

The initials shown on this Plate afford a good idea of the increasing attention bestowed on beauty of form, coupled with that imperial magnificence which the use of gold lettering on a purple ground could not fail to insure. They are derived from a magnificent lectionary, containing the Epistles and Gospels of the year, now in the Imperial Library at Paris—" Ancien Fonds Latin, Supplement, No. 688."

VIII. CENTURY, No. 6,

Gives further illustrations of Carlovingian splendour, from the same source as those shown on the preceding Plate.

IX. CENTURY, No. 1.

From the Coronation Book of the Anglo-Saxon Kings. Cott. Tib. A 2. (*See* note, page 23.)

IX. CENTURY, No. 2.

Figures 1, 2, 3, 4, 5, and 6, are taken from the Bible of Louis le Debonnaire, son and successor of Charlemagne; and 7 and 8 are from the Gospels, once highly prized by François II. of France. (*See* page 29.)

IX. CENTURY, No. 3.

Figures 3, 4, 5, are from the Bible of Charles le Chauve, or Bald, one of the grandsons of Charlemagne; and Figures 1, 2, 6, 7, 8, from the Gospels of Lothaire. Both of these manuscripts are in the Imperial Library of France. (*See* page 29.)

IX. CENTURY, No. 4.

Figures 1, 2, 3, and 5, are from the "Sacramentaire" of Metz; and Figures 4, 6, and 7, from the Gospels of Mans. (*See* page 29.)

IX. CENTURY, No. 5.

Figures 1, 2, 3, 4, 5, 6, and 8, are from the Bible of Charles the Bald, to which we have already alluded, and Figure 7 is from the Gospels of Lothaire. (*See* page 29.)

IX. CENTURY, No. 6.

For this, and the following, Plate we are indebted to the magnificent Latin Bible of the British Museum collection, known as Add. MSS., No. 10,546.

IX. CENTURY, No. 7.

These letters, and the ornaments which decorate them, are no less agreeable in design both as regards colour and form, than those upon the preceding Plate from the same source.

X. CENTURY, No. 1.

From the Fragments of Charles the Bald's Bible. Harl. 7,551.

X. CENTURY, No. 2.

These initials are all derived from French manuscripts, and exhibit, more especially in the foliated portions of the letter Q at the lower left-hand corner of the Plate, a rapid approximation towards the style of ornament so general and popular during the greater part of the 12th century.

X. CENTURY, No. 3.

These borders, which are further developments of the principle of foliation noted in the last Plate, have all been taken from the very remarkable Bible of St. Martial of Limoges, preserved in the Imperial Library of France. (*See* page 30.)

X. CENTURY, No. 4.

All from the Gospels of Canute. Reg. I. D. G. A noble specimen of Winchester (Hyde Abbey) work. (*See* page 23.)

XI. CENTURY, No. 1.

Nos. 1, 2, and 3 from Harl. 76 ; Nos. 4 and 5 from Egerton 608.

XI. CENTURY, No. 2.

From the British Museum MSS., Harleian collection No. 7,183 ; consisting of a selection of passages in Latin from the New Testament, exhibits a clearly transitional style of ornament from the Anglo-Saxon, to that which is generally known in architecture as pure Romanesque. The intricate interlacings of the former style are still retained ; but a distinct recognition of the principle of foliation derived rather direct from nature than through the antique, is also evidenced. The colours are inharmonious, and the work is apparently German.

XI. CENTURY, No. 3,

Is from the same MSS. as the previous Plate.

XI. CENTURY, No. 4.

These letters, equally eccentric in form and colour, are derived from the peculiar "Evangeliaire of Mont Majour," preserved in the Imperial Library at Paris. They have been figured by Count Bastard.

XII. CENTURY, No. 1.

We now arrive at that graceful class of lettering, which, under a yet more perfect form, attained to such remarkable perfection during the 13th century. Our alphabets have been selected from the Harleian MSS., No. 2,800, which contains in three large folio volumes a series of lives of Saints for the whole year. The volume formerly belonged to the Monastery of St. Mary and St. Nicholas, at Arnstein, in the diocese of Treves. The initial letters throughout are for the most part executed in red, with the grounds of the scroll-work, of which they are composed, filled in with light blue and green, after the usual German manner of the 12th century. The drawing of the altogether conventional foliage is good throughout the whole work, which is ascribed by Sir Frederic Madden to "about the year 1190."

XII. CENTURY, No. 2.

These specimens are taken from a manuscript in the Royal Library of the British Museum, under the mark 1 C VII., containing the books of Joshua, Judges, and Ruth, in the Vulgate version, with St. Jerome's prologues, and attributed by Sir Frederic Madden to the middle of the 12th century. Such examples are certainly preferable models in point of tone to those afforded by the preceding Plate ; and we may look with much satisfaction upon this manuscript, since it demonstrates how free and graceful a style of ornament may be associated, with strict archæological propriety, with the cumbrous, but well-balanced forms of contemporary Norman architecture.

XII. CENTURY, No. 3.

Mr. Henry Shaw, in his beautiful work on illuminated manuscripts, has devoted no less than eight plates, giving an entire alphabet of initial letters, to the illustration of the remarkable MS. which is well known as the Harleian No. 2,800, and which has furnished the material for the Plate under notice, as well as for our No. 1 of the same century. Sir Frederic Madden considers the MS. to be "written in the class of character which came into use at the close of the 12th century, and which formed the link between the round open letter of the preceding century and a half, and the square or Gothic letter of a later period."

XII. CENTURY, No. 4.

It is for form rather than colour that these cleverly-designed borders can be safely looked upon as models. They suffice, however, to show the flexibility of the florid style of foliation which was the immediate precursor of the beautiful style of ornament which we generally recognize in this country as Early English. The manuscript from which these patterns have been chosen is in the Harleian collection, No. 3,045.

XII. CENTURY, No. 5,

Is from the same source as No. 2 in this century. It is interesting to compare Figure 1 with the same letter of the 9th century in the Bible of Charles the Bald ("Bible de St. Denis"). The general outline of the two is identical, while in the later of the two, foliation and isomorphic form take the place of knotwork with lacertine convolution and extremities. It is impossible to doubt that the earlier specimen formed the model for the later.

XII. CENTURY, No. 6.

These examples of initials and ornament of the same class, but less agreeable in colour than those given in the last Plate, are derived from the British Museum, Harleian collection No. 3,045,—a very fine book, not a little creditable to the skill, imagination, and patience of Hrabinus de Cruch.

XII. CENTURY, No. 7,

From the same MSS., supplies us with a grand specimen, in the initial letter M, of the complications of form which, whether in their early or late styles, have always proved grateful to the taste of the Germans.

XII. CENTURY, No. 8.

No. 1 from Reg. 2 C 10 ; Nos. 2, 3, and 4, from Harl. 3,045.

XII. CENTURY, No. 9.

All from Reg. 2 A 22.

XIII. CENTURY, No. 1,

Gives us a legible, but rather too square alphabet, derived from a copy of Gratian's Decretals (or Canons of the Church), in the Arundel collection (No. 490) of the British Museum. This is unquestionably one of the earliest copies of this celebrated collection of Gratian's, which was compiled by him about the middle of the 12th century.

XIII. CENTURY, No. 2.

In the last Plate may be noticed a deviation from the mode of designing shown upon previous Plates, in the introduction of free strokes and flourishes of the pen, altogether outside, and occasionally independent, of the ornamental letters. The present Plate, derived from a set of Lives of the Saints in the British Museum (Bibl. Reg. 20 D 7), written in French, shows the practice in an advancing stage of eccentricity. It was never very popular in England, but in Italy, France, and ultimately in Flanders, it became, as we shall hereafter have occasion to see, exceedingly popular.

XIII. CENTURY, No. 3.

In the noble "Image du Monde" (B. M. Sloane 2,435), from which this Plate has been taken, we meet with none of the florid pen-work of the two preceding Plates ; all here is compatible with the stern severity of the satirist, "who holds, as 'twere, the mirror up to Nature." In its solid, opaque colouring, heightened with white, burnished gold grounds, and strong black outline, this manuscript furnishes us with a beautiful example of the style which became most popular in this country.

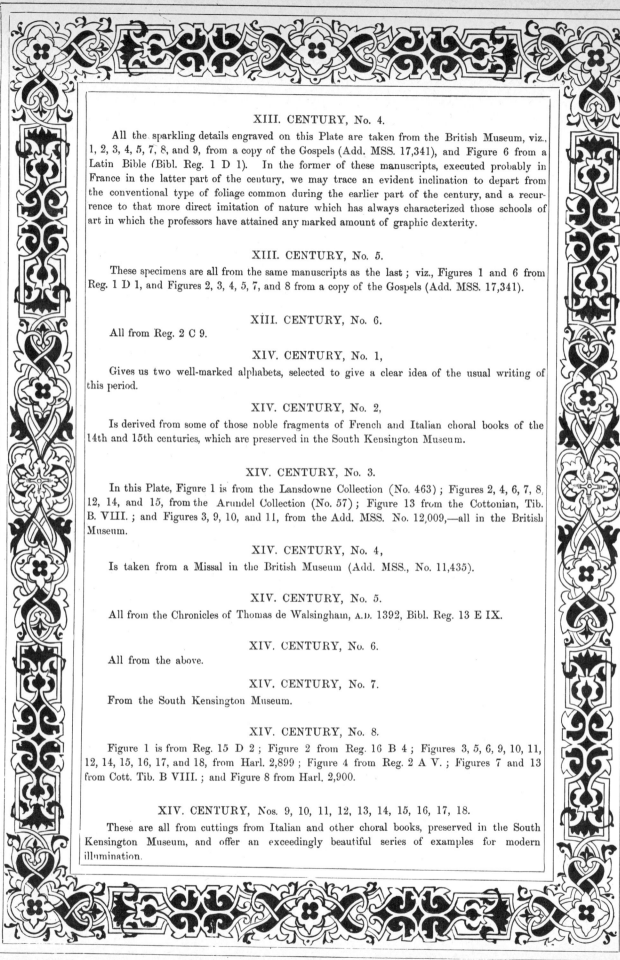

XIII. CENTURY, No. 4.

All the sparkling details engraved on this Plate are taken from the British Museum, viz., 1, 2, 3, 4, 5, 7, 8, and 9, from a copy of the Gospels (Add. MSS. 17,341), and Figure 6 from a Latin Bible (Bibl. Reg. 1 D 1). In the former of these manuscripts, executed probably in France in the latter part of the century, we may trace an evident inclination to depart from the conventional type of foliage common during the earlier part of the century, and a recurrence to that more direct imitation of nature which has always characterized those schools of art in which the professors have attained any marked amount of graphic dexterity.

XIII. CENTURY, No. 5.

These specimens are all from the same manuscripts as the last; viz., Figures 1 and 6 from Reg. 1 D 1, and Figures 2, 3, 4, 5, 7, and 8 from a copy of the Gospels (Add. MSS. 17,341).

XIII. CENTURY, No. 6.

All from Reg. 2 C 9.

XIV. CENTURY, No. 1,

Gives us two well-marked alphabets, selected to give a clear idea of the usual writing of this period.

XIV. CENTURY, No. 2,

Is derived from some of those noble fragments of French and Italian choral books of the 14th and 15th centuries, which are preserved in the South Kensington Museum.

XIV. CENTURY, No. 3.

In this Plate, Figure 1 is from the Lansdowne Collection (No. 463); Figures 2, 4, 6, 7, 8, 12, 14, and 15, from the Arundel Collection (No. 57); Figure 13 from the Cottonian, Tib. B. VIII.; and Figures 3, 9, 10, and 11, from the Add. MSS. No. 12,009,—all in the British Museum.

XIV. CENTURY, No. 4,

Is taken from a Missal in the British Museum (Add. MSS., No. 11,435).

XIV. CENTURY, No. 5.

All from the Chronicles of Thomas de Walsingham, A.D. 1392, Bibl. Reg. 13 E IX.

XIV. CENTURY, No. 6.

All from the above.

XIV. CENTURY, No. 7.

From the South Kensington Museum.

XIV. CENTURY, No. 8.

Figure 1 is from Reg. 15 D 2; Figure 2 from Reg. 16 B 4; Figures 3, 5, 6, 9, 10, 11, 12, 14, 15, 16, 17, and 18, from Harl. 2,899; Figure 4 from Reg. 2 A V.; Figures 7 and 13 from Cott. Tib. B VIII.; and Figure 8 from Harl. 2,900.

XIV. CENTURY, Nos. 9, 10, 11, 12, 13, 14, 15, 16, 17, 18.

These are all from cuttings from Italian and other choral books, preserved in the South Kensington Museum, and offer an exceedingly beautiful series of examples for modern illumination.

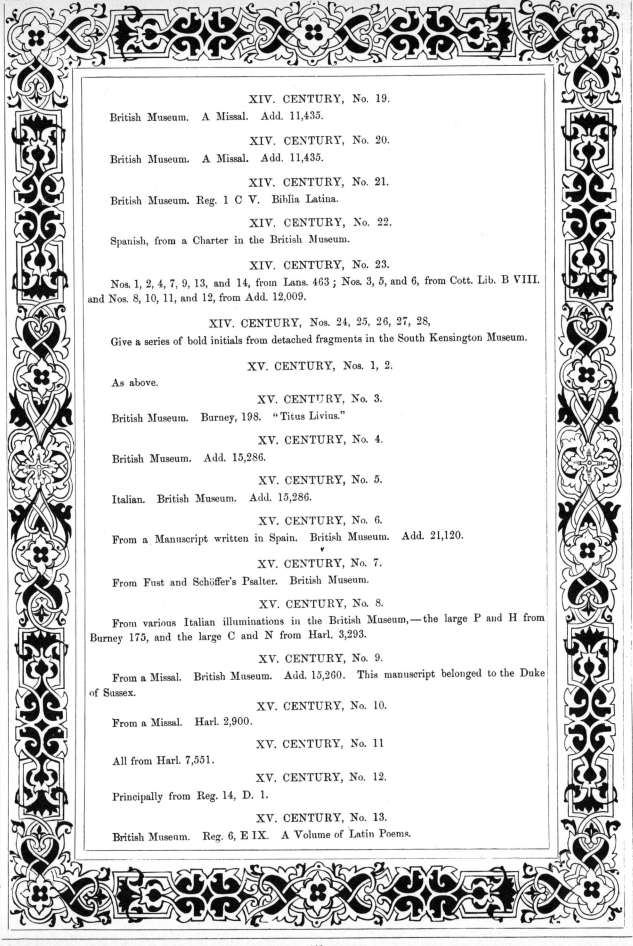

XIV. CENTURY, No. 19.

British Museum.   A Missal.   Add. 11,435.

XIV. CENTURY, No. 20.

British Museum.   A Missal.   Add. 11,435.

XIV. CENTURY, No. 21.

British Museum. Reg. 1 C V.   Biblia Latina.

XIV. CENTURY, No. 22.

Spanish, from a Charter in the British Museum.

XIV. CENTURY, No. 23.

Nos. 1, 2, 4, 7, 9, 13, and 14, from Lans. 463 ; Nos. 3, 5, and 6, from Cott. Lib. B VIII. and Nos. 8, 10, 11, and 12, from Add. 12,009.

XIV. CENTURY, Nos. 24, 25, 26, 27, 28,

Give a series of bold initials from detached fragments in the South Kensington Museum.

XV. CENTURY, Nos. 1, 2.

As above.

XV. CENTURY, No. 3.

British Museum.   Burney, 198.   "Titus Livius."

XV. CENTURY, No. 4.

British Museum.   Add. 15,286.

XV. CENTURY, No. 5.

Italian.   British Museum.   Add. 15,286.

XV. CENTURY, No. 6.

From a Manuscript written in Spain.   British Museum.   Add. 21,120.

XV. CENTURY, No. 7.

From Fust and Schöffer's Psalter.   British Museum.

XV. CENTURY, No. 8.

From various Italian illuminations in the British Museum,—the large P and H from Burney 175, and the large C and N from Harl. 3,293.

XV. CENTURY, No. 9.

From a Missal.   British Museum.   Add. 15,260.   This manuscript belonged to the Duke of Sussex.

XV. CENTURY, No. 10.

From a Missal.   Harl. 2,900.

XV. CENTURY, No. 11

All from Harl. 7,551.

XV. CENTURY, No. 12.

Principally from Reg. 14, D. 1.

XV. CENTURY, No. 13.

British Museum.   Reg. 6, E IX.   A Volume of Latin Poems.

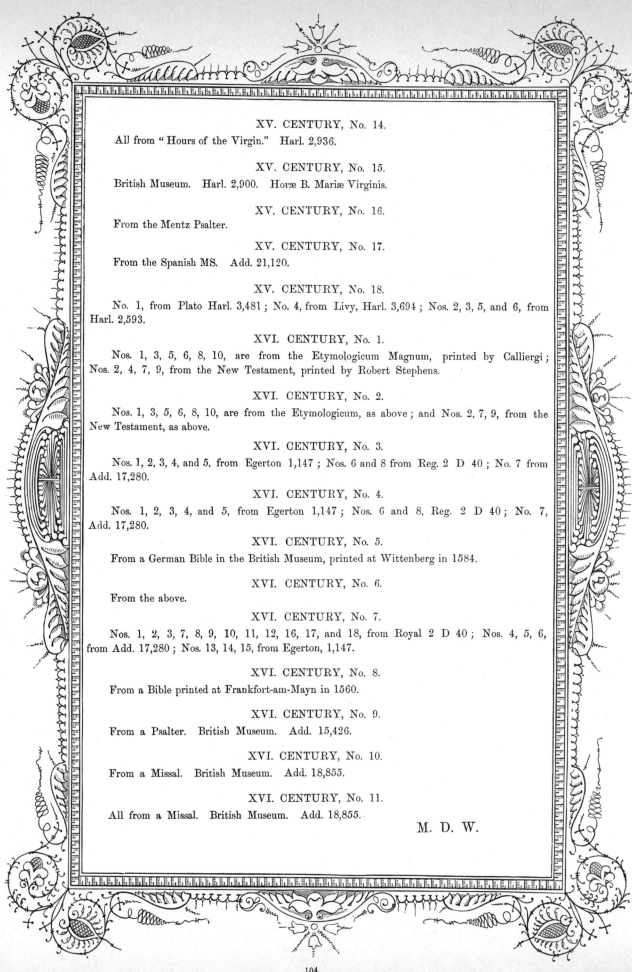

XV. CENTURY, No. 14.

All from "Hours of the Virgin." Harl. 2,936.

XV. CENTURY, No. 15.

British Museum. Harl. 2,900. Horæ B. Mariæ Virginis.

XV. CENTURY, No. 16.

From the Mentz Psalter.

XV. CENTURY, No. 17.

From the Spanish MS. Add. 21,120.

XV. CENTURY, No. 18.

No. 1, from Plato Harl. 3,481 ; No. 4, from Livy, Harl. 3,694 ; Nos. 2, 3, 5, and 6, from Harl. 2,593.

XVI. CENTURY, No. 1.

Nos. 1, 3, 5, 6, 8, 10, are from the Etymologicum Magnum, printed by Calliergi ; Nos. 2, 4, 7, 9, from the New Testament, printed by Robert Stephens.

XVI. CENTURY, No. 2.

Nos. 1, 3, 5, 6, 8, 10, are from the Etymologicum, as above ; and Nos. 2, 7, 9, from the New Testament, as above.

XVI. CENTURY, No. 3.

Nos. 1, 2, 3, 4, and 5, from Egerton 1,147 ; Nos. 6 and 8 from Reg. 2 D 40 ; No. 7 from Add. 17,280.

XVI. CENTURY, No. 4.

Nos. 1, 2, 3, 4, and 5, from Egerton 1,147 ; Nos. 6 and 8, Reg. 2 D 40 ; No. 7, Add. 17,280.

XVI. CENTURY, No. 5.

From a German Bible in the British Museum, printed at Wittenberg in 1584.

XVI. CENTURY, No. 6.

From the above.

XVI. CENTURY, No. 7.

Nos. 1, 2, 3, 7, 8, 9, 10, 11, 12, 16, 17, and 18, from Royal 2 D 40 ; Nos. 4, 5, 6, from Add. 17,280 ; Nos. 13, 14, 15, from Egerton, 1,147.

XVI. CENTURY, No. 8.

From a Bible printed at Frankfort-am-Mayn in 1560.

XVI. CENTURY, No. 9.

From a Psalter. British Museum. Add. 15,426.

XVI. CENTURY, No. 10.

From a Missal. British Museum. Add. 18,855.

XVI. CENTURY, No. 11.

All from a Missal. British Museum. Add. 18,855.

M. D. W.

A A B C C
O E F G H
J L M N H
P Q R S S
S T U

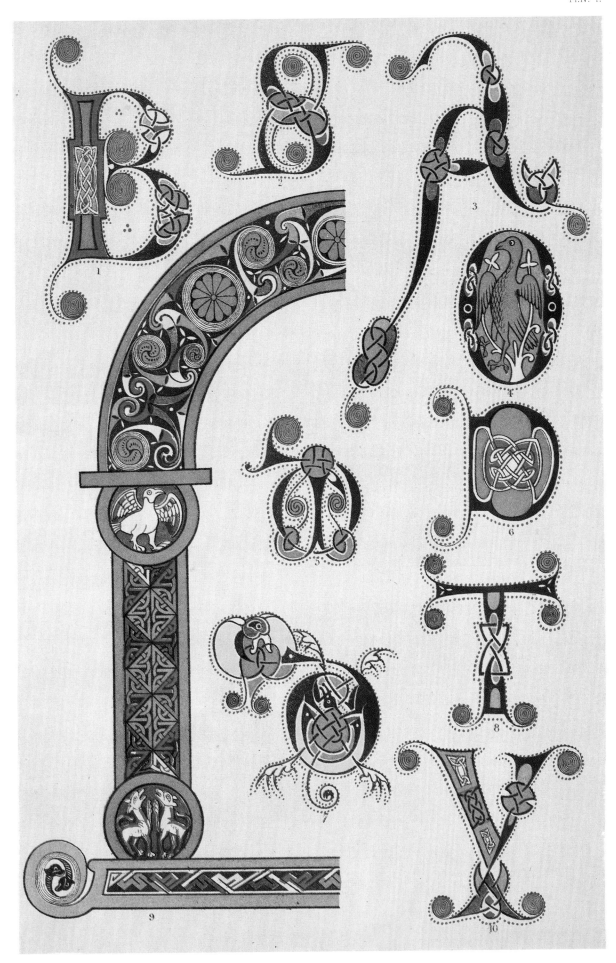

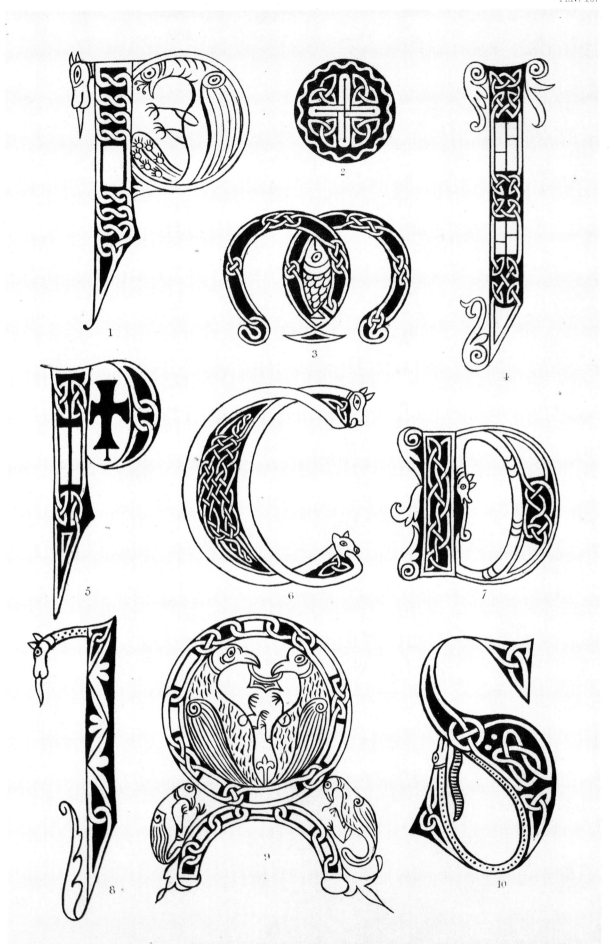

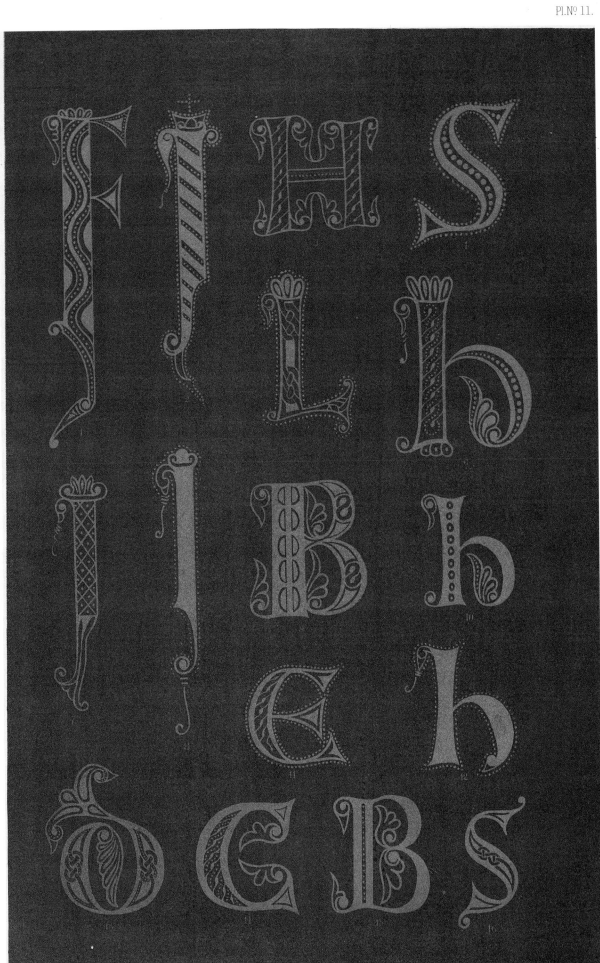

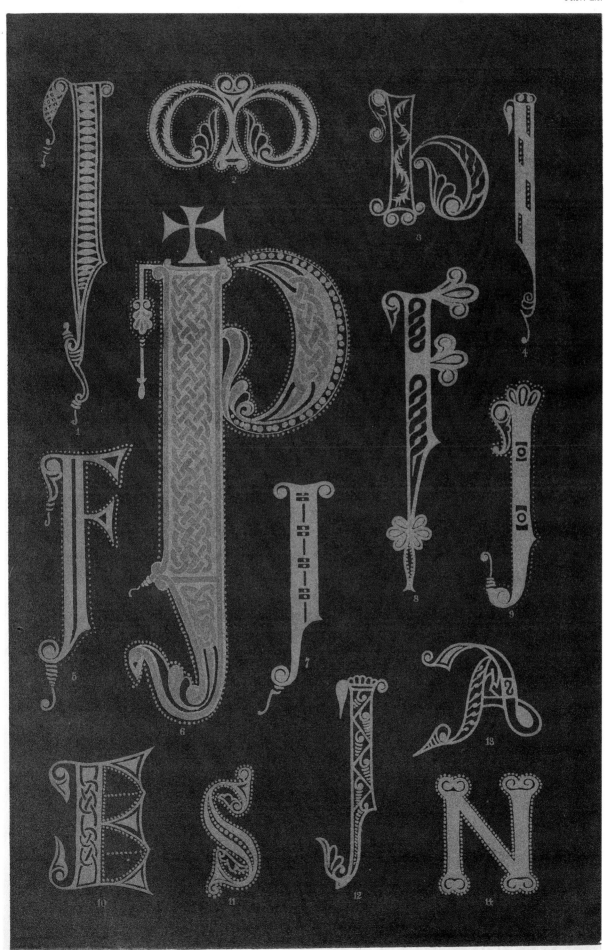

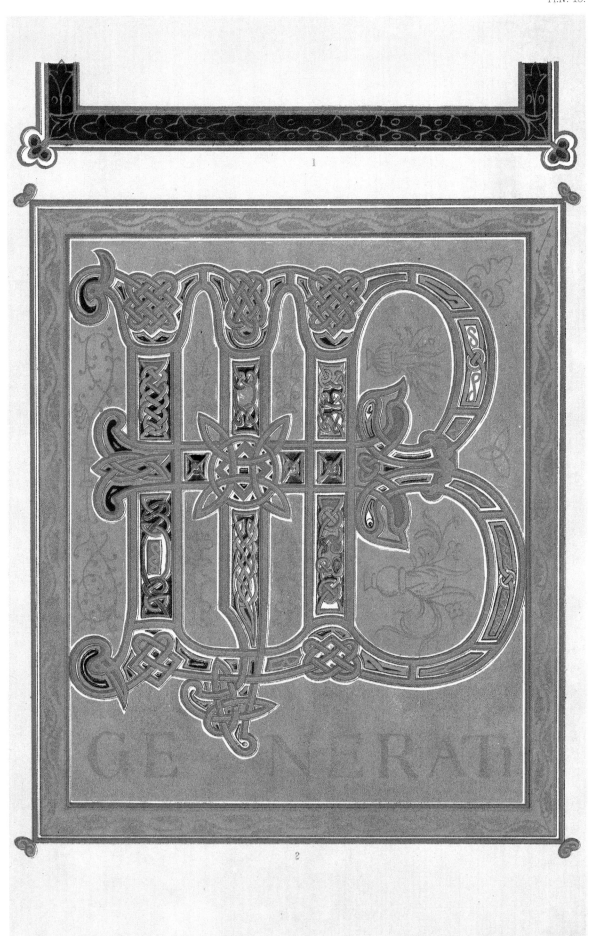

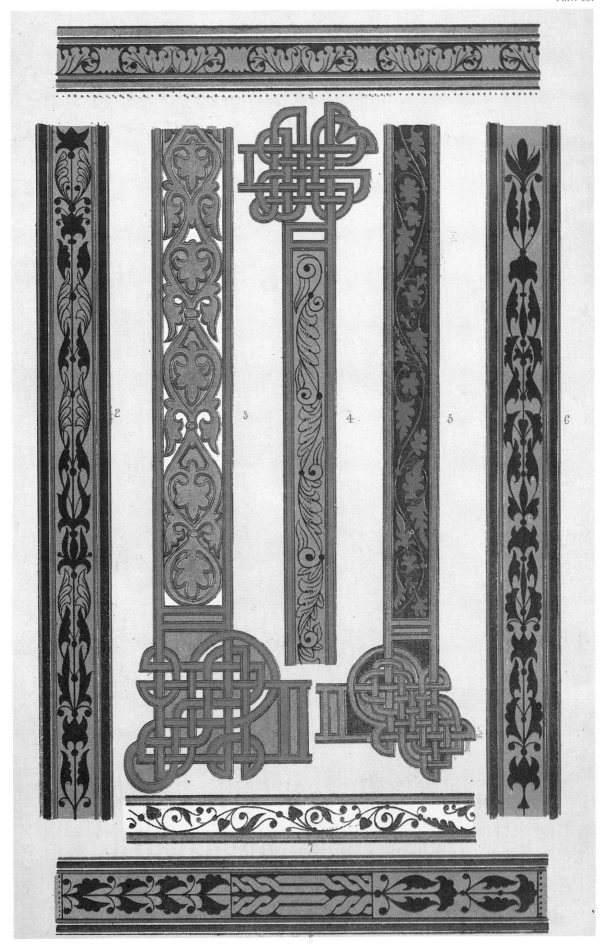

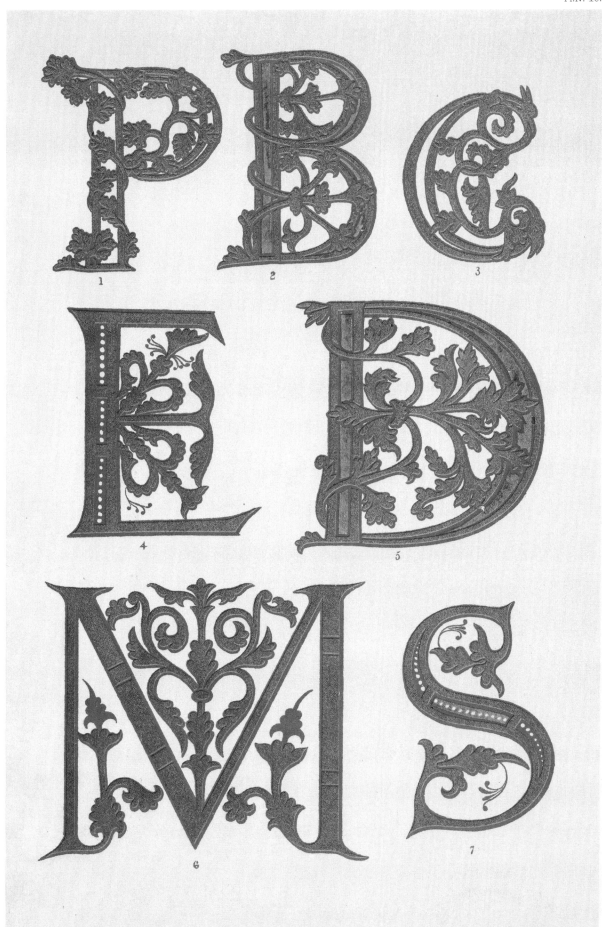

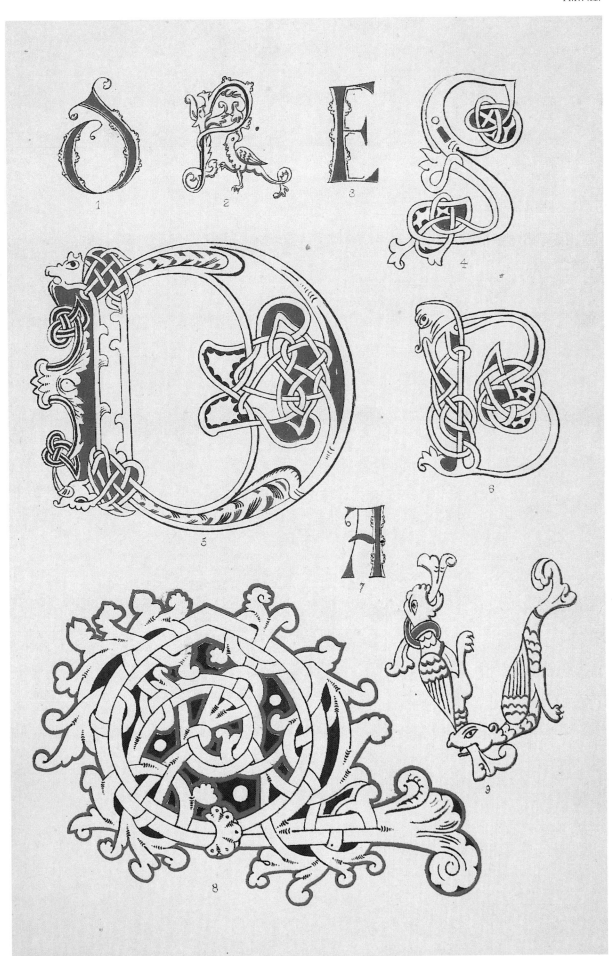

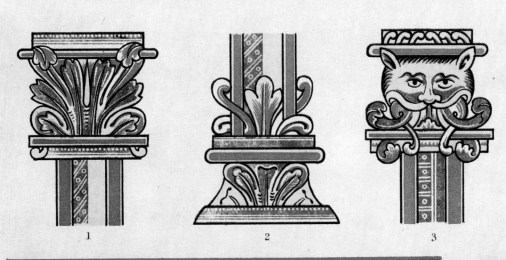

1

2

3

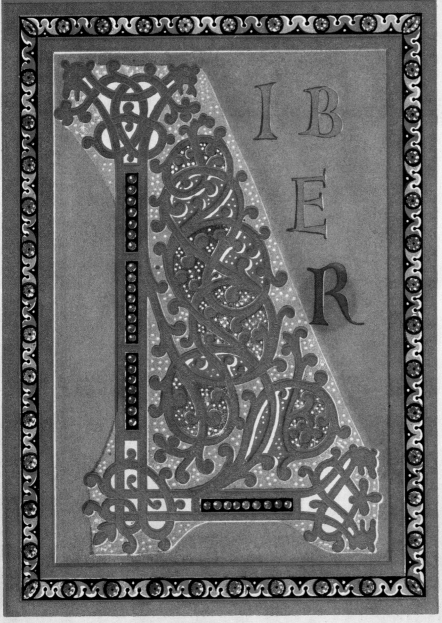

4

5

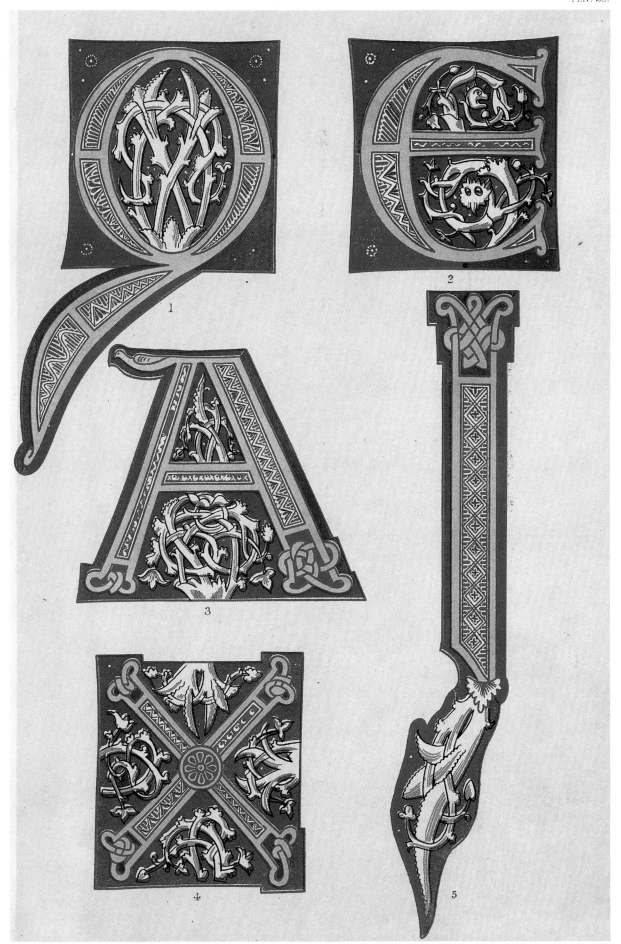

R A A B C D
O E E E F F
F G H I I J
L L M M M O N
N O P Q R S
T T U X Y Z
a b c d e f g h i k l m n o p q r s ſ t
t u v w x y z

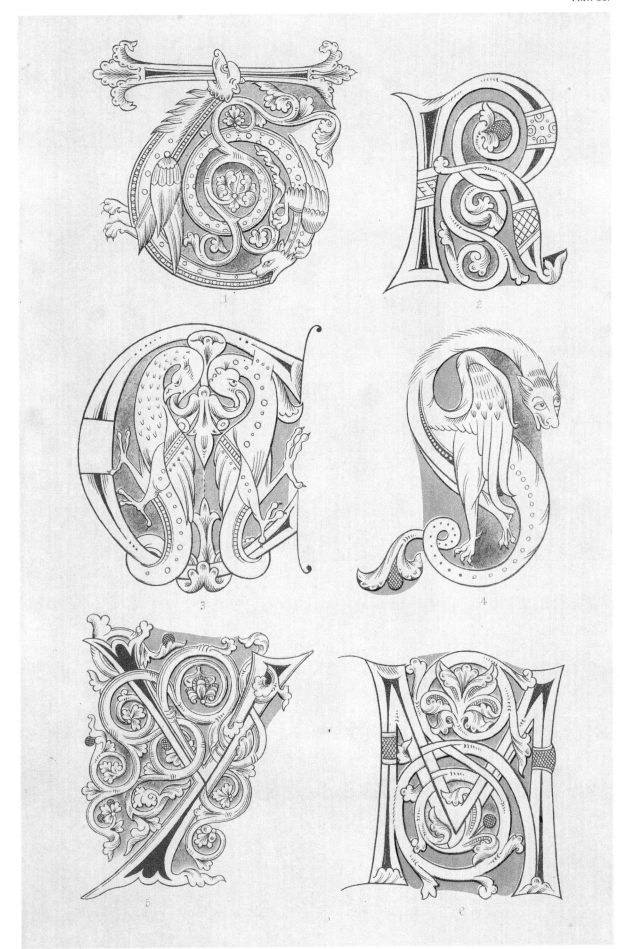

1   2   3   4   5

6

7

8

9   10

1

2

3

1

2

3

4

1

2

3

4

5

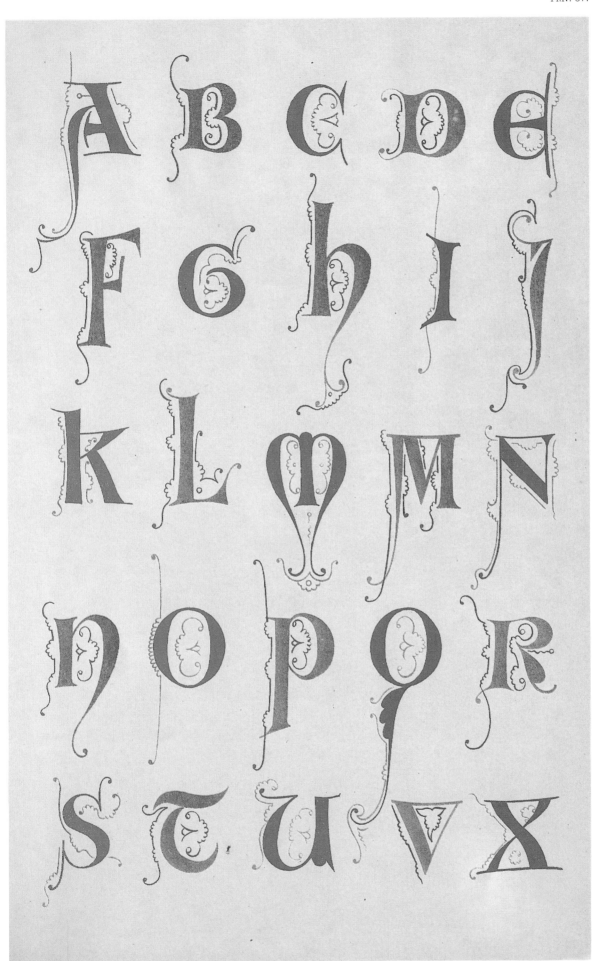

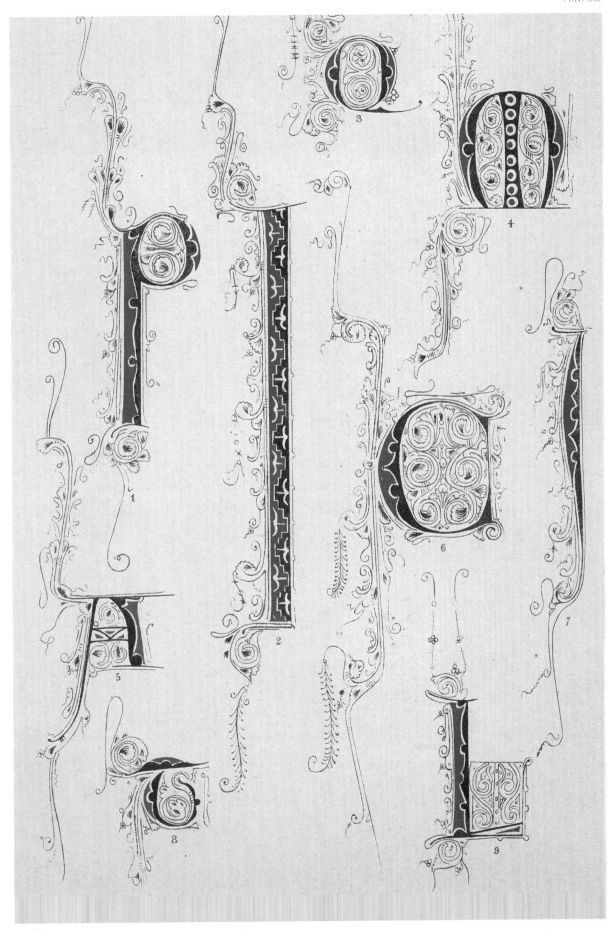

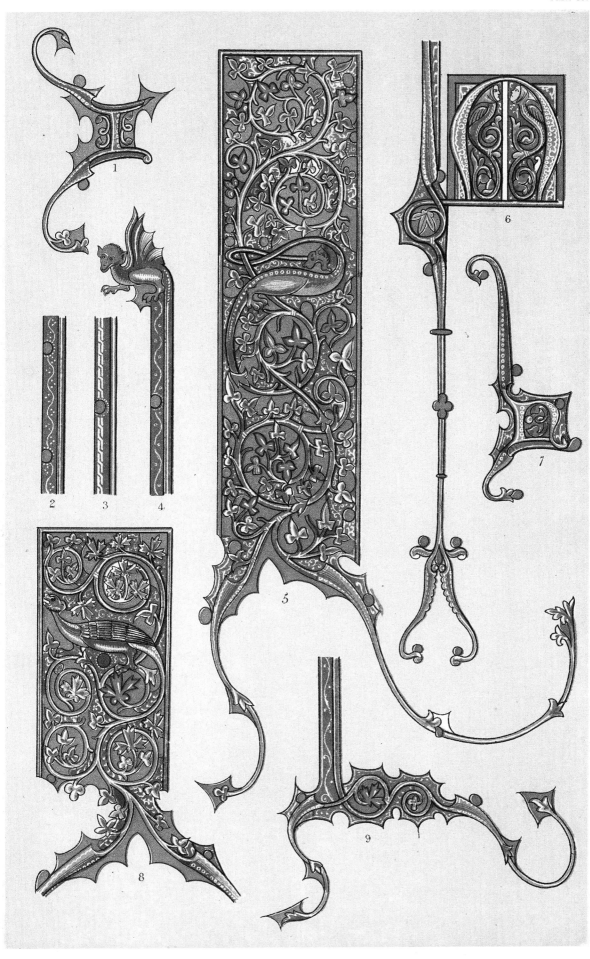

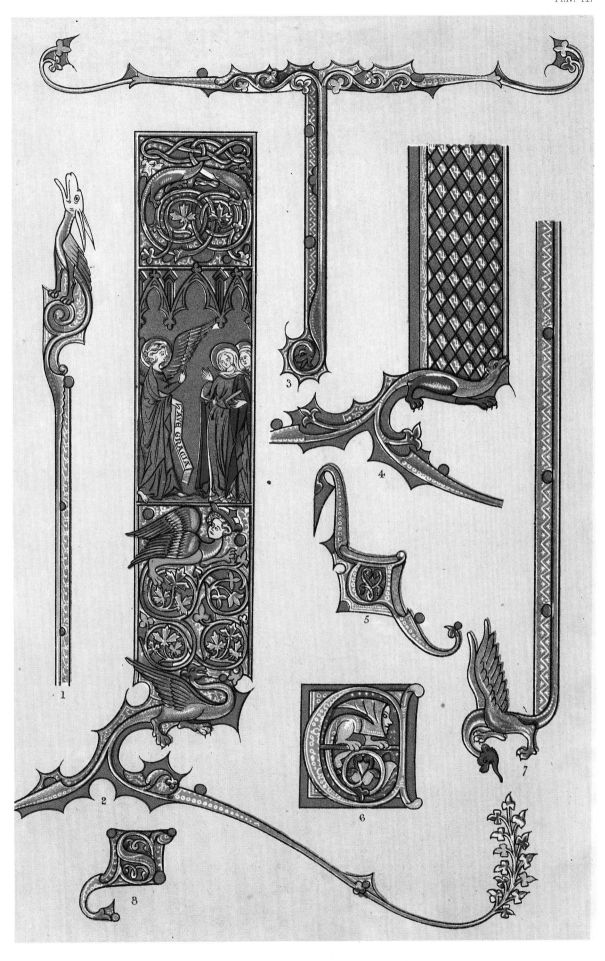

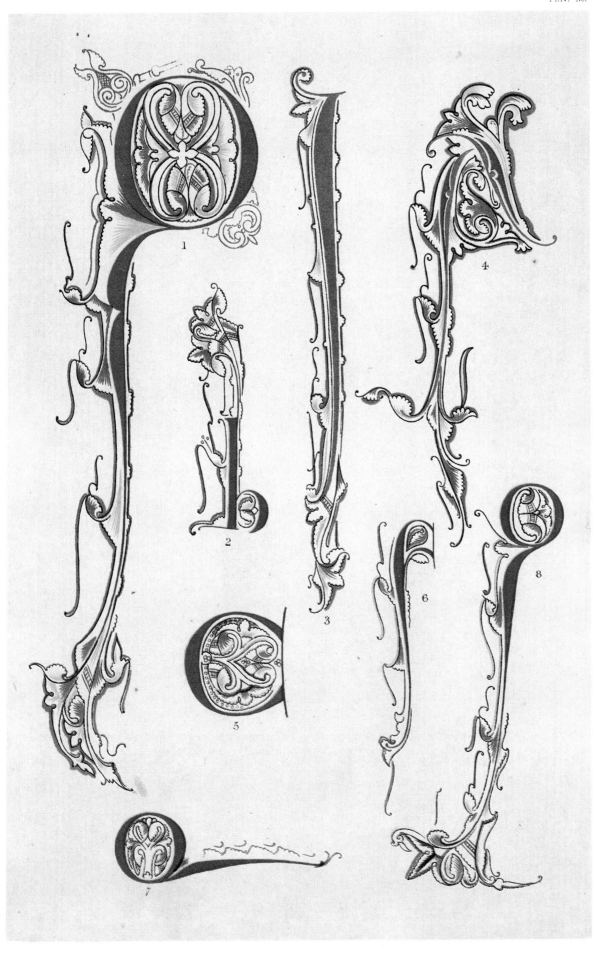

ABCDEF
GHIKLM
NOPQRS
TUVWY

abcdefghijklmno
pqrſstuvwxyz

1

2

3

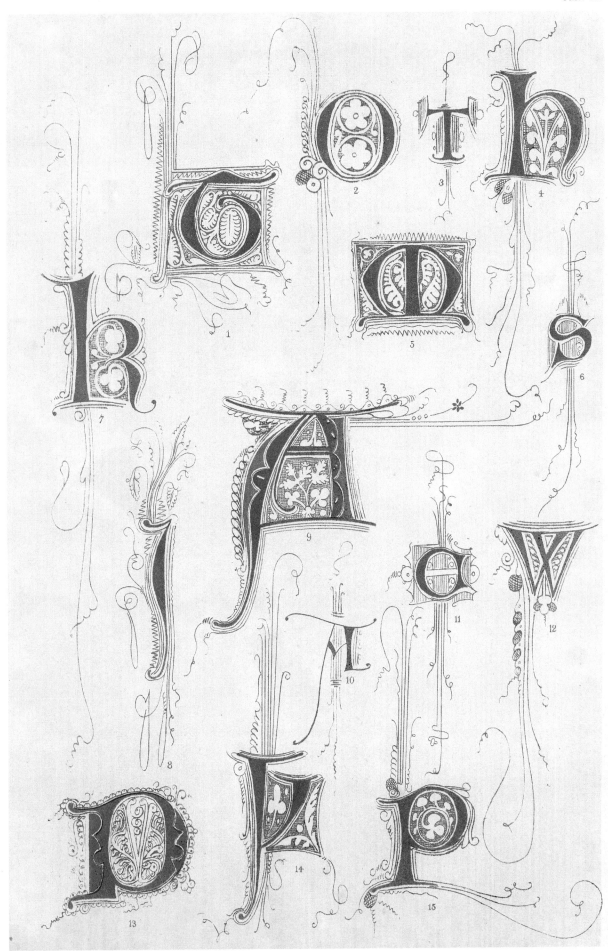

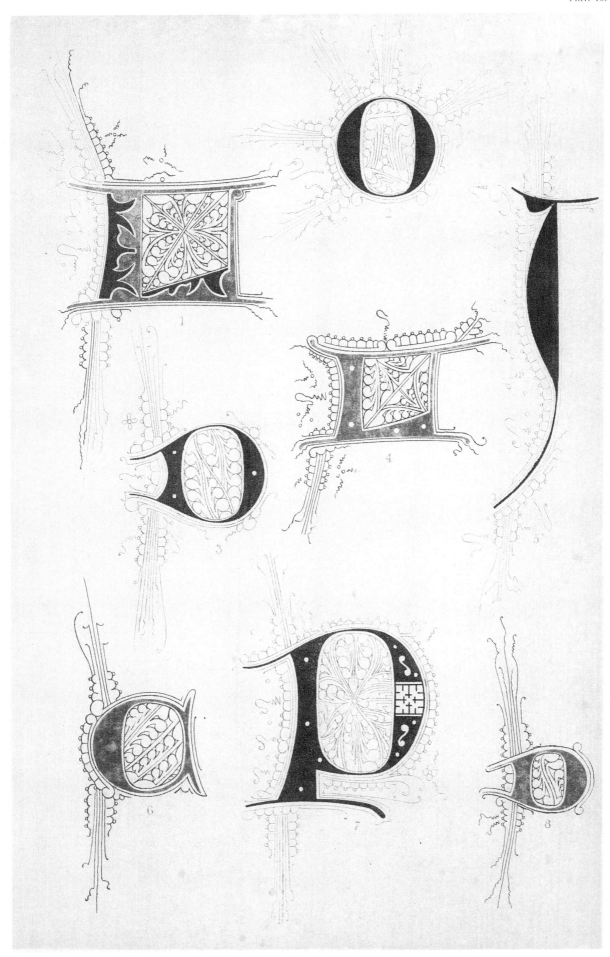

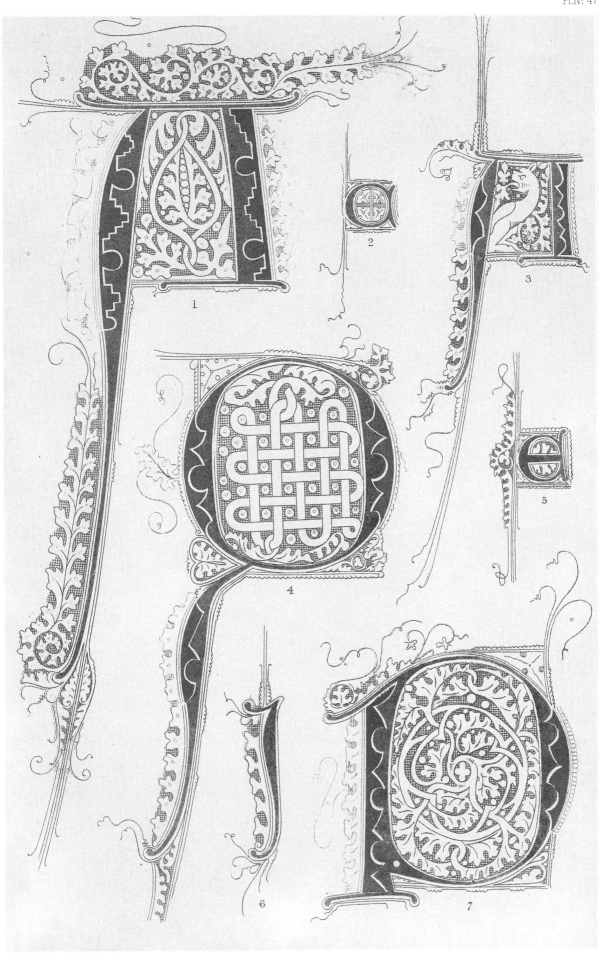

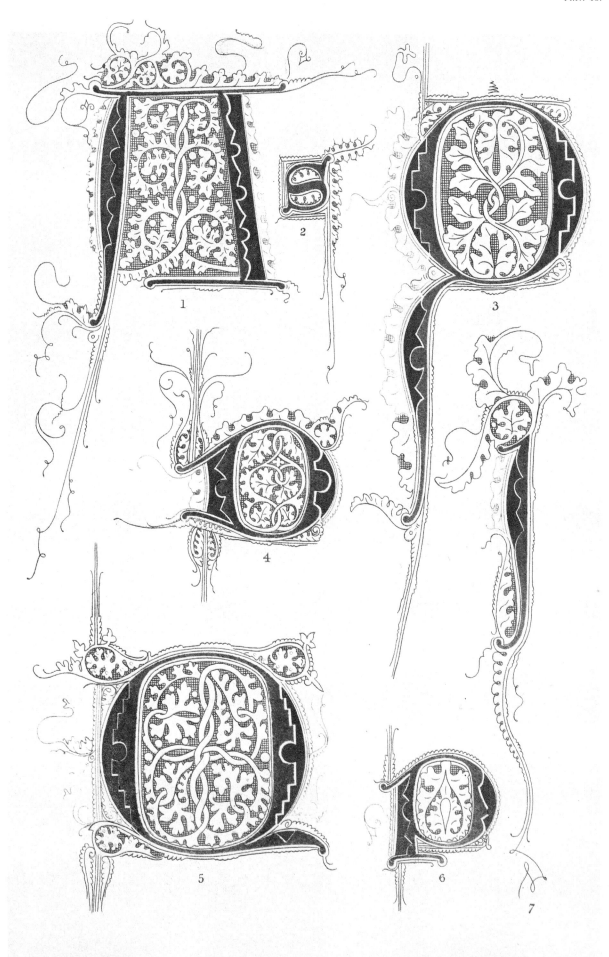

1

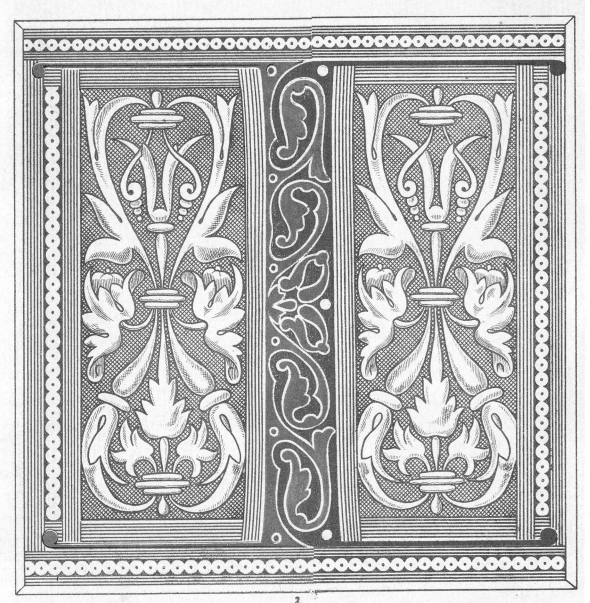

2

3

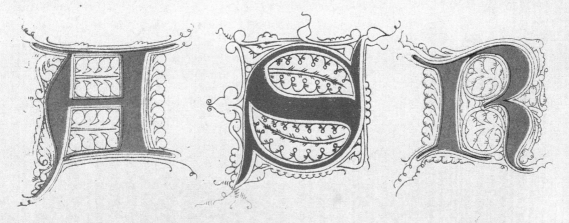

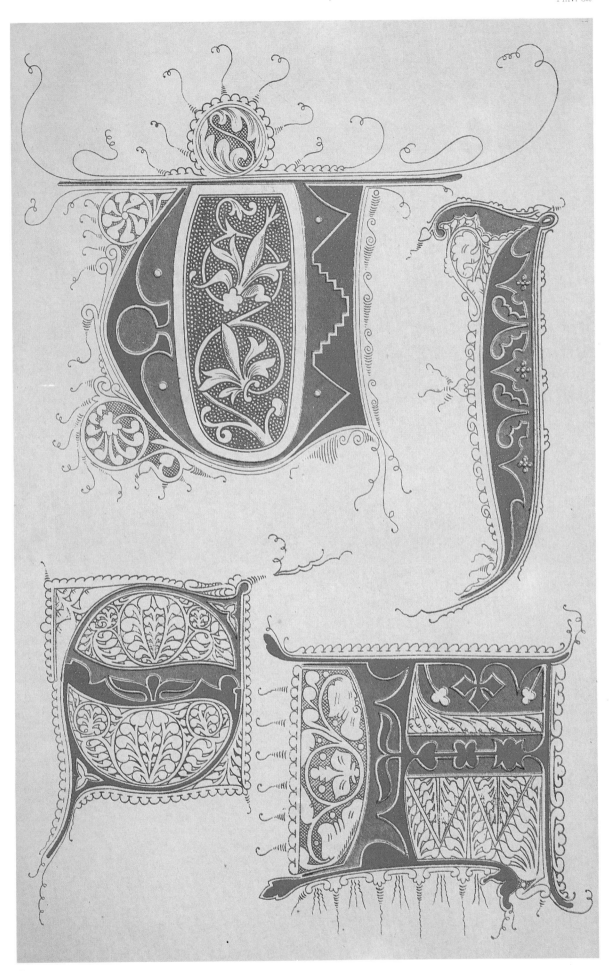

1

2

1

2

1

2

3

1

2

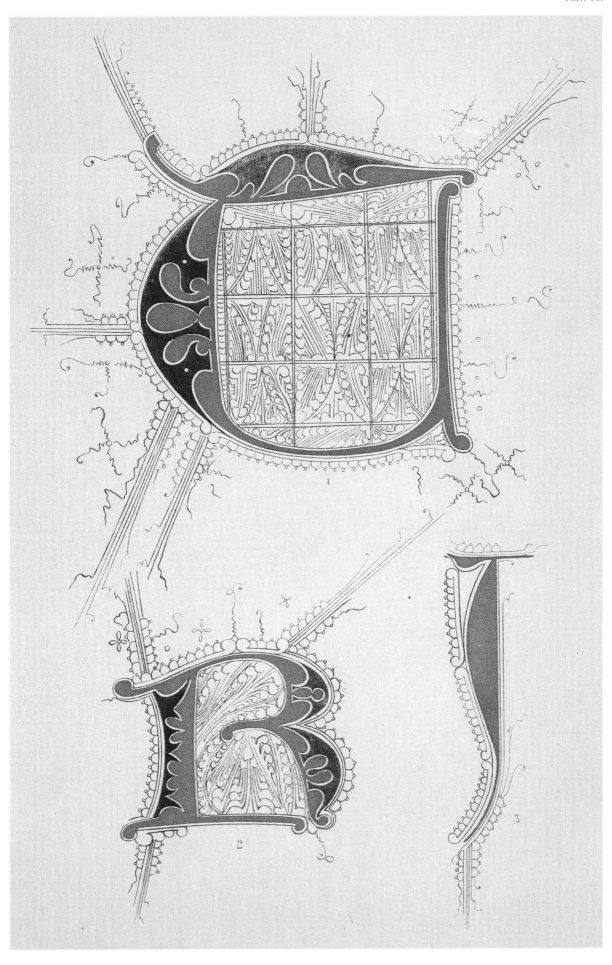

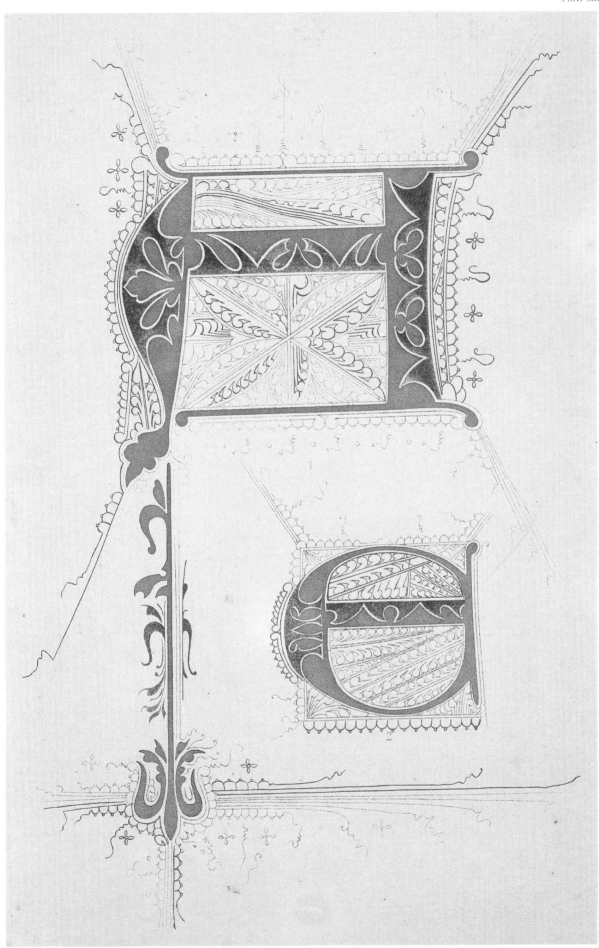

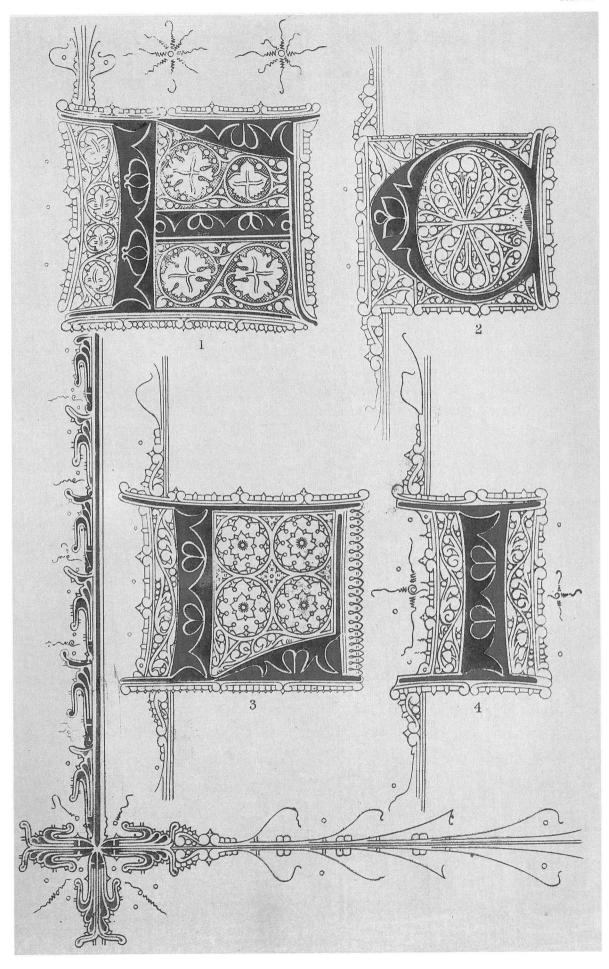

ABCDDE

AGHILM

NOPQRS

TUY

abcdefghijklmnop
qrstuvy

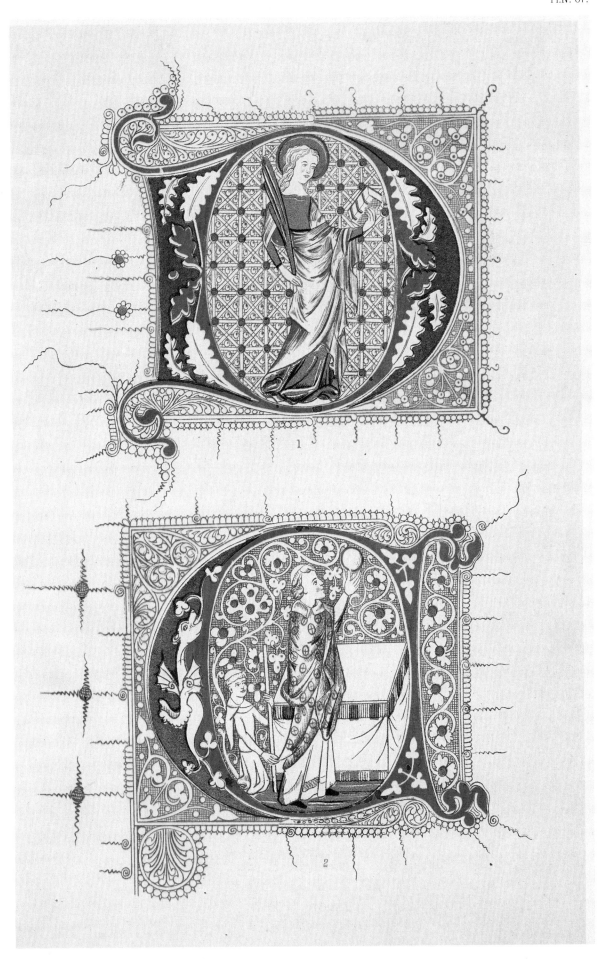

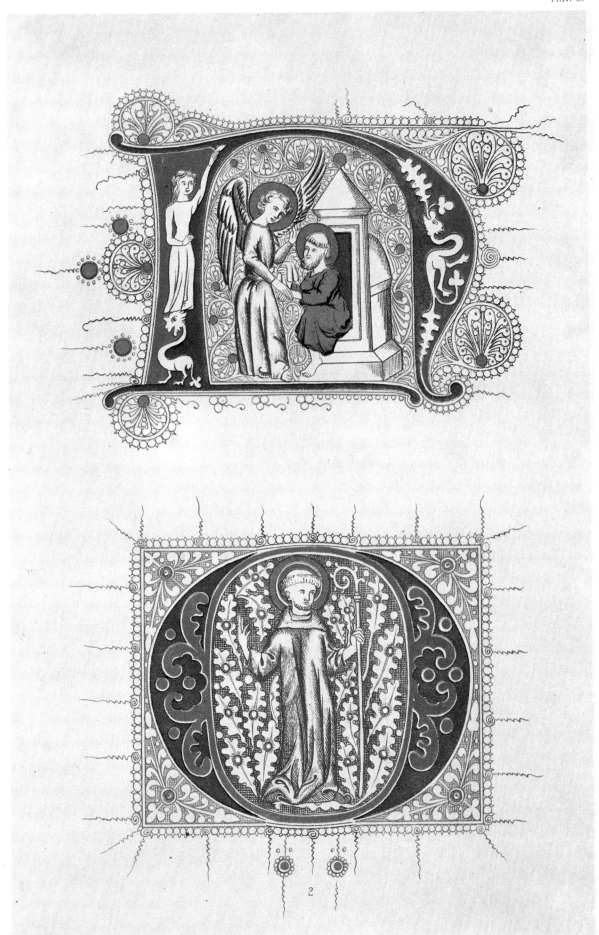

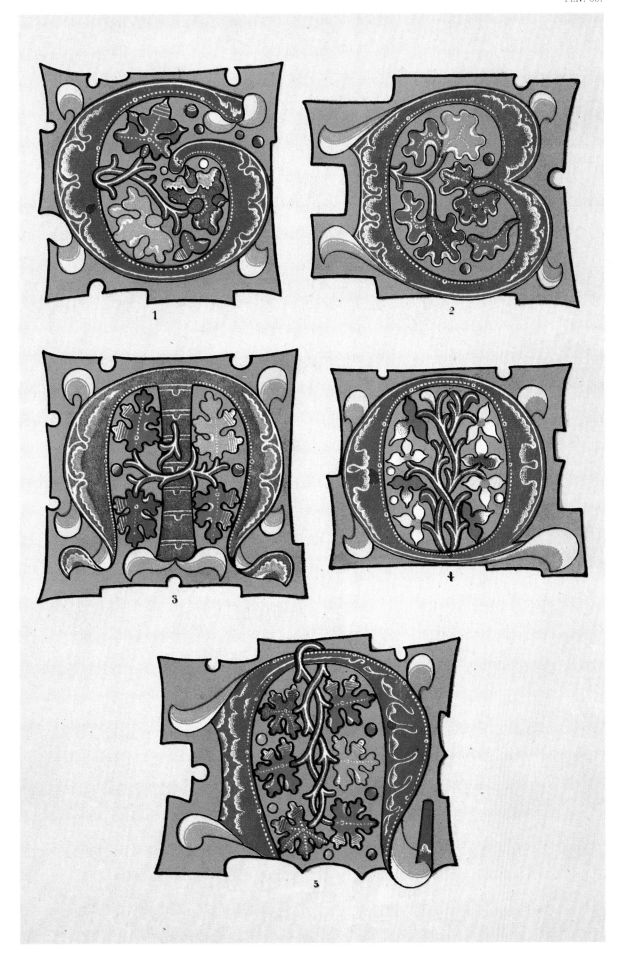

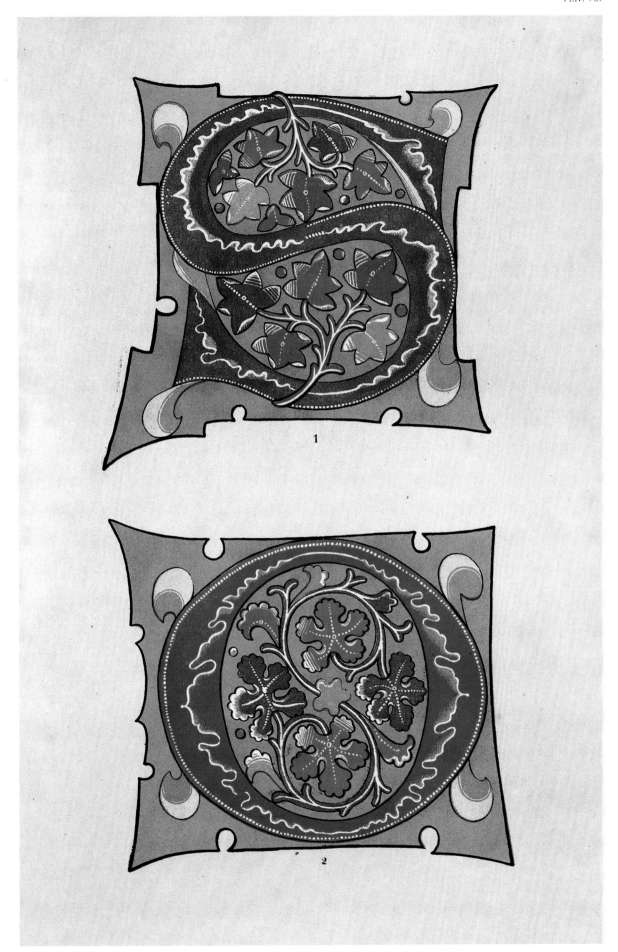

1

2

ABCDEFGHI
LMNOPQRS
TUVW

aabcdefghilmnopqr2
fstuvxy

1

ABCDEFGHIL
MNOPQRSTYZ

abcdefghilmnopqrf
stuvwyz

2

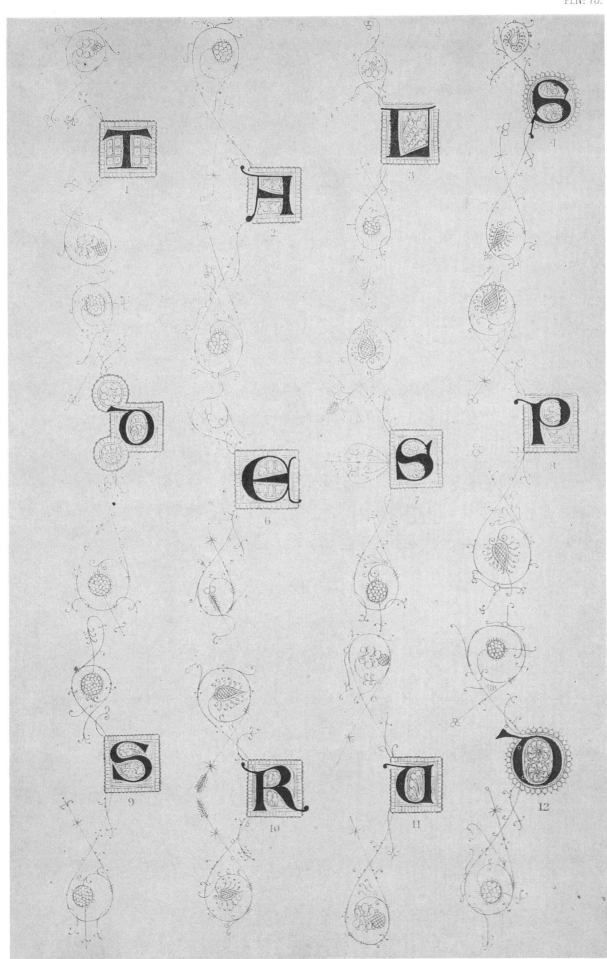

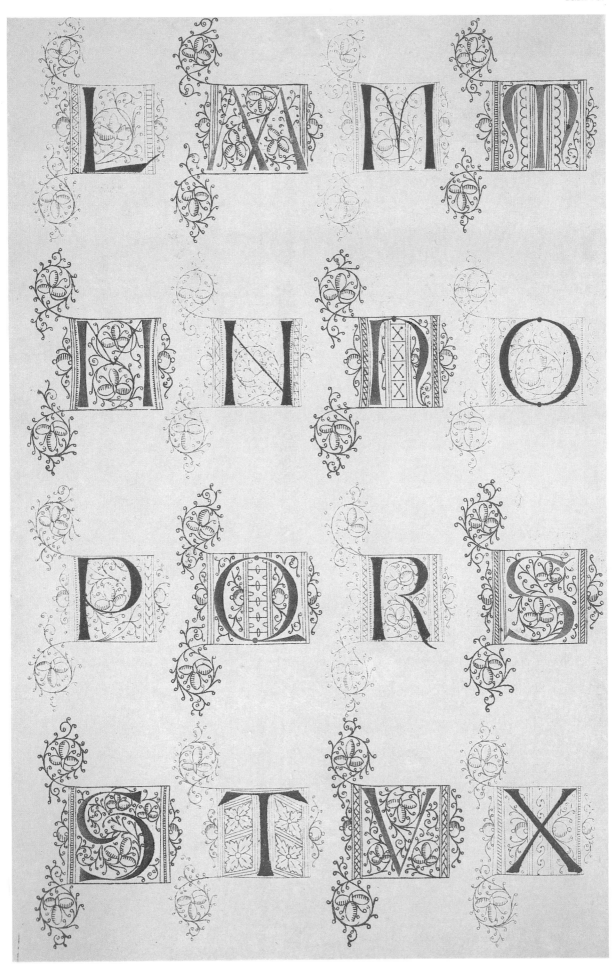

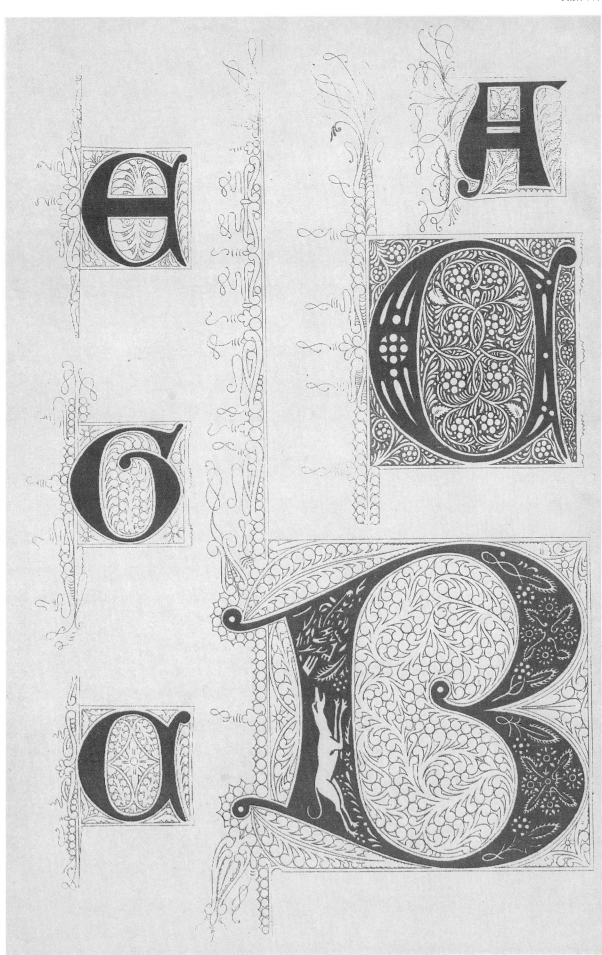

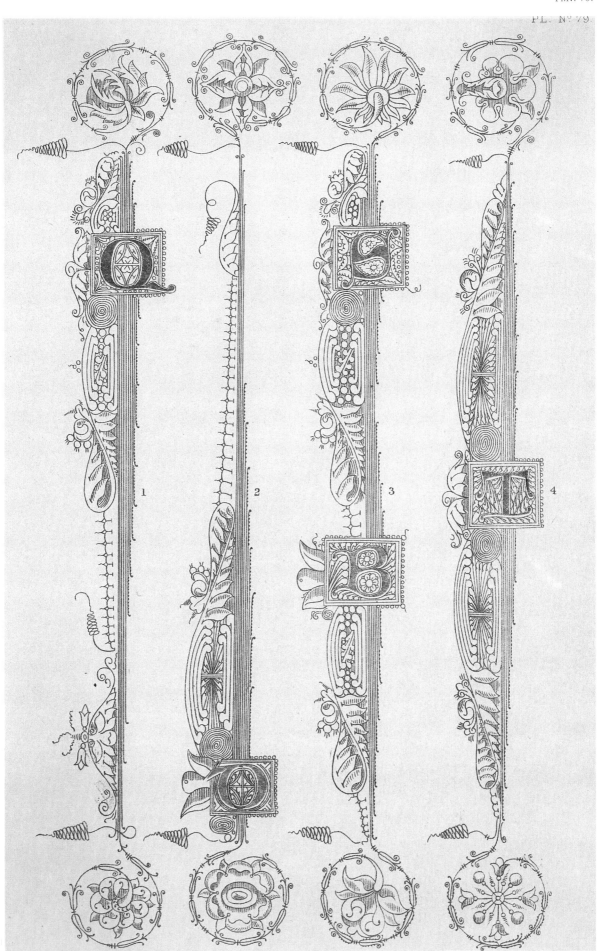

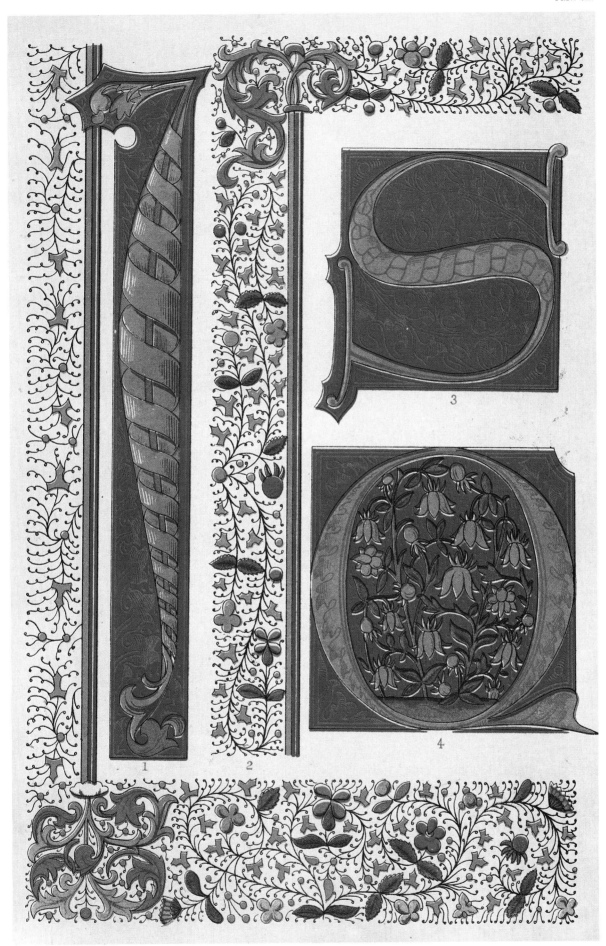

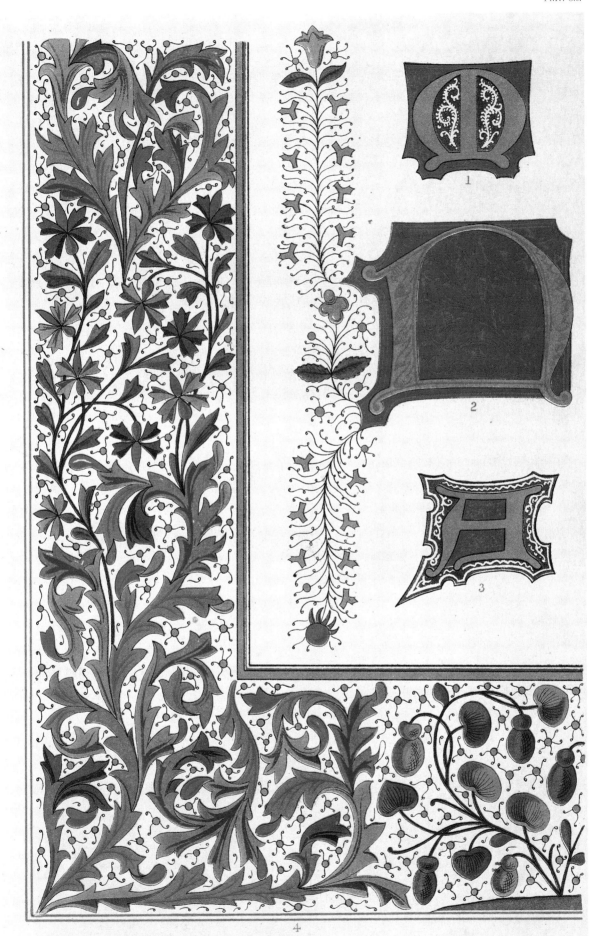

1

2

3

4

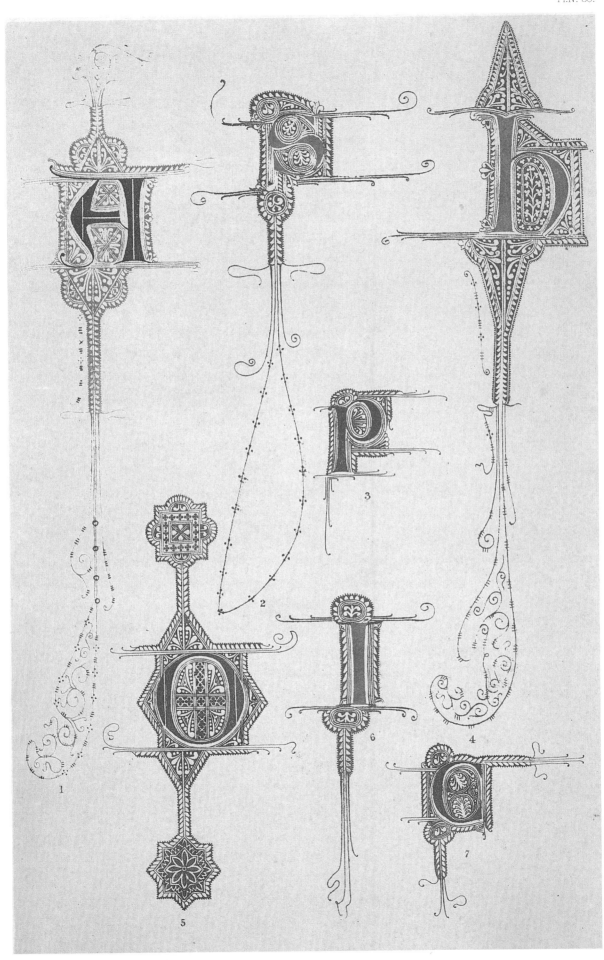

1

2

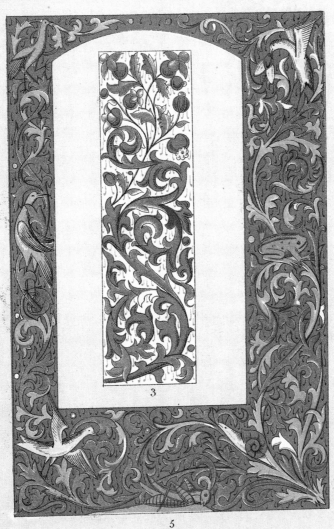

3

4

5

6

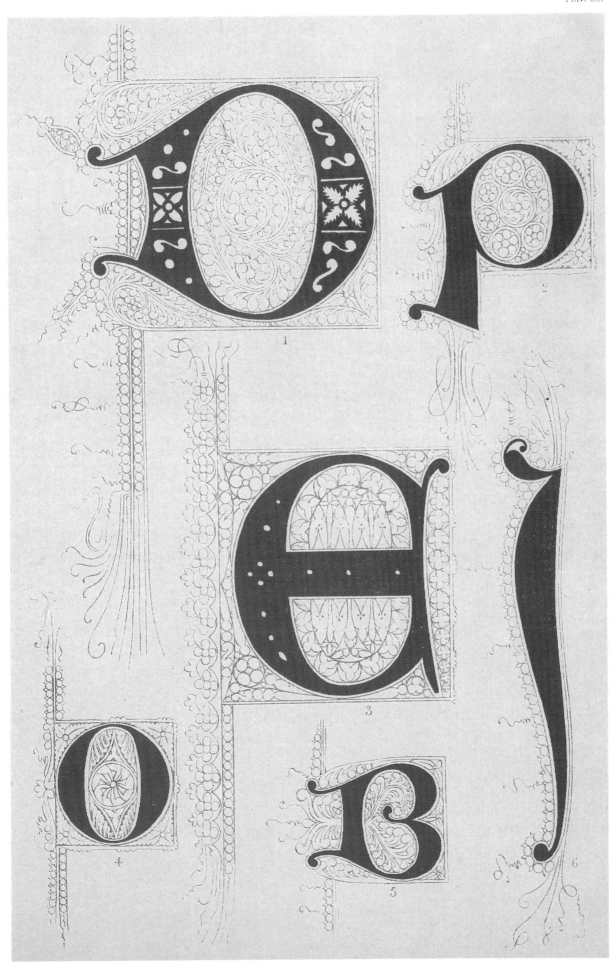

1

2

3

4

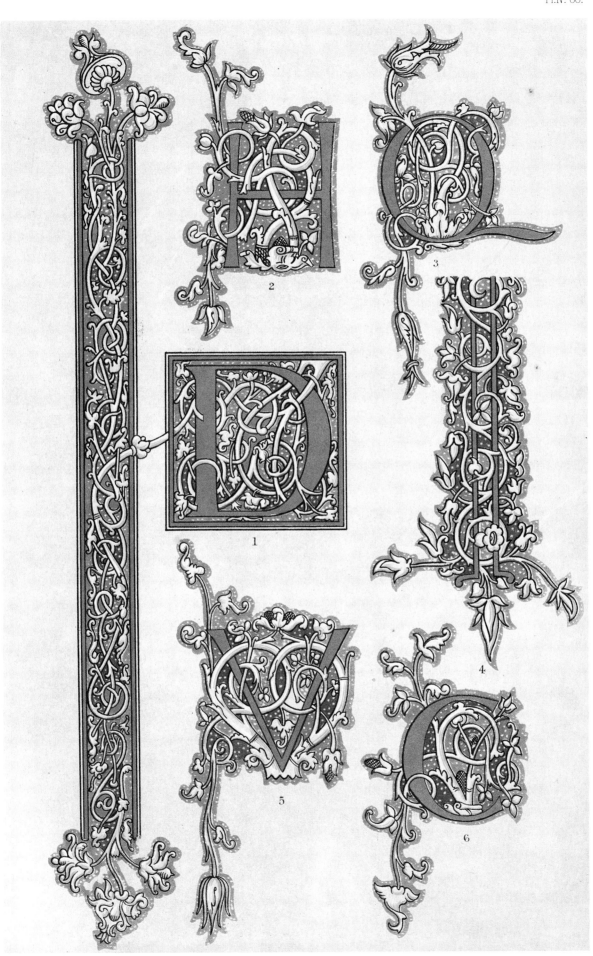

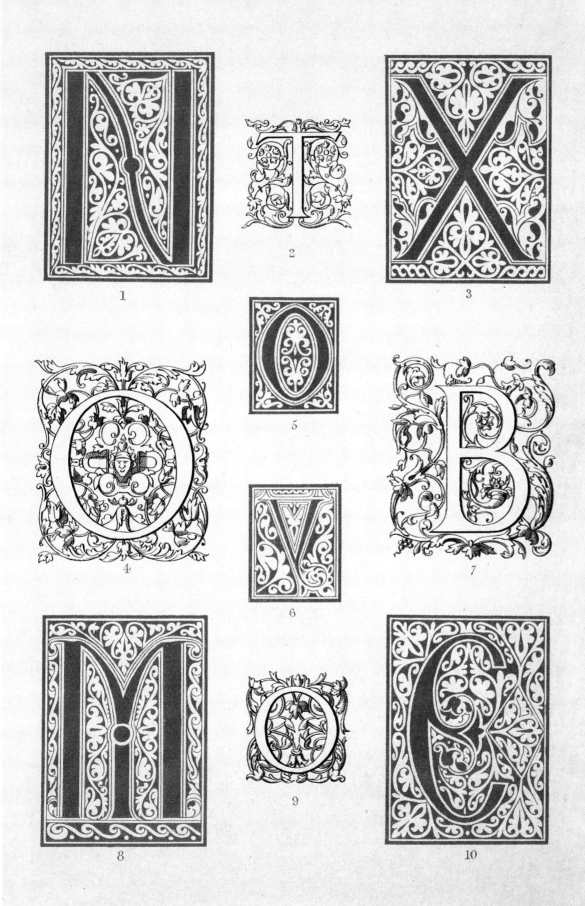

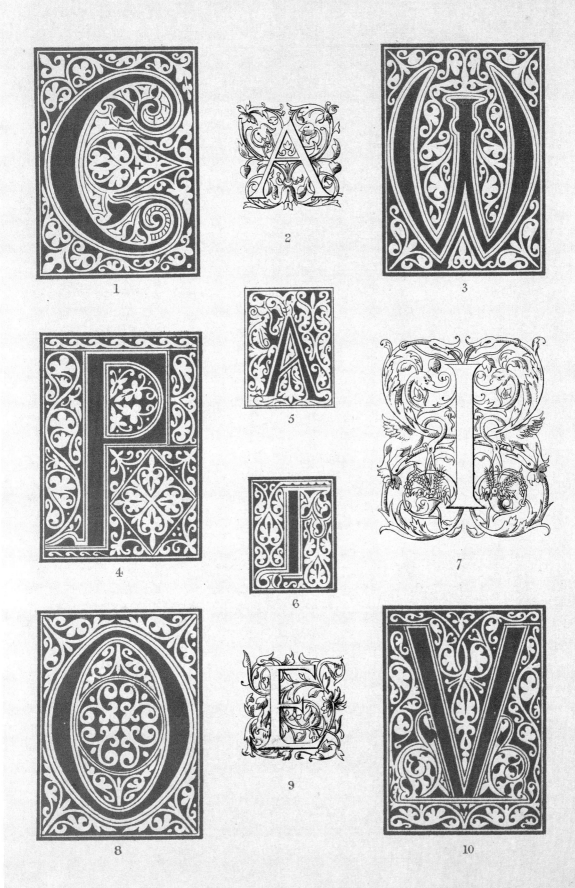

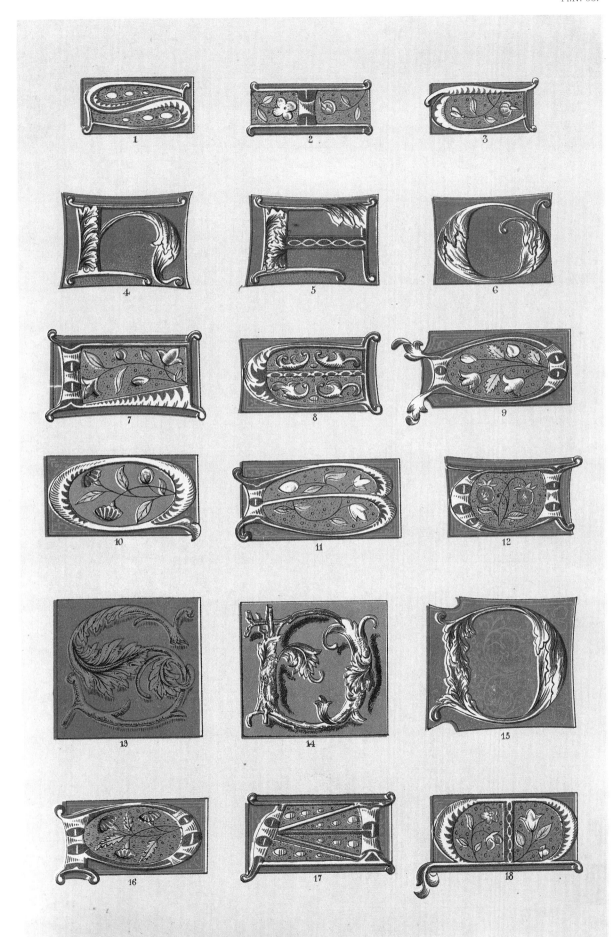

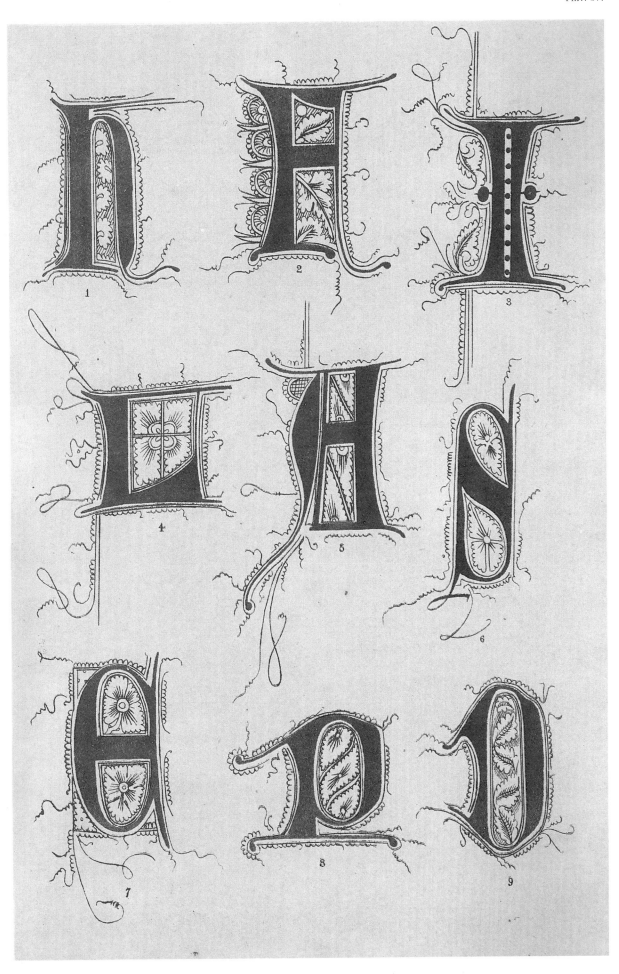